Just The facts101

Textbook Key Facts

Bundle: Business 10E

CW00607237

Table of Contents

Index: Answers

Just The Facts101

Exam Prep for

Bundle: Business 10E

Just The Facts101 Exam Prep is your link from
the textbook and lecture to your exams.

**Just The Facts101 Exam Preps are unauthorized and comprehensive reviews
of your textbooks.**

All material provided by CTI Publications (c) 2019

Textbook publishers and textbook authors do not participate in or contribute to these reviews.

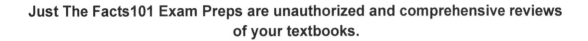

Just The Facts101 Exam Prep

eAIN 459720

Foundations of Business

A business, also known as an enterprise, agency or a firm, is an entity involved in the provision of goods and/or services to consumers. Businesses are prevalent in capitalist economies, where most of them are privately owned and provide goods and services to customers in exchange for other goods, services, or money.

:: Alchemical processes ::

In chemistry, a _____ is a special type of homogeneous mixture composed of two or more substances. In such a mixture, a solute is a substance dissolved in another substance, known as a solvent. The mixing process of a _____ happens at a scale where the effects of chemical polarity are involved, resulting in interactions that are specific to solvation. The _____ assumes the phase of the solvent when the solvent is the larger fraction of the mixture, as is commonly the case. The concentration of a solute in a _____ is the mass of that solute expressed as a percentage of the mass of the whole _____ . The term aqueous _____ is when one of the solvents is water.

Exam Probability: **High**

1. *Answer choices:*

(see index for correct answer)

- a. Fixation
- b. Solution
- c. Unity of opposites
- d. Putrefaction

Guidance: level 1

:: Derivatives (finance) ::

_____ is any bodily activity that enhances or maintains physical fitness and overall health and wellness. It is performed for various reasons, to aid growth and improve strength, preventing aging, developing muscles and the cardiovascular system, honing athletic skills, weight loss or maintenance, improving health and also for enjoyment. Many individuals choose to _____ outdoors where they can congregate in groups, socialize, and enhance well-being.

Exam Probability: **Medium**

2. *Answer choices:*

(see index for correct answer)

- a. Exercise
- b. Strike price
- c. Credit derivative
- d. Imarex

Guidance: level 1

:: Debt ::

_____ is when something, usually money, is owed by one party, the borrower or _____ or, to a second party, the lender or creditor. _____ is a deferred payment, or series of payments, that is owed in the future, which is what differentiates it from an immediate purchase. The _____ may be owed by sovereign state or country, local government, company, or an individual. Commercial _____ is generally subject to contractual terms regarding the amount and timing of repayments of principal and interest. Loans, bonds, notes, and mortgages are all types of _____ . The term can also be used metaphorically to cover moral obligations and other interactions not based on economic value. For example, in Western cultures, a person who has been helped by a second person is sometimes said to owe a " _____ of gratitude" to the second person.

Exam Probability: **Medium**

3. *Answer choices:*

(see index for correct answer)

- a. Troubled Debt Restructuring
- b. Debt
- c. Exchangeable bond
- d. Legal liability

Guidance: level 1

:: Employment ::

_____ is a relationship between two parties, usually based on a contract where work is paid for, where one party, which may be a corporation, for profit, not-for-profit organization, co-operative or other entity is the employer and the other is the employee. Employees work in return for payment, which may be in the form of an hourly wage, by piecework or an annual salary, depending on the type of work an employee does or which sector she or he is working in. Employees in some fields or sectors may receive gratuities, bonus payment or stock options. In some types of _____ , employees may receive benefits in addition to payment. Benefits can include health insurance, housing, disability insurance or use of a gym. _____ is typically governed by _____ laws, regulations or legal contracts.

Exam Probability: **High**

4. *Answer choices:*

(see index for correct answer)

- a. Extreme careerism
- b. Working parent
- c. Employment
- d. Split shift

Guidance: level 1

:: Marketing analytics ::

_____ is a long-term, forward-looking approach to planning with the fundamental goal of achieving a sustainable competitive advantage. Strategic planning involves an analysis of the company's strategic initial situation prior to the formulation, evaluation and selection of market-oriented competitive position that contributes to the company's goals and marketing objectives.

Exam Probability: **Medium**

5. *Answer choices:*

(see index for correct answer)

- a. Perceptual map
- b. Marketing mix modeling
- c. Marketing operations management
- d. Sumall

Guidance: level 1

:: Business law ::

A _____ is a business entity created by two or more parties, generally characterized by shared ownership, shared returns and risks, and shared governance. Companies typically pursue _____ s for one of four reasons: to access a new market, particularly emerging markets; to gain scale efficiencies by combining assets and operations; to share risk for major investments or projects; or to access skills and capabilities.

6. *Answer choices:*

(see index for correct answer)

- a. Voidable floating charge
- b. Equity of redemption
- c. Court auction
- d. Joint venture

Guidance: level 1

:: Credit cards ::

The _____ Company, also known as Amex, is an American multinational financial services corporation headquartered in Three World Financial Center in New York City. The company was founded in 1850 and is one of the 30 components of the Dow Jones Industrial Average. The company is best known for its charge card, credit card, and traveler's cheque businesses.

Exam Probability: **Low**

7. *Answer choices:*

(see index for correct answer)

- a. American Express
- b. Access

- c. CardLab
- d. Offshore credit card

Guidance: level 1

:: Competition (economics) ::

_____ arises whenever at least two parties strive for a goal which cannot be shared: where one's gain is the other's loss .

Exam Probability: **High**

8. *Answer choices:*

(see index for correct answer)

- a. Regulatory competition
- b. Tax competition
- c. Competition
- d. Category killer

Guidance: level 1

:: Macroeconomics ::

A foreign _____ is an investment in the form of a controlling ownership in a business in one country by an entity based in another country. It is thus distinguished from a foreign portfolio investment by a notion of direct control.

Exam Probability: **High**

9. *Answer choices:*

(see index for correct answer)

- a. Direct investment
- b. Net economic welfare
- c. Recursive competitive equilibrium
- d. Economic recovery

Guidance: level 1

:: Systems theory ::

A _____ is a group of interacting or interrelated entities that form a unified whole. A _____ is delineated by its spatial and temporal boundaries, surrounded and influenced by its environment, described by its structure and purpose and expressed in its functioning.

Exam Probability: **Low**

10. *Answer choices:*

(see index for correct answer)

- a. Viable System Model
- b. transient state
- c. Black box
- d. equifinality

Guidance: level 1

:: Television commercials ::

_____ is a characteristic that distinguishes physical entities that have biological processes, such as signaling and self-sustaining processes, from those that do not, either because such functions have ceased , or because they never had such functions and are classified as inanimate. Various forms of _____ exist, such as plants, animals, fungi, protists, archaea, and bacteria. The criteria can at times be ambiguous and may or may not define viruses, viroids, or potential synthetic _____ as "living". Biology is the science concerned with the study of _____ .

Exam Probability: **High**

11. *Answer choices:*
(see index for correct answer)

- a. Dreamer
- b. TenderCrisp
- c. CM Yoko

- d. Life

Guidance: level 1

:: ::

_____ is the study and management of exchange relationships. _____ is the business process of creating relationships with and satisfying customers. With its focus on the customer, _____ is one of the premier components of business management.

Exam Probability: **Low**

12. *Answer choices:*
(see index for correct answer)

- a. Character
- b. empathy
- c. similarity-attraction theory
- d. interpersonal communication

Guidance: level 1

:: Management accounting ::

_____ s are costs that change as the quantity of the good or service that a business produces changes. _____ s are the sum of marginal costs over all units produced. They can also be considered normal costs. Fixed costs and _____ s make up the two components of total cost. Direct costs are costs that can easily be associated with a particular cost object. However, not all _____ s are direct costs. For example, variable manufacturing overhead costs are _____ s that are indirect costs, not direct costs. _____ s are sometimes called unit-level costs as they vary with the number of units produced.

Exam Probability: **Low**

13. *Answer choices:*

(see index for correct answer)

- a. Variable cost
- b. Fixed assets management
- c. Owner earnings
- d. Standard cost

Guidance: level 1

:: Business terms ::

A _____ is a short statement of why an organization exists, what its overall goal is, identifying the goal of its operations: what kind of product or service it provides, its primary customers or market, and its geographical region of operation. It may include a short statement of such fundamental matters as the organization's values or philosophies, a business's main competitive advantages, or a desired future state—the "vision".

Exam Probability: **Low**

14. *Answer choices:*

(see index for correct answer)

- a. Mission statement
- b. organizational capital
- c. year-to-date
- d. Strategic partner

Guidance: level 1

:: Management ::

A _____ is a formal written document containing business goals, the methods on how these goals can be attained, and the time frame within which these goals need to be achieved. It also describes the nature of the business, background information on the organization, the organization's financial projections, and the strategies it intends to implement to achieve the stated targets. In its entirety, this document serves as a road map that provides direction to the business.

15. *Answer choices:*

(see index for correct answer)

- a. Social risk management
- b. Operations management
- c. Business plan
- d. Quality

Guidance: level 1

:: Strategic management ::

_____ is a strategic planning technique used to help a person or organization identify strengths, weaknesses, opportunities, and threats related to business competition or project planning. It is intended to specify the objectives of the business venture or project and identify the internal and external factors that are favorable and unfavorable to achieving those objectives. Users of a _____ often ask and answer questions to generate meaningful information for each category to make the tool useful and identify their competitive advantage. SWOT has been described as the tried-and-true tool of strategic analysis.

Exam Probability: **High**

16. *Answer choices:*

(see index for correct answer)

- a. Earlyvangelist
- b. Nicolas De Santis
- c. Structure follows strategy
- d. SWOT analysis

Guidance: level 1

:: Project management ::

In political science, an _____ is a means by which a petition signed by a certain minimum number of registered voters can force a government to choose to either enact a law or hold a public vote in parliament in what is called indirect _____ , or under direct _____ , the proposition is immediately put to a plebiscite or referendum, in what is called a Popular initiated Referendum or citizen-initiated referendum).

Exam Probability: **Low**

17. *Answer choices:*
(see index for correct answer)

- a. Problem domain analysis
- b. Aggregate planning
- c. Effective Development Group
- d. Global Alliance for Project Performance Standards

Guidance: level 1

:: Marketing ::

_____ or stock is the goods and materials that a business holds for the ultimate goal of resale .

Exam Probability: **Low**

18. *Answer choices:*

(see index for correct answer)

- a. Art Infusion
- b. Geographical pricing
- c. Marketspace
- d. Product planning

Guidance: level 1

:: Business models ::

_____ es are privately owned corporations, partnerships, or sole proprietorships that have fewer employees and/or less annual revenue than a regular-sized business or corporation. Businesses are defined as "small" in terms of being able to apply for government support and qualify for preferential tax policy varies depending on the country and industry.

_____ es range from fifteen employees under the Australian Fair Work Act 2009, fifty employees according to the definition used by the European Union, and fewer than five hundred employees to qualify for many U.S. _____ Administration programs. While _____ es can also be classified according to other methods, such as annual revenues, shipments, sales, assets, or by annual gross or net revenue or net profits, the number of employees is one of the most widely used measures.

Exam Probability: **High**

19. *Answer choices:*

(see index for correct answer)

- a. Technology push
- b. Dependent growth business model
- c. Copy to China
- d. Organizational architecture

Guidance: level 1

:: Globalization-related theories ::

_____ is an economic system based on the private ownership of the means of production and their operation for profit. Characteristics central to _____ include private property, capital accumulation, wage labor, voluntary exchange, a price system, and competitive markets. In a capitalist market economy, decision-making and investment are determined by every owner of wealth, property or production ability in financial and capital markets, whereas prices and the distribution of goods and services are mainly determined by competition in goods and services markets.

Exam Probability: **High**

20. *Answer choices:*

(see index for correct answer)

- a. post-industrial
- b. Economic Development
- c. Capitalism

Guidance: level 1

:: Industrial Revolution ::

The _____ , now also known as the First _____ , was the transition to new manufacturing processes in Europe and the US, in the period from about 1760 to sometime between 1820 and 1840. This transition included going from hand production methods to machines, new chemical manufacturing and iron production processes, the increasing use of steam power and water power, the development of machine tools and the rise of the mechanized factory system. The _____ also led to an unprecedented rise in the rate of population growth.

21. *Answer choices:*

(see index for correct answer)

- a. Weaving shed
- b. Industrial Revolution
- c. Upper Priory Cotton Mill
- d. Hulett

Guidance: level 1

:: Management ::

_____ is the practice of initiating, planning, executing, controlling, and closing the work of a team to achieve specific goals and meet specific success criteria at the specified time.

Exam Probability: **Low**

22. *Answer choices:*

(see index for correct answer)

- a. Perth leadership outcome model
- b. Real property administrator
- c. Commercial management
- d. Defensive expenditures

:: Actuarial science ::

_____ is the possibility of losing something of value. Values can be gained or lost when taking _____ resulting from a given action or inaction, foreseen or unforeseen . _____ can also be defined as the intentional interaction with uncertainty. Uncertainty is a potential, unpredictable, and uncontrollable outcome; _____ is a consequence of action taken in spite of uncertainty.

Exam Probability: **High**

23. *Answer choices:*

(see index for correct answer)

- a. Disease
- b. Risk
- c. Fictional actuaries
- d. Cohort

:: Service industries ::

_____ are the economic services provided by the finance industry, which encompasses a broad range of businesses that manage money, including credit unions, banks, credit-card companies, insurance companies, accountancy companies, consumer-finance companies, stock brokerages, investment funds, individual managers and some government-sponsored enterprises. _____ companies are present in all economically developed geographic locations and tend to cluster in local, national, regional and international financial centers such as London, New York City, and Tokyo.

Exam Probability: **High**

24. *Answer choices:*

(see index for correct answer)

- a. Financial services
- b. Tourism
- c. Financial services in Japan
- d. Pension Administration

Guidance: level 1

:: ::

_____ is an abstract concept of management of complex systems according to a set of rules and trends. In systems theory, these types of rules exist in various fields of biology and society, but the term has slightly different meanings according to context. For example.

25. *Answer choices:*

(see index for correct answer)

- a. imperative
- b. surface-level diversity
- c. Regulation
- d. open system

Guidance: level 1

:: Logistics ::

_____ is generally the detailed organization and implementation of a complex operation. In a general business sense, _____ is the management of the flow of things between the point of origin and the point of consumption in order to meet requirements of customers or corporations. The resources managed in _____ may include tangible goods such as materials, equipment, and supplies, as well as food and other consumable items. The _____ of physical items usually involves the integration of information flow, materials handling, production, packaging, inventory, transportation, warehousing, and often security.

26. *Answer choices:*

(see index for correct answer)

- a. Distribution resource planning
- b. Freightos
- c. Liquid logistics
- d. Logistics

Guidance: level 1

:: Business ::

_____ is the activity of making one's living or making money by producing or buying and selling products . Simply put, it is "any activity or enterprise entered into for profit. It does not mean it is a company, a corporation, partnership, or have any such formal organization, but it can range from a street peddler to General Motors."

Exam Probability: **Medium**

27. *Answer choices:*
(see index for correct answer)

- a. Absentee business owner
- b. Encore fellowships
- c. Business
- d. Employee experience management

Guidance: level 1

:: Stochastic processes ::

_____ is a system of rules that are created and enforced through social or governmental institutions to regulate behavior. It has been defined both as "the Science of Justice" and "the Art of Justice". _____ is a system that regulates and ensures that individuals or a community adhere to the will of the state. State-enforced _____ s can be made by a collective legislature or by a single legislator, resulting in statutes, by the executive through decrees and regulations, or established by judges through precedent, normally in common _____ jurisdictions. Private individuals can create legally binding contracts, including arbitration agreements that may elect to accept alternative arbitration to the normal court process. The formation of _____ s themselves may be influenced by a constitution, written or tacit, and the rights encoded therein. The _____ shapes politics, economics, history and society in various ways and serves as a mediator of relations between people.

Exam Probability: **High**

28. *Answer choices:*

(see index for correct answer)

- a. Continuous-time stochastic process
- b. Brownian bridge
- c. Feller process
- d. Law

Guidance: level 1

:: Payments ::

A _____ is the trade of value from one party to another for goods, or services, or to fulfill a legal obligation.

Exam Probability: Low

29. *Answer choices:*

(see index for correct answer)

- a. County payments
- b. Payment
- c. Market transition payments
- d. Thirty pieces of silver

Guidance: level 1

:: Scientific method ::

In the social sciences and life sciences, a _____ is a research method involving an up-close, in-depth, and detailed examination of a subject of study , as well as its related contextual conditions.

Exam Probability: Low

30. *Answer choices:*

(see index for correct answer)

- a. explanatory research
- b. Preference test
- c. Case study
- d. pilot project

Guidance: level 1

:: Manufacturing ::

A _____ is an object used to extend the ability of an individual to modify features of the surrounding environment. Although many animals use simple _____ s, only human beings, whose use of stone _____ s dates back hundreds of millennia, use _____ s to make other _____ s. The set of _____ s needed to perform different tasks that are part of the same activity is called gear or equipment.

Exam Probability: **Low**

31. *Answer choices:*

(see index for correct answer)

- a. International Material Data System
- b. Tool
- c. Optical comparator
- d. Engineering bill of materials

Guidance: level 1

_____ is a means of protection from financial loss. It is a form of risk management, primarily used to hedge against the risk of a contingent or uncertain loss

Exam Probability: **High**

32. *Answer choices:*

(see index for correct answer)

- a. interpersonal communication
- b. Insurance
- c. co-culture
- d. hierarchical perspective

Guidance: level 1

:: Business ::

_____ is a trade policy that does not restrict imports or exports; it can also be understood as the free market idea applied to international trade. In government, _____ is predominantly advocated by political parties that hold liberal economic positions while economically left-wing and nationalist political parties generally support protectionism, the opposite of _____ .

Exam Probability: **Low**

33. *Answer choices:*

(see index for correct answer)

- a. SONGZIO
- b. Attention marketing
- c. Open-book contract
- d. Backward invention

Guidance: level 1

:: Generally Accepted Accounting Principles ::

An _____ or profit and loss account is one of the financial statements of a company and shows the company's revenues and expenses during a particular period.

Exam Probability: **High**

34. *Answer choices:*

(see index for correct answer)

- a. Normal balance
- b. Net income
- c. Gross profit
- d. Deferred income

Guidance: level 1

:: Regression analysis ::

A _____ often refers to a set of documented requirements to be satisfied by a material, design, product, or service. A _____ is often a type of technical standard.

Exam Probability: **High**

35. *Answer choices:*

(see index for correct answer)

- a. Generalized least squares
- b. Specification
- c. Heckman correction
- d. Total sum of squares

Guidance: level 1

:: Rhetoric ::

_____ is the pattern of narrative development that aims to make vivid a place, object, character, or group. _____ is one of four rhetorical modes , along with exposition, argumentation, and narration. In practice it would be difficult to write literature that drew on just one of the four basic modes.

36. *Answer choices:*

(see index for correct answer)

- a. Anacoenosis
- b. Procatalepsis
- c. Rhetoric to Alexander
- d. Dialogus de oratoribus

Guidance: level 1

:: ::

_____ is the collection of mechanisms, processes and relations by which corporations are controlled and operated. Governance structures and principles identify the distribution of rights and responsibilities among different participants in the corporation and include the rules and procedures for making decisions in corporate affairs. _____ is necessary because of the possibility of conflicts of interests between stakeholders, primarily between shareholders and upper management or among shareholders.

37. *Answer choices:*

(see index for correct answer)

- a. hierarchical perspective

- b. cultural
- c. Corporate governance
- d. corporate values

Guidance: level 1

:: Social security ::

_____ is "any government system that provides monetary assistance to people with an inadequate or no income." In the United States, this is usually called welfare or a social safety net, especially when talking about Canada and European countries.

Exam Probability: **Low**

38. *Answer choices:*

(see index for correct answer)

- a. Employees%27 State Insurance
- b. Child benefit
- c. Student benefit
- d. Social security

Guidance: level 1

:: Classification systems ::

_____ is the practice of comparing business processes and performance metrics to industry bests and best practices from other companies. Dimensions typically measured are quality, time and cost.

Exam Probability: **Medium**

39. *Answer choices:*

(see index for correct answer)

- a. Schedule for Affective Disorders and Schizophrenia
- b. Classification of percussion instruments
- c. Benchmarking
- d. Transformed cladistics

Guidance: level 1

:: Management ::

The term _____ refers to measures designed to increase the degree of autonomy and self-determination in people and in communities in order to enable them to represent their interests in a responsible and self-determined way, acting on their own authority. It is the process of becoming stronger and more confident, especially in controlling one`s life and claiming one`s rights. _____ as action refers both to the process of self- _____ and to professional support of people, which enables them to overcome their sense of powerlessness and lack of influence, and to recognize and use their resources. To do work with power.

40. *Answer choices:*

(see index for correct answer)

- a. Supply chain sustainability
- b. Shrinkage
- c. Scenario planning
- d. Empowerment

Guidance: level 1

:: Management ::

A _____ is a method or technique that has been generally accepted as superior to any alternatives because it produces results that are superior to those achieved by other means or because it has become a standard way of doing things, e.g., a standard way of complying with legal or ethical requirements.

41. *Answer choices:*

(see index for correct answer)

- a. Central administration
- b. Best practice
- c. Purchasing management

- d. Innovation leadership

Guidance: level 1

:: Supply chain management terms ::

In business and finance, _____ is a system of organizations, people, activities, information, and resources involved inmoving a product or service from supplier to customer. _____ activities involve the transformation of natural resources, raw materials, and components into a finished product that is delivered to the end customer. In sophisticated _____ systems, used products may re-enter the _____ at any point where residual value is recyclable. _____ s link value chains.

Exam Probability: **Medium**

42. *Answer choices:*
(see index for correct answer)

- a. Supply chain
- b. Final assembly schedule
- c. Work in process
- d. Overstock

Guidance: level 1

:: Non-profit technology ::

Instituto del Tercer Mundo is a Non-Governmental Organization that performs information, communication and education activities. _____ , which was established in 1989, shares the same secretariat and coordinating personnel as Social Watch and is based in Montevideo, Uruguay.

Exam Probability: **Low**

43. *Answer choices:*

(see index for correct answer)

- a. E2D International
- b. John G. McNutt
- c. ITeM
- d. The Planetary Society

Guidance: level 1

:: ::

_____ or accountancy is the measurement, processing, and communication of financial information about economic entities such as businesses and corporations. The modern field was established by the Italian mathematician Luca Pacioli in 1494. _____ , which has been called the "language of business", measures the results of an organization's economic activities and conveys this information to a variety of users, including investors, creditors, management, and regulators. Practitioners of _____ are known as accountants. The terms " _____ " and "financial reporting" are often used as synonyms.

44. *Answer choices:*

(see index for correct answer)

- a. process perspective
- b. interpersonal communication
- c. Accounting
- d. information systems assessment

Guidance: level 1

:: Financial statements ::

In financial accounting, a _____ or statement of financial position or statement of financial condition is a summary of the financial balances of an individual or organization, whether it be a sole proprietorship, a business partnership, a corporation, private limited company or other organization such as Government or not-for-profit entity. Assets, liabilities and ownership equity are listed as of a specific date, such as the end of its financial year. A _____ is often described as a "snapshot of a company's financial condition". Of the four basic financial statements, the _____ is the only statement which applies to a single point in time of a business' calendar year.

45. *Answer choices:*

(see index for correct answer)

- a. Statement on Auditing Standards No. 55
- b. Balance sheet
- c. Consolidated financial statement
- d. Financial report

Guidance: level 1

:: ::

A _____ is any person who contracts to acquire an asset in return for some form of consideration.

Exam Probability: **Medium**

46. *Answer choices:*

(see index for correct answer)

- a. process perspective
- b. Buyer
- c. cultural
- d. similarity-attraction theory

Guidance: level 1

:: Analysis ::

_____ is the process of breaking a complex topic or substance into smaller parts in order to gain a better understanding of it. The technique has been applied in the study of mathematics and logic since before Aristotle , though _____ as a formal concept is a relatively recent development.

Exam Probability: **Medium**

47. *Answer choices:*

(see index for correct answer)

- a. Gompertz constant
- b. Analysis
- c. Dialogical analysis
- d. Analytical quality control

Guidance: level 1

:: Business ::

- a. Demand
- b. Rational addiction
- c. Slutsky equation
- d. Induced consumption

Guidance: level 1

:: Management ::

_____ is the identification, evaluation, and prioritization of risks followed by coordinated and economical application of resources to minimize, monitor, and control the probability or impact of unfortunate events or to maximize the realization of opportunities.

Exam Probability: **Medium**

51. *Answer choices:*

(see index for correct answer)

- a. Product breakdown structure
- b. Management buyout
- c. Certified management consultant
- d. Risk management

Guidance: level 1

:: Evaluation ::

A _____ is an evaluation of a publication, service, or company such as a movie , video game , musical composition , book ; a piece of hardware like a car, home appliance, or computer; or an event or performance, such as a live music concert, play, musical theater show, dance show, or art exhibition. In addition to a critical evaluation, the _____ 's author may assign the work a rating to indicate its relative merit. More loosely, an author may _____ current events, trends, or items in the news. A compilation of _____ s may itself be called a _____ . The New York _____ of Books, for instance, is a collection of essays on literature, culture, and current affairs. National _____ , founded by William F. Buckley, Jr., is an influential conservative magazine, and Monthly _____ is a long-running socialist periodical.

Exam Probability: **Medium**

52. *Answer choices:*

(see index for correct answer)

- a. Scale of one to ten
- b. Educational assessment
- c. Evaluation Assurance Level
- d. Encomium

Guidance: level 1

:: Finance ::

_____ is a field that is concerned with the allocation of assets and liabilities over space and time, often under conditions of risk or uncertainty. _____ can also be defined as the art of money management. Participants in the market aim to price assets based on their risk level, fundamental value, and their expected rate of return. _____ can be split into three sub-categories: public _____ , corporate _____ and personal _____ .

Exam Probability: **Low**

53. *Answer choices:*

(see index for correct answer)

- a. Finance
- b. Chartered Financial Planner
- c. Total value of ownership
- d. Ministry of Finance

Guidance: level 1

:: Market research ::

A _____ is a small, but demographically diverse group of people and whose reactions are studied especially in market research or political analysis in guided or open discussions about a new product or something else to determine the reactions that can be expected from a larger population. It is a form of qualitative research consisting of interviews in which a group of people are asked about their perceptions, opinions, beliefs, and attitudes towards a product, service, concept, advertisement, idea, or packaging. Questions are asked in an interactive group setting where participants are free to talk with other group members. During this process, the researcher either takes notes or records the vital points he or she is getting from the group. Researchers should select members of the _____ carefully for effective and authoritative responses.

Exam Probability: **Medium**

54. *Answer choices:*

(see index for correct answer)

- a. Marketing research
- b. Global environmental analysis
- c. Focus group
- d. Industry analyst

Guidance: level 1

:: Workplace ::

_____ is asystematic determination of a subject's merit, worth and significance, using criteria governed by a set of standards. It can assist an organization, program, design, project or any other intervention or initiative to assess any aim, realisable concept/proposal, or any alternative, to help in decision-making; or to ascertain the degree of achievement or value in regard to the aim and objectives and results of any such action that has been completed. The primary purpose of _____ , in addition to gaining insight into prior or existing initiatives, is to enable reflection and assist in the identification of future change.

Exam Probability: **Medium**

55. *Answer choices:*

(see index for correct answer)

- a. Workplace incivility
- b. Evaluation
- c. Workplace deviance
- d. Workplace friendship

Guidance: level 1

:: Loans ::

In finance, a _____ is the lending of money by one or more individuals, organizations, or other entities to other individuals, organizations etc. The recipient incurs a debt, and is usually liable to pay interest on that debt until it is repaid, and also to repay the principal amount borrowed.

56. *Answer choices:*

(see index for correct answer)

- a. amortizing bond
- b. Government-backed loan
- c. Mortgage Assumption Value
- d. Loan

Guidance: level 1

:: International trade ::

_____ or globalisation is the process of interaction and integration among people, companies, and governments worldwide. As a complex and multifaceted phenomenon, _____ is considered by some as a form of capitalist expansion which entails the integration of local and national economies into a global, unregulated market economy. _____ has grown due to advances in transportation and communication technology. With the increased global interactions comes the growth of international trade, ideas, and culture. _____ is primarily an economic process of interaction and integration that's associated with social and cultural aspects. However, conflicts and diplomacy are also large parts of the history of _____ , and modern _____ .

Exam Probability: **Medium**

57. *Answer choices:*

(see index for correct answer)

- a. Globalization
- b. Cross-border cooperation
- c. Trade route
- d. Northwest Cattle Project

Guidance: level 1

:: International trade ::

_____ involves the transfer of goods or services from one person or entity to another, often in exchange for money. A system or network that allows _____ is called a market.

Exam Probability: **High**

58. *Answer choices:*

(see index for correct answer)

- a. OPEC
- b. Bilateral trade
- c. London Customs Convention
- d. Northwest Cattle Project

Guidance: level 1

:: Goods ::

In most contexts, the concept of _____ denotes the conduct that should be preferred when posed with a choice between possible actions. _____ is generally considered to be the opposite of evil, and is of interest in the study of morality, ethics, religion and philosophy. The specific meaning and etymology of the term and its associated translations among ancient and contemporary languages show substantial variation in its inflection and meaning depending on circumstances of place, history, religious, or philosophical context.

Exam Probability: **Medium**

59. *Answer choices:*
(see index for correct answer)

- a. Experience good
- b. Credence good
- c. Global public good
- d. Good

Guidance: level 1

Management

Management is the administration of an organization, whether it is a business, a not-for-profit organization, or government body. Management includes the activities of setting the strategy of an organization and coordinating the efforts of its employees (or of volunteers) to accomplish its objectives through the application of available resources, such as financial, natural, technological, and human resources.

:: Evaluation ::

A _____ is an evaluation of a publication, service, or company such as a movie , video game , musical composition , book ; a piece of hardware like a car, home appliance, or computer; or an event or performance, such as a live music concert, play, musical theater show, dance show, or art exhibition. In addition to a critical evaluation, the _____ 's author may assign the work a rating to indicate its relative merit. More loosely, an author may _____ current events, trends, or items in the news. A compilation of _____ s may itself be called a _____ . The New York _____ of Books, for instance, is a collection of essays on literature, culture, and current affairs. National _____ , founded by William F. Buckley, Jr., is an influential conservative magazine, and Monthly _____ is a long-running socialist periodical.

Exam Probability: **Medium**

1. *Answer choices:*

(see index for correct answer)

- a. Transferable skills analysis
- b. Educational assessment
- c. Appraisal
- d. Program evaluation

Guidance: level 1

:: Business terms ::

A _____ is a short statement of why an organization exists, what its overall goal is, identifying the goal of its operations: what kind of product or service it provides, its primary customers or market, and its geographical region of operation. It may include a short statement of such fundamental matters as the organization's values or philosophies, a business's main competitive advantages, or a desired future state—the "vision".

2. *Answer choices:*

(see index for correct answer)

- a. organizational capital
- b. noncommercial
- c. back office
- d. Strategic partner

Guidance: level 1

:: Management ::

_____ is a method of quality control which employs statistical methods to monitor and control a process. This helps to ensure that the process operates efficiently, producing more specification-conforming products with less waste . SPC can be applied to any process where the "conforming product" output can be measured. Key tools used in SPC include run charts, control charts, a focus on continuous improvement, and the design of experiments. An example of a process where SPC is applied is manufacturing lines.

3. *Answer choices:*

(see index for correct answer)

- a. Fall guy
- b. Statistical process control
- c. Event chain methodology
- d. Evidence-based management

Guidance: level 1

:: Belief ::

_____ is the study of general and fundamental questions about existence, knowledge, values, reason, mind, and language. Such questions are often posed as problems to be studied or resolved. The term was probably coined by Pythagoras . Philosophical methods include questioning, critical discussion, rational argument, and systematic presentation. Classic philosophical questions include: Is it possible to know anything and to prove it What is most real Philosophers also pose more practical and concrete questions such as: Is there a best way to live Is it better to be just or unjust Do humans have free will

4. *Answer choices:*

(see index for correct answer)

- a. Urdoxa
- b. Transubstantiation
- c. Eschatological verification
- d. Philosophy

Guidance: level 1

:: Information systems ::

_____ is the process of creating, sharing, using and managing the knowledge and information of an organisation. It refers to a multidisciplinary approach to achieving organisational objectives by making the best use of knowledge.

Exam Probability: **Low**

5. *Answer choices:*

(see index for correct answer)

- a. Semantic desktop
- b. Enhanced publication
- c. Information Processes and Technology
- d. DIKW Pyramid

Guidance: level 1

:: Goods ::

In most contexts, the concept of _____ denotes the conduct that should be preferred when posed with a choice between possible actions. _____ is generally considered to be the opposite of evil, and is of interest in the study of morality, ethics, religion and philosophy. The specific meaning and etymology of the term and its associated translations among ancient and contemporary languages show substantial variation in its inflection and meaning depending on circumstances of place, history, religious, or philosophical context.

Exam Probability: **High**

6. *Answer choices:*
(see index for correct answer)

- a. Public good
- b. Private good
- c. Yellow goods
- d. Inferior good

Guidance: level 1

:: Electronic feedback ::

_____ occurs when outputs of a system are routed back as inputs as part of a chain of cause-and-effect that forms a circuit or loop. The system can then be said to feed back into itself. The notion of cause-and-effect has to be handled carefully when applied to _____ systems.

Exam Probability: **High**

7. *Answer choices:*

(see index for correct answer)

- a. Positive feedback
- b. Feedback

Guidance: level 1

:: Game theory ::

To _____ is to make a deal between different parties where each party gives up part of their demand. In arguments, _____ is a concept of finding agreement through communication, through a mutual acceptance of terms—often involving variations from an original goal or desires.

Exam Probability: **Medium**

8. *Answer choices:*

(see index for correct answer)

- a. Compromise
- b. Pirate game
- c. Axiom of projective determinacy
- d. Mutual knowledge

Guidance: level 1

:: ::

_____ involves decision making. It can include judging the merits of multiple options and selecting one or more of them. One can make a _____ between imagined options or between real options followed by the corresponding action. For example, a traveler might choose a route for a journey based on the preference of arriving at a given destination as soon as possible. The preferred route can then follow from information such as the length of each of the possible routes, traffic conditions, etc. The arrival at a _____ can include more complex motivators such as cognition, instinct, and feeling.

Exam Probability: **Medium**

9. *Answer choices:*

(see index for correct answer)

- a. information systems assessment
- b. Sarbanes-Oxley act of 2002
- c. personal values
- d. Choice

:: Critical thinking ::

An _____ is a set of statements usually constructed to describe a set of facts which clarifies the causes, context, and consequences of those facts. This description of the facts et cetera may establish rules or laws, and may clarify the existing rules or laws in relation to any objects, or phenomena examined. The components of an _____ can be implicit, and interwoven with one another.

Exam Probability: **High**

10. *Answer choices:*

(see index for correct answer)

- a. Interpretive discussion
- b. Project Reason
- c. Informal logic
- d. Explanation

:: ::

_____ is the process of making predictions of the future based on past and present data and most commonly by analysis of trends. A commonplace example might be estimation of some variable of interest at some specified future date. Prediction is a similar, but more general term. Both might refer to formal statistical methods employing time series, cross-sectional or longitudinal data, or alternatively to less formal judgmental methods. Usage can differ between areas of application: for example, in hydrology the terms "forecast" and "_____" are sometimes reserved for estimates of values at certain specific future times, while the term "prediction" is used for more general estimates, such as the number of times floods will occur over a long period.

Exam Probability: **Medium**

11. *Answer choices:*

(see index for correct answer)

- a. cultural
- b. deep-level diversity
- c. open system
- d. Character

Guidance: level 1

:: Management ::

In the field of management, _____ involves the formulation and implementation of the major goals and initiatives taken by an organization's top management on behalf of owners, based on consideration of resources and an assessment of the internal and external environments in which the organization operates.

Exam Probability: **Low**

12. *Answer choices:*

(see index for correct answer)

- a. Concept of operations
- b. PhD in management
- c. Risk management
- d. Strategic management

Guidance: level 1

:: ::

_____ is the stock of habits, knowledge, social and personality attributes embodied in the ability to perform labor so as to produce economic value.

Exam Probability: **High**

13. *Answer choices:*

(see index for correct answer)

- a. co-culture
- b. imperative
- c. Human capital
- d. process perspective

Guidance: level 1

:: ::

_____ is the consumption and saving opportunity gained by an entity within a specified timeframe, which is generally expressed in monetary terms. For households and individuals, " _____ is the sum of all the wages, salaries, profits, interest payments, rents, and other forms of earnings received in a given period of time."

Exam Probability: **Medium**

14. *Answer choices:*
(see index for correct answer)

- a. cultural
- b. Income
- c. similarity-attraction theory
- d. functional perspective

:: ::

_____ , known in Europe as research and technological development , refers to innovative activities undertaken by corporations or governments in developing new services or products, or improving existing services or products. _____ constitutes the first stage of development of a potential new service or the production process.

Exam Probability: **Medium**

15. *Answer choices:*

(see index for correct answer)

- a. hierarchical perspective
- b. imperative
- c. Character
- d. Research and development

:: ::

_____ is the exchange of capital, goods, and services across international borders or territories.

Exam Probability: **Medium**

16. *Answer choices:*

(see index for correct answer)

- a. hierarchical
- b. interpersonal communication
- c. International trade
- d. Sarbanes-Oxley act of 2002

Guidance: level 1

:: Management ::

The term _____ refers to measures designed to increase the degree of autonomy and self-determination in people and in communities in order to enable them to represent their interests in a responsible and self-determined way, acting on their own authority. It is the process of becoming stronger and more confident, especially in controlling one`s life and claiming one`s rights. _____ as action refers both to the process of self- _____ and to professional support of people, which enables them to overcome their sense of powerlessness and lack of influence, and to recognize and use their resources. To do work with power.

Exam Probability: **High**

17. *Answer choices:*

- a. Smiling curve
- b. Empowerment
- c. Swarm Development Group
- d. Logistics support analysis

Guidance: level 1

:: Lean manufacturing ::

A continual improvement process, also often called a _____ process , is an ongoing effort to improve products, services, or processes. These efforts can seek "incremental" improvement over time or "breakthrough" improvement all at once. Delivery processes are constantly evaluated and improved in the light of their efficiency, effectiveness and flexibility.

Exam Probability: **High**

18. *Answer choices:*

- a. Autonomation
- b. Setsuban Kanri
- c. Lean services
- d. Continuous improvement

:: Workplace ::

A _____ is a process through which feedback from an employee's subordinates, colleagues, and supervisor, as well as a self-evaluation by the employee themselves is gathered. Such feedback can also include, when relevant, feedback from external sources who interact with the employee, such as customers and suppliers or other interested stakeholders. _____ is so named because it solicits feedback regarding an employee's behavior from a variety of points of view . It therefore may be contrasted with "downward feedback" , or "upward feedback" delivered to supervisory or management employees by subordinates only.

Exam Probability: **Medium**

19. *Answer choices:*

(see index for correct answer)

- a. Evaluation
- b. Open allocation
- c. Workplace conflict
- d. Workplace deviance

:: Leadership ::

_____ is a theory of leadership where a leader works with teams to identify needed change, creating a vision to guide the change through inspiration, and executing the change in tandem with committed members of a group; it is an integral part of the Full Range Leadership Model. _____ serves to enhance the motivation, morale, and job performance of followers through a variety of mechanisms; these include connecting the follower's sense of identity and self to a project and to the collective identity of the organization; being a role model for followers in order to inspire them and to raise their interest in the project; challenging followers to take greater ownership for their work, and understanding the strengths and weaknesses of followers, allowing the leader to align followers with tasks that enhance their performance.

Exam Probability: **High**

20. *Answer choices:*

(see index for correct answer)

- a. Evolutionary leadership theory
- b. Coro
- c. Transactional leadership
- d. Sex differences in leadership

Guidance: level 1

:: Project management ::

_____ and Theory Y are theories of human work motivation and management. They were created by Douglas McGregor while he was working at the MIT Sloan School of Management in the 1950s, and developed further in the 1960s. McGregor's work was rooted in motivation theory alongside the works of Abraham Maslow, who created the hierarchy of needs. The two theories proposed by McGregor describe contrasting models of workforce motivation applied by managers in human resource management, organizational behavior, organizational communication and organizational development. _____ explains the importance of heightened supervision, external rewards, and penalties, while Theory Y highlights the motivating role of job satisfaction and encourages workers to approach tasks without direct supervision. Management use of _____ and Theory Y can affect employee motivation and productivity in different ways, and managers may choose to implement strategies from both theories into their practices.

Exam Probability: **Medium**

21. *Answer choices:*

(see index for correct answer)

- a. Soft Costs
- b. Project
- c. overdue
- d. Opportunity management

Guidance: level 1

:: Market research ::

_____ is an organized effort to gather information about target markets or customers. It is a very important component of business strategy. The term is commonly interchanged with marketing research; however, expert practitioners may wish to draw a distinction, in that marketing research is concerned specifically about marketing processes, while _____ is concerned specifically with markets.

Exam Probability: **High**

22. *Answer choices:*

(see index for correct answer)

- a. Market research
- b. The Ehrenberg-Bass Institute for Marketing Science
- c. Online panel
- d. Brand elections

Guidance: level 1

:: Project management ::

A _____ is a source or supply from which a benefit is produced and it has some utility. _____ s can broadly be classified upon their availability—they are classified into renewable and non-renewable _____ s.Examples of non renewable _____ s are coal ,crude oil natural gas nuclear energy etc. Examples of renewable _____ s are air,water,wind,solar energy etc. They can also be classified as actual and potential on the basis of level of development and use, on the basis of origin they can be classified as biotic and abiotic, and on the basis of their distribution, as ubiquitous and localized . An item becomes a _____ with time and developing technology. Typically, _____ s are materials, energy, services, staff, knowledge, or other assets that are transformed to produce benefit and in the process may be consumed or made unavailable. Benefits of _____ utilization may include increased wealth, proper functioning of a system, or enhanced well-being. From a human perspective a natural _____ is anything obtained from the environment to satisfy human needs and wants. From a broader biological or ecological perspective a _____ satisfies the needs of a living organism .

Exam Probability: **Low**

23. *Answer choices:*

(see index for correct answer)

- a. Project Management South Africa
- b. Integrated product team
- c. Resource
- d. Test and evaluation master plan

Guidance: level 1

:: ::

A _____ is an individual or institution that legally owns one or more shares of stock in a public or private corporation. _____ s may be referred to as members of a corporation. Legally, a person is not a _____ in a corporation until their name and other details are entered in the corporation's register of _____ s or members.

24. *Answer choices:*

(see index for correct answer)

- a. process perspective
- b. cultural
- c. Shareholder
- d. information systems assessment

Guidance: level 1

:: Data analysis ::

In statistics, the _____ is a measure that is used to quantify the amount of variation or dispersion of a set of data values. A low _____ indicates that the data points tend to be close to the mean of the set, while a high _____ indicates that the data points are spread out over a wider range of values.

25. *Answer choices:*

(see index for correct answer)

- a. Experimental uncertainty analysis
- b. Standard deviation
- c. Barnardisation
- d. Exponential smoothing

Guidance: level 1

:: Management accounting ::

_____ s are costs that change as the quantity of the good or service that a business produces changes. _____ s are the sum of marginal costs over all units produced. They can also be considered normal costs. Fixed costs and _____ s make up the two components of total cost. Direct costs are costs that can easily be associated with a particular cost object. However, not all _____ s are direct costs. For example, variable manufacturing overhead costs are _____ s that are indirect costs, not direct costs. _____ s are sometimes called unit-level costs as they vary with the number of units produced.

Exam Probability: **Medium**

26. *Answer choices:*

(see index for correct answer)

- a. Management control system
- b. Fixed assets management

- c. Variable cost
- d. Backflush accounting

:: Rhetoric ::

_____ is the pattern of narrative development that aims to make vivid a place, object, character, or group. _____ is one of four rhetorical modes , along with exposition, argumentation, and narration. In practice it would be difficult to write literature that drew on just one of the four basic modes.

Exam Probability: **Low**

27. *Answer choices:*

(see index for correct answer)

- a. Parachesis
- b. Pathos
- c. Description
- d. Antithetic parallelism

:: Management ::

_____ is a process by which entities review the quality of all factors involved in production. ISO 9000 defines _____ as "A part of quality management focused on fulfilling quality requirements".

Exam Probability: **High**

28. *Answer choices:*

(see index for correct answer)

- a. Quality control
- b. Staff management
- c. Supply chain optimization
- d. Earned value management

Guidance: level 1

:: Organizational theory ::

Decentralisation is the process by which the activities of an organization, particularly those regarding planning and decision making, are distributed or delegated away from a central, authoritative location or group. Concepts of _____ have been applied to group dynamics and management science in private businesses and organizations, political science, law and public administration, economics, money and technology.

Exam Probability: **High**

29. *Answer choices:*

- a. Bureaucracy
- b. Decentralization
- c. Imprinting
- d. resource dependence

Guidance: level 1

:: Decision theory ::

A _____ is a deliberate system of principles to guide decisions and achieve rational outcomes. A _____ is a statement of intent, and is implemented as a procedure or protocol. Policies are generally adopted by a governance body within an organization. Policies can assist in both subjective and objective decision making. Policies to assist in subjective decision making usually assist senior management with decisions that must be based on the relative merits of a number of factors, and as a result are often hard to test objectively, e.g. work-life balance _____ . In contrast policies to assist in objective decision making are usually operational in nature and can be objectively tested, e.g. password _____ .

Exam Probability: **Medium**

30. *Answer choices:*

- a. Policy

- b. Applied information economics
- c. Two-moment decision model
- d. Bulk Dispatch Lapse

Guidance: level 1

:: Marketing techniques ::

In industry, product lifecycle management is the process of managing the entire lifecycle of a product from inception, through engineering design and manufacture, to service and disposal of manufactured products. PLM integrates people, data, processes and business systems and provides a product information backbone for companies and their extended enterprise.

Exam Probability: **Medium**

31. *Answer choices:*

(see index for correct answer)

- a. AISDALSLove
- b. Unique perceived benefit
- c. Prize
- d. Intent marketing

Guidance: level 1

:: Human resource management ::

_____ is a core function of human resource management and it is related to the specification of contents, methods and relationship of jobs in order to satisfy technological and organizational requirements as well as the social and personal requirements of the job holder or the employee. Its principles are geared towards how the nature of a person's job affects their attitudes and behavior at work, particularly relating to characteristics such as skill variety and autonomy. The aim of a _____ is to improve job satisfaction, to improve through-put, to improve quality and to reduce employee problems .

Exam Probability: **Low**

32. *Answer choices:*

(see index for correct answer)

- a. Talent supply chain management
- b. Job design
- c. Administrative services organization
- d. Skills management

Guidance: level 1

:: Labour relations ::

_____ is a field of study that can have different meanings depending on the context in which it is used. In an international context, it is a subfield of labor history that studies the human relations with regard to work – in its broadest sense – and how this connects to questions of social inequality. It explicitly encompasses unregulated, historical, and non-Western forms of labor. Here, _____ define "for or with whom one works and under what rules. These rules determine the type of work, type and amount of remuneration, working hours, degrees of physical and psychological strain, as well as the degree of freedom and autonomy associated with the work."

Exam Probability: **Low**

33. *Answer choices:*

(see index for correct answer)

- a. Negotiated cartelism
- b. Labor relations
- c. Acas
- d. Boulwarism

Guidance: level 1

:: ::

In communications and information processing, _____ is a system of rules to convert information—such as a letter, word, sound, image, or gesture—into another form or representation, sometimes shortened or secret, for communication through a communication channel or storage in a storage medium. An early example is the invention of language, which enabled a person, through speech, to communicate what they saw, heard, felt, or thought to others. But speech limits the range of communication to the distance a voice can carry, and limits the audience to those present when the speech is uttered. The invention of writing, which converted spoken language into visual symbols, extended the range of communication across space and time.

Exam Probability: **Low**

34. *Answer choices:*

(see index for correct answer)

- a. cultural
- b. open system
- c. similarity-attraction theory
- d. process perspective

Guidance: level 1

:: Time management ::

_____ is the process of planning and exercising conscious control of time spent on specific activities, especially to increase effectiveness, efficiency, and productivity. It involves a juggling act of various demands upon a person relating to work, social life, family, hobbies, personal interests and commitments with the finiteness of time. Using time effectively gives the person "choice" on spending/managing activities at their own time and expediency.

Exam Probability: **Medium**

35. *Answer choices:*

(see index for correct answer)

- a. Sufficient unto the day is the evil thereof
- b. HabitRPG
- c. Maestro concept
- d. Time perception

Guidance: level 1

:: ::

An _____ is a contingent motivator. Traditional _____ s are extrinsic motivators which reward actions to yield a desired outcome. The effectiveness of traditional _____ s has changed as the needs of Western society have evolved. While the traditional _____ model is effective when there is a defined procedure and goal for a task, Western society started to require a higher volume of critical thinkers, so the traditional model became less effective. Institutions are now following a trend in implementing strategies that rely on intrinsic motivations rather than the extrinsic motivations that the traditional _____ s foster.

Exam Probability: **Low**

36. *Answer choices:*

(see index for correct answer)

- a. personal values
- b. hierarchical
- c. information systems assessment
- d. Incentive

Guidance: level 1

:: Product management ::

_____ s, also known as Shewhart charts or process-behavior charts, are a statistical process control tool used to determine if a manufacturing or business process is in a state of control.

37. *Answer choices:*

(see index for correct answer)

- a. Trademark look
- b. Control chart
- c. Trademark distinctiveness
- d. Whole product

Guidance: level 1

:: Unemployment ::

In economics, a _____ is a business cycle contraction when there is a general decline in economic activity. Macroeconomic indicators such as GDP , investment spending, capacity utilization, household income, business profits, and inflation fall, while bankruptcies and the unemployment rate rise. In the United Kingdom, it is defined as a negative economic growth for two consecutive quarters.

Exam Probability: **High**

38. *Answer choices:*

(see index for correct answer)

- a. Organization Workshop
- b. Wage curve

- c. Outplacement
- d. Recession

Guidance: level 1

:: Employment ::

_____ is a relationship between two parties, usually based on a contract where work is paid for, where one party, which may be a corporation, for profit, not-for-profit organization, co-operative or other entity is the employer and the other is the employee. Employees work in return for payment, which may be in the form of an hourly wage, by piecework or an annual salary, depending on the type of work an employee does or which sector she or he is working in. Employees in some fields or sectors may receive gratuities, bonus payment or stock options. In some types of _____ , employees may receive benefits in addition to payment. Benefits can include health insurance, housing, disability insurance or use of a gym. _____ is typically governed by _____ laws, regulations or legal contracts.

Exam Probability: **Medium**

39. *Answer choices:*

(see index for correct answer)

- a. PATCOB
- b. Attendance allowance
- c. Cyberloafing
- d. Contingent workforce

:: Power (social and political) ::

_____ is a form of reverence gained by a leader who has strong interpersonal relationship skills. _____ , as an aspect of personal power, becomes particularly important as organizational leadership becomes increasingly about collaboration and influence, rather than command and control.

Exam Probability: **Medium**

40. *Answer choices:*
(see index for correct answer)

- a. Expert power
- b. need for power
- c. Referent power

:: Workplace ::

A _____ , also referred to as a performance review, performance evaluation, development discussion, or employee appraisal is a method by which the job performance of an employee is documented and evaluated. _____ s are a part of career development and consist of regular reviews of employee performance within organizations.

Exam Probability: **Low**

41. *Answer choices:*

(see index for correct answer)

- a. Workplace listening
- b. performance review
- c. Work etiquette
- d. Workplace aggression

Guidance: level 1

:: Human resource management ::

_____ are the people who make up the workforce of an organization, business sector, or economy. "Human capital" is sometimes used synonymously with " _____ ", although human capital typically refers to a narrower effect . Likewise, other terms sometimes used include manpower, talent, labor, personnel, or simply people.

Exam Probability: **Medium**

42. *Answer choices:*

(see index for correct answer)

- a. Vendor on premises
- b. Illness rate
- c. Disciplinary probation
- d. Human resources

Guidance: level 1

:: ::

An _____ is a process where candidates are examined to determine their suitability for specific types of employment, especially management or military command. The candidates' personality and aptitudes are determined by techniques including interviews, group exercises, presentations, examinations and psychometric testing.

Exam Probability: **High**

43. *Answer choices:*

(see index for correct answer)

- a. similarity-attraction theory
- b. Assessment center
- c. surface-level diversity
- d. cultural

:: Reputation management ::

_____ or image of a social entity is an opinion about that entity, typically as a result of social evaluation on a set of criteria.

Exam Probability: **Low**

44. *Answer choices:*

(see index for correct answer)

- a. BrandYourself
- b. Raph Levien
- c. Meta-moderation system
- d. Reputation

:: Workplace ::

_____ is a systematic determination of a subject's merit, worth and significance, using criteria governed by a set of standards. It can assist an organization, program, design, project or any other intervention or initiative to assess any aim, realisable concept/proposal, or any alternative, to help in decision-making; or to ascertain the degree of achievement or value in regard to the aim and objectives and results of any such action that has been completed. The primary purpose of _____ , in addition to gaining insight into prior or existing initiatives, is to enable reflection and assist in the identification of future change.

Exam Probability: **Medium**

45. *Answer choices:*

(see index for correct answer)

- a. Hostile environment sexual harassment
- b. Workplace friendship
- c. Workplace aggression
- d. Evaluation

Guidance: level 1

:: Labor rights ::

A _____ is a wrong or hardship suffered, real or supposed, which forms legitimate grounds of complaint. In the past, the word meant the infliction or cause of hardship.

46. *Answer choices:*

(see index for correct answer)

- a. Grievance
- b. China Labor Watch
- c. The Hyatt 100
- d. Swift raids

Guidance: level 1

:: ::

_____ is a means of protection from financial loss. It is a form of risk management, primarily used to hedge against the risk of a contingent or uncertain loss

Exam Probability: **Low**

47. *Answer choices:*

(see index for correct answer)

- a. interpersonal communication
- b. personal values
- c. open system
- d. Sarbanes-Oxley act of 2002

:: Hospitality management ::

A _____ is an establishment that provides paid lodging on a short-term basis. Facilities provided may range from a modest-quality mattress in a small room to large suites with bigger, higher-quality beds, a dresser, a refrigerator and other kitchen facilities, upholstered chairs, a flat screen television, and en-suite bathrooms. Small, lower-priced _____ s may offer only the most basic guest services and facilities. Larger, higher-priced _____ s may provide additional guest facilities such as a swimming pool, business centre , childcare, conference and event facilities, tennis or basketball courts, gymnasium, restaurants, day spa, and social function services. _____ rooms are usually numbered to allow guests to identify their room. Some boutique, high-end _____ s have custom decorated rooms. Some _____ s offer meals as part of a room and board arrangement. In the United Kingdom, a _____ is required by law to serve food and drinks to all guests within certain stated hours. In Japan, capsule _____ s provide a tiny room suitable only for sleeping and shared bathroom facilities.

Exam Probability: **Low**

48. *Answer choices:*

(see index for correct answer)

- a. BSc. HCM
- b. Hospitality consulting
- c. Hotel
- d. RateGain

:: Management ::

A _____ describes the rationale of how an organization creates, delivers, and captures value, in economic, social, cultural or other contexts. The process of _____ construction and modification is also called _____ innovation and forms a part of business strategy.

Exam Probability: **High**

49. *Answer choices:*

(see index for correct answer)

- a. Bed management
- b. Business model
- c. Business rule mining
- d. Quick response manufacturing

:: Strategic alliances ::

A _____ is an agreement between two or more parties to pursue a set of agreed upon objectives needed while remaining independent organizations. A _____ will usually fall short of a legal partnership entity, agency, or corporate affiliate relationship. Typically, two companies form a _____ when each possesses one or more business assets or have expertise that will help the other by enhancing their businesses. _____ s can develop in outsourcing relationships where the parties desire to achieve long-term win-win benefits and innovation based on mutually desired outcomes.

Exam Probability: **Low**

50. *Answer choices:*

(see index for correct answer)

- a. International joint venture
- b. Bridge Alliance
- c. Cross-licensing
- d. Strategic alliance

Guidance: level 1

:: Psychometrics ::

_____ is a dynamic, structured, interactive process where a neutral third party assists disputing parties in resolving conflict through the use of specialized communication and negotiation techniques. All participants in _____ are encouraged to actively participate in the process. _____ is a "party-centered" process in that it is focused primarily upon the needs, rights, and interests of the parties. The mediator uses a wide variety of techniques to guide the process in a constructive direction and to help the parties find their optimal solution. A mediator is facilitative in that she/he manages the interaction between parties and facilitates open communication. _____ is also evaluative in that the mediator analyzes issues and relevant norms, while refraining from providing prescriptive advice to the parties.

Exam Probability: **Medium**

51. *Answer choices:*

(see index for correct answer)

- a. Computerized classification test
- b. Francis Galton
- c. Objective test
- d. Multistage testing

Guidance: level 1

:: Statistical terminology ::

_____ is the ability to avoid wasting materials, energy, efforts, money, and time in doing something or in producing a desired result. In a more general sense, it is the ability to do things well, successfully, and without waste. In more mathematical or scientific terms, it is a measure of the extent to which input is well used for an intended task or function . It often specifically comprises the capability of a specific application of effort to produce a specific outcome with a minimum amount or quantity of waste, expense, or unnecessary effort. _____ refers to very different inputs and outputs in different fields and industries.

Exam Probability: **High**

52. *Answer choices:*

(see index for correct answer)

- a. Degrees of freedom
- b. Collectively exhaustive
- c. Univariate
- d. Univariate distribution

Guidance: level 1

:: ::

A _____ is an approximate imitation of the operation of a process or system; the act of simulating first requires a model is developed. This model is a well-defined description of the simulated subject, and represents its key characteristics, such as its behaviour, functions and abstract or physical properties. The model represents the system itself, whereas the _____ represents its operation over time.

Exam Probability: **Medium**

53. *Answer choices:*

(see index for correct answer)

- a. interpersonal communication
- b. hierarchical perspective
- c. personal values
- d. Simulation

Guidance: level 1

:: Business process ::

A _____ or business method is a collection of related, structured activities or tasks by people or equipment which in a specific sequence produce a service or product for a particular customer or customers. _____ es occur at all organizational levels and may or may not be visible to the customers. A _____ may often be visualized as a flowchart of a sequence of activities with interleaving decision points or as a process matrix of a sequence of activities with relevance rules based on data in the process. The benefits of using _____ es include improved customer satisfaction and improved agility for reacting to rapid market change. Process-oriented organizations break down the barriers of structural departments and try to avoid functional silos.

Exam Probability: **High**

54. *Answer choices:*

(see index for correct answer)

- a. Business logic
- b. Bizagi
- c. Business process
- d. Outsourced document processing

Guidance: level 1

:: Packaging ::

In work place, _____ or job _____ means good ranking with the hypothesized conception of requirements of a role. There are two types of job _____ s: contextual and task. Task _____ is related to cognitive ability while contextual _____ is dependent upon personality. Task _____ are behavioral roles that are recognized in job descriptions and by remuneration systems, they are directly related to organizational _____ , whereas, contextual _____ are value based and additional behavioral roles that are not recognized in job descriptions and covered by compensation; they are extra roles that are indirectly related to organizational _____ . Citizenship _____ like contextual _____ means a set of individual activity/contribution that supports the organizational culture.

Exam Probability: **High**

55. *Answer choices:*

(see index for correct answer)

- a. Doypack
- b. Shrink bands
- c. Plain cigarette packaging
- d. Performance

Guidance: level 1

:: Organizational theory ::

A _____ is an organizational theory that claims that there is no best way to organize a corporation, to lead a company, or to make decisions. Instead, the optimal course of action is contingent upon the internal and external situation. A contingent leader effectively applies their own style of leadership to the right situation.

Exam Probability: **Medium**

56. *Answer choices:*

(see index for correct answer)

- a. Bureaucratic inertia
- b. Conflict
- c. Organisational semiotics
- d. Organizational change fatigue

Guidance: level 1

:: Majority–minority relations ::

_____ , also known as reservation in India and Nepal, positive discrimination / action in the United Kingdom, and employment equity in Canada and South Africa, is the policy of promoting the education and employment of members of groups that are known to have previously suffered from discrimination. Historically and internationally, support for _____ has sought to achieve goals such as bridging inequalities in employment and pay, increasing access to education, promoting diversity, and redressing apparent past wrongs, harms, or hindrances.

57. *Answer choices:*

(see index for correct answer)

- a. positive discrimination
- b. cultural dissonance
- c. Affirmative action

Guidance: level 1

:: Human resource management ::

_____ , also known as management by results , was first popularized by Peter Drucker in his 1954 book The Practice of Management. _____ is the process of defining specific objectives within an organization that management can convey to organization members, then deciding on how to achieve each objective in sequence. This process allows managers to take work that needs to be done one step at a time to allow for a calm, yet productive work environment. This process also helps organization members to see their accomplishments as they achieve each objective, which reinforces a positive work environment and a sense of achievement. An important part of MBO is the measurement and comparison of an employee's actual performance with the standards set. Ideally, when employees themselves have been involved with the goal-setting and choosing the course of action to be followed by them, they are more likely to fulfill their responsibilities.According to George S. Odiorne, the system of _____ can be described as a process whereby the superior and subordinate jointly identify common goals, define each individual's major areas of responsibility in terms of the results expected of him or her, and use these measures as guides for operating the unit and assessing the contribution of each of its members.

58. *Answer choices:*

(see index for correct answer)

- a. Chartered Institute of Personnel and Development
- b. E-HRM
- c. At-will employment
- d. Illness rate

Guidance: level 1

:: Marketing ::

_____ is based on a marketing concept which can be adopted by an organization as a strategy for business expansion. Where implemented, a franchisor licenses its know-how, procedures, intellectual property, use of its business model, brand, and rights to sell its branded products and services to a franchisee. In return the franchisee pays certain fees and agrees to comply with certain obligations, typically set out in a Franchise Agreement.

Exam Probability: **Medium**

59. *Answer choices:*

(see index for correct answer)

- a. The customer is always right
- b. Book of business

- c. Content creation
- d. Franchising

Guidance: level 1

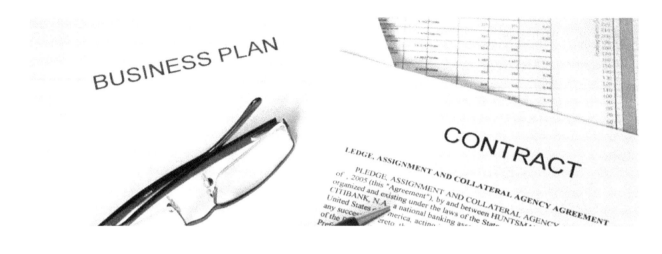

Business law

Corporate law (also known as business law) is the body of law governing the rights, relations, and conduct of persons, companies, organizations and businesses. It refers to the legal practice relating to, or the theory of corporations. Corporate law often describes the law relating to matters which derive directly from the life-cycle of a corporation. It thus encompasses the formation, funding, governance, and death of a corporation.

:: Business law ::

A _____ is a business entity created by two or more parties, generally characterized by shared ownership, shared returns and risks, and shared governance. Companies typically pursue _____ s for one of four reasons: to access a new market, particularly emerging markets; to gain scale efficiencies by combining assets and operations; to share risk for major investments or projects; or to access skills and capabilities.

Exam Probability: **High**

- a. Valuation using the Market Penetration Model
- b. Joint venture
- c. Trading while insolvent
- d. Output contract

Guidance: level 1

:: Business law ::

A _____ is a form of security interest granted over an item of property to secure the payment of a debt or performance of some other obligation. The owner of the property, who grants the _____ , is referred to as the _____ ee and the person who has the benefit of the _____ is referred to as the _____ or or _____ holder.

Exam Probability: **Medium**

- a. Wrongful trading
- b. Negative option billing
- c. Company mortgage
- d. Unfair competition

:: Law ::

_____ is a body of law which defines the role, powers, and structure of different entities within a state, namely, the executive, the parliament or legislature, and the judiciary; as well as the basic rights of citizens and, in federal countries such as the United States and Canada, the relationship between the central government and state, provincial, or territorial governments.

Exam Probability: **High**

3. *Answer choices:*

(see index for correct answer)

- a. Comparative law
- b. Legal case

:: ::

A _____ is a formal presentation of a matter such as a complaint, indictment or bill of exchange. In early-medieval England, juries of _____ would hear inquests in order to establish whether someone should be presented for a crime.

Exam Probability: **Medium**

4. *Answer choices:*

(see index for correct answer)

- a. imperative
- b. similarity-attraction theory
- c. personal values
- d. Presentment

Guidance: level 1

:: Contract law ::

_____ , also called an anticipatory breach, is a term in the law of contracts that describes a declaration by the promising party to a contract that he or she does not intend to live up to his or her obligations under the contract.

Exam Probability: **Medium**

5. *Answer choices:*

(see index for correct answer)

- a. Franchisor
- b. Multimarket contact
- c. Anticipatory repudiation
- d. Warranty tolling

Guidance: level 1

:: Judgment (law) ::

In law, a _____ is a judgment entered by a court for one party and against another party summarily, i.e., without a full trial. Such a judgment may be issued on the merits of an entire case, or on discrete issues in that case.

Exam Probability: **Low**

6. *Answer choices:*
(see index for correct answer)

- a. judgment as a matter of law
- b. Entry of judgment

Guidance: level 1

The _____ is an intergovernmental organization that is concerned with the regulation of international trade between nations. The WTO officially commenced on 1 January 1995 under the Marrakesh Agreement, signed by 124 nations on 15 April 1994, replacing the General Agreement on Tariffs and Trade , which commenced in 1948. It is the largest international economic organization in the world.

Exam Probability: **Medium**

7. *Answer choices:*

(see index for correct answer)

- a. interpersonal communication
- b. functional perspective
- c. co-culture
- d. hierarchical perspective

Guidance: level 1

:: Clauses of the United States Constitution ::

The _____ describes an enumerated power listed in the United States Constitution . The clause states that the United States Congress shall have power "To regulate Commerce with foreign Nations, and among the several States, and with the Indian Tribes." Courts and commentators have tended to discuss each of these three areas of commerce as a separate power granted to Congress. It is common to see the individual components of the _____ referred to under specific terms: the Foreign _____ , the Interstate _____ , and the Indian _____ .

Exam Probability: **High**

8. *Answer choices:*

(see index for correct answer)

- a. Double Jeopardy Clause
- b. Full faith and credit
- c. Full Faith and Credit Clause

Guidance: level 1

:: Business law ::

In the United States, the United Kingdom, Australia, Canada and South Africa, _____ relates to the doctrines of the law of agency. It is relevant particularly in corporate law and constitutional law. _____ refers to a situation where a reasonable third party would understand that an agent had authority to act. This means a principal is bound by the agent's actions, even if the agent had no actual authority, whether express or implied. It raises an estoppel because the third party is given an assurance, which he relies on and would be inequitable for the principal to deny the authority given. _____ can legally be found, even if actual authority has not been given.

Exam Probability: **High**

9. *Answer choices:*

(see index for correct answer)

- a. Practicing without a license
- b. Leave of absence
- c. Financial Security Law of France
- d. Undervalue transaction

Guidance: level 1

:: ::

A _____ loan or, simply, _____ is used either by purchasers of real property to raise funds to buy real estate, or alternatively by existing property owners to raise funds for any purpose, while putting a lien on the property being _____ d. The loan is "secured" on the borrower's property through a process known as _____ origination. This means that a legal mechanism is put into place which allows the lender to take possession and sell the secured property to pay off the loan in the event the borrower defaults on the loan or otherwise fails to abide by its terms. The word _____ is derived from a Law French term used in Britain in the Middle Ages meaning "death pledge" and refers to the pledge ending when either the obligation is fulfilled or the property is taken through foreclosure. A _____ can also be described as "a borrower giving consideration in the form of a collateral for a benefit ".

Exam Probability: **High**

10. *Answer choices:*

(see index for correct answer)

- a. cultural
- b. information systems assessment
- c. Mortgage
- d. surface-level diversity

Guidance: level 1

:: Legal terms ::

_____ , or exemplary damages, are damages assessed in order to punish the defendant for outrageous conduct and/or to reform or deter the defendant and others from engaging in conduct similar to that which formed the basis of the lawsuit. Although the purpose of _____ is not to compensate the plaintiff, the plaintiff will receive all or some of the _____ award.

Exam Probability: **Low**

11. *Answer choices:*

(see index for correct answer)

- a. Precommitment
- b. Person of interest
- c. Punitive damages
- d. Guarantor

Guidance: level 1

:: Business law ::

An _____ is a clause in a contract that requires the parties to resolve their disputes through an arbitration process. Although such a clause may or may not specify that arbitration occur within a specific jurisdiction, it always binds the parties to a type of resolution outside the courts, and is therefore considered a kind of forum selection clause.

Exam Probability: **Low**

12. *Answer choices:*

(see index for correct answer)

- a. Arbitration clause
- b. Tax patent
- c. Facilitating payment
- d. Voting trust

Guidance: level 1

:: ::

Credit is the trust which allows one party to provide money or resources to another party wherein the second party does not reimburse the first party immediately , but promises either to repay or return those resources at a later date. In other words, credit is a method of making reciprocity formal, legally enforceable, and extensible to a large group of unrelated people.

Exam Probability: **Low**

13. *Answer choices:*

(see index for correct answer)

- a. open system
- b. cultural
- c. Consumer credit
- d. process perspective

:: Real estate ::

_____ , real estate, realty, or immovable property In English common law refers to landed properties belonging to some person. It include all structures, crops, buildings, machinery, wells, dams, ponds, mines, canals, and roads, among other things. The term is historic, arising from the now-discontinued form of action, which distinguish between _____ disputes and personal property disputes. Personal property was, and continues to refer to all properties that are not real properties.

Exam Probability: **Low**

14. *Answer choices:*

(see index for correct answer)

- a. Real property
- b. Gated community
- c. mezzanine financing
- d. Dominant estate

:: Financial regulatory authorities of the United States ::

The _____ is the revenue service of the United States federal government. The government agency is a bureau of the Department of the Treasury, and is under the immediate direction of the Commissioner of Internal Revenue, who is appointed to a five-year term by the President of the United States. The IRS is responsible for collecting taxes and administering the Internal Revenue Code, the main body of federal statutory tax law of the United States. The duties of the IRS include providing tax assistance to taxpayers and pursuing and resolving instances of erroneous or fraudulent tax filings. The IRS has also overseen various benefits programs, and enforces portions of the Affordable Care Act.

Exam Probability: **High**

15. *Answer choices:*

(see index for correct answer)

- a. Office of Thrift Supervision
- b. Federal Reserve Board
- c. Office of the Comptroller of the Currency
- d. Internal Revenue Service

Guidance: level 1

:: Contract law ::

Offer and acceptance analysis is a traditional approach in contract law. The offer and acceptance formula, developed in the 19th century, identifies a moment of formation when the parties are of one mind. This classical approach to contract formation has been modified by developments in the law of estoppel, misleading conduct, misrepresentation and unjust enrichment.

Exam Probability: **High**

16. *Answer choices:*

(see index for correct answer)

- a. Extended warranty
- b. Offeree
- c. Penal damages
- d. Beneficial interest

Guidance: level 1

:: ::

_____ is an insurance that covers the whole or a part of the risk of a person incurring medical expenses, spreading the risk over a large number of persons. By estimating the overall risk of health care and health system expenses over the risk pool, an insurer can develop a routine finance structure, such as a monthly premium or payroll tax, to provide the money to pay for the health care benefits specified in the insurance agreement. The benefit is administered by a central organization such as a government agency, private business, or not-for-profit entity.

17. *Answer choices:*

(see index for correct answer)

- a. similarity-attraction theory
- b. Health insurance
- c. cultural
- d. imperative

Guidance: level 1

:: ::

The _____ of 1933, also known as the 1933 Act, the _____ , the Truth in _____ , the Federal _____ , and the `33 Act, was enacted by the United States Congress on May 27, 1933, during the Great Depression, after the stock market crash of 1929. Legislated pursuant to the Interstate Commerce Clause of the Constitution, it requires every offer or sale of securities that uses the means and instrumentalities of interstate commerce to be registered with the SEC pursuant to the 1933 Act, unless an exemption from registration exists under the law. The term "means and instrumentalities of interstate commerce" is extremely broad and it is virtually impossible to avoid the operation of the statute by attempting to offer or sell a security without using an "instrumentality" of interstate commerce. Any use of a telephone, for example, or the mails would probably be enough to subject the transaction to the statute.

18. *Answer choices:*

- a. imperative
- b. corporate values
- c. deep-level diversity
- d. Securities Act

Guidance: level 1

:: ::

_____ refers to a business or organization attempting to acquire goods or services to accomplish its goals. Although there are several organizations that attempt to set standards in the _____ process, processes can vary greatly between organizations. Typically the word " _____ " is not used interchangeably with the word "procurement", since procurement typically includes expediting, supplier quality, and transportation and logistics in addition to _____ .

Exam Probability: **High**

19. *Answer choices:*

- a. personal values
- b. interpersonal communication
- c. deep-level diversity

- d. hierarchical

Guidance: level 1

:: Business law ::

A _____ , also known as the sole trader, individual entrepreneurship or proprietorship, is a type of enterprise that is owned and run by one person and in which there is no legal distinction between the owner and the business entity. A sole trader does not necessarily work `alone`—it is possible for the sole trader to employ other people.

Exam Probability: **Low**

20. *Answer choices:*

(see index for correct answer)

- a. Uniform Partnership Act
- b. Limited partnership
- c. Perfection
- d. Sole proprietorship

Guidance: level 1

:: ::

In common law legal systems, _____ is a principle or rule established in a previous legal case that is either binding on or persuasive for a court or other tribunal when deciding subsequent cases with similar issues or facts. Common-law legal systems place great value on deciding cases according to consistent principled rules, so that similar facts will yield similar and predictable outcomes, and observance of _____ is the mechanism by which that goal is attained. The principle by which judges are bound to _____ s is known as stare decisis. Common-law _____ is a third kind of law, on equal footing with statutory law and delegated legislation or regulatory law

.

Exam Probability: **Medium**

21. *Answer choices:*

(see index for correct answer)

- a. similarity-attraction theory
- b. Precedent
- c. empathy
- d. interpersonal communication

Guidance: level 1

:: ::

_____ is the administration of an organization, whether it is a business, a not-for-profit organization, or government body. _____ includes the activities of setting the strategy of an organization and coordinating the efforts of its employees to accomplish its objectives through the application of available resources, such as financial, natural, technological, and human resources. The term " _____ " may also refer to those people who manage an organization.

Exam Probability: **Medium**

22. *Answer choices:*

(see index for correct answer)

- a. personal values
- b. Management
- c. corporate values
- d. surface-level diversity

Guidance: level 1

:: Contract law ::

In the law of contracts, the _____ , also referred to as an unequivocal and absolute acceptance requirement, states that an offer must be accepted exactly with no modifications. The offeror is the master of one`s own offer. An attempt to accept the offer on different terms instead creates a counter-offer, and this constitutes a rejection of the original offer.

23. *Answer choices:*

(see index for correct answer)

- a. Breach of contract
- b. Doctrine of concurrent delay
- c. Neo-classical contract
- d. Mirror image rule

Guidance: level 1

:: Information technology audit ::

_____ is the act of using a computer to take or alter electronic data, or to gain unlawful use of a computer or system. In the United States, _____ is specifically proscribed by the _____ and Abuse Act, which criminalizes computer-related acts under federal jurisdiction. Types of _____ include.

Exam Probability: **Low**

24. *Answer choices:*

(see index for correct answer)

- a. ACL
- b. David Coderre

- c. Computer fraud
- d. NCC Group

Guidance: level 1

:: ::

In contract law, rescission is an equitable remedy which allows a contractual party to cancel the contract. Parties may _____ if they are the victims of a vitiating factor, such as misrepresentation, mistake, duress, or undue influence. Rescission is the unwinding of a transaction. This is done to bring the parties, as far as possible, back to the position in which they were before they entered into a contract .

Exam Probability: **High**

25. *Answer choices:*

(see index for correct answer)

- a. personal values
- b. similarity-attraction theory
- c. deep-level diversity
- d. corporate values

Guidance: level 1

:: ::

_____ is a legal term which, in its broadest sense, is a synonym for anyone in a position of trust and so can refer to any person who holds property, authority, or a position of trust or responsibility for the benefit of another. A _____ can also refer to a person who is allowed to do certain tasks but not able to gain income. Although in the strictest sense of the term a _____ is the holder of property on behalf of a beneficiary, the more expansive sense encompasses persons who serve, for example, on the board of _____ s of an institution that operates for a charity, for the benefit of the general public, or a person in the local government.

Exam Probability: **Low**

26. *Answer choices:*

(see index for correct answer)

- a. functional perspective
- b. hierarchical perspective
- c. Trustee
- d. surface-level diversity

Guidance: level 1

:: ::

Advertising is a marketing communication that employs an openly sponsored, non-personal message to promote or sell a product, service or idea. Sponsors of advertising are typically businesses wishing to promote their products or services. Advertising is differentiated from public relations in that an advertiser pays for and has control over the message. It differs from personal selling in that the message is non-personal, i.e., not directed to a particular individual. Advertising is communicated through various mass media, including traditional media such as newspapers, magazines, television, radio, outdoor advertising or direct mail; and new media such as search results, blogs, social media, websites or text messages. The actual presentation of the message in a medium is referred to as an _____ , or "ad" or advert for short.

Exam Probability: **Medium**

27. *Answer choices:*

(see index for correct answer)

- a. Advertisement
- b. process perspective
- c. hierarchical perspective
- d. empathy

Guidance: level 1

:: ::

A contract is a legally-binding agreement which recognises and governs the rights and duties of the parties to the agreement. A contract is legally enforceable because it meets the requirements and approval of the law. An agreement typically involves the exchange of goods, services, money, or promises of any of those. In the event of breach of contract, the law awards the injured party access to legal remedies such as damages and cancellation.

Exam Probability: **Medium**

28. *Answer choices:*

(see index for correct answer)

- a. hierarchical perspective
- b. process perspective
- c. Contract law
- d. Character

Guidance: level 1

:: Legal reasoning ::

_____ is a Latin expression meaning on its first encounter or at first sight. The literal translation would be "at first face" or "at first appearance", from the feminine forms of primus and facies, both in the ablative case. In modern, colloquial and conversational English, a common translation would be "on the face of it". The term _____ is used in modern legal English to signify that upon initial examination, sufficient corroborating evidence appears to exist to support a case. In common law jurisdictions, _____ denotes evidence that, unless rebutted, would be sufficient to prove a particular proposition or fact. The term is used similarly in academic philosophy. Most legal proceedings, in most jurisdictions, require a _____ case to exist, following which proceedings may then commence to test it, and create a ruling.

Exam Probability: **Low**

29. *Answer choices:*

(see index for correct answer)

- a. Prima facie
- b. deliberation
- c. Reasonable man

Guidance: level 1

:: ::

_____ , or auditory perception, is the ability to perceive sounds by detecting vibrations, changes in the pressure of the surrounding medium through time, through an organ such as the ear. The academic field concerned with _____ is auditory science.

Exam Probability: **Medium**

30. *Answer choices:*

(see index for correct answer)

- a. empathy
- b. co-culture
- c. open system
- d. Hearing

Guidance: level 1

:: Contract law ::

An _____ is a contract, the terms of which have been agreed by spoken communication. This is in contrast to a written contract, where the contract is a written document. There may be written, or other physical evidence, of an _____ – for example where the parties write down what they have agreed – but the contract itself is not a written one.

Exam Probability: **Medium**

31. *Answer choices:*

(see index for correct answer)

- a. Shrink wrap contract
- b. Oral contract
- c. Seaworthiness
- d. Acceleration clause

Guidance: level 1

:: Arbitration law ::

The United States Arbitration Act , more commonly referred to as the _____ or FAA, is an act of Congress that provides for judicial facilitation of private dispute resolution through arbitration. It applies in both state courts and federal courts, as was held constitutional in Southland Corp. v. Keating. It applies where the transaction contemplated by the parties "involves" interstate commerce and is predicated on an exercise of the Commerce Clause powers granted to Congress in the U.S. Constitution.

Exam Probability: **Medium**

32. *Answer choices:*

(see index for correct answer)

- a. James A. Graham
- b. Convention on the Recognition and Enforcement of Foreign Arbitral Awards

- c. Title 9 of the United States Code
- d. Federal Arbitration Act

Guidance: level 1

:: Services management and marketing ::

A _____ or servicemark is a trademark used in the United States and several other countries to identify a service rather than a product.

Exam Probability: **Medium**

33. *Answer choices:*

(see index for correct answer)

- a. Service delivery framework
- b. Service mark
- c. Industrialization of services business model
- d. Night service

Guidance: level 1

:: ::

A _____ is a person or firm who arranges transactions between a buyer and a seller for a commission when the deal is executed. A _____ who also acts as a seller or as a buyer becomes a principal party to the deal. Neither role should be confused with that of an agent—one who acts on behalf of a principal party in a deal.

Exam Probability: **Medium**

34. *Answer choices:*

(see index for correct answer)

- a. open system
- b. Broker
- c. imperative
- d. corporate values

Guidance: level 1

:: ::

In law, an _____ is the process in which cases are reviewed, where parties request a formal change to an official decision. _____ s function both as a process for error correction as well as a process of clarifying and interpreting law. Although appellate courts have existed for thousands of years, common law countries did not incorporate an affirmative right to _____ into their jurisprudence until the 19th century.

Exam Probability: **High**

35. *Answer choices:*

(see index for correct answer)

- a. corporate values
- b. Appeal
- c. imperative
- d. surface-level diversity

Guidance: level 1

:: ::

_____ , in United States trademark law, is a statutory cause of action that permits a party to petition the Trademark Trial and Appeal Board of the Patent and Trademark Office to cancel a trademark registration that "may disparage or falsely suggest a connection with persons, living or dead, institutions, beliefs, or national symbols, or bring them into contempt or disrepute." Unlike claims regarding the validity of the mark, a _____ claim can be brought "at any time," subject to equitable defenses such as laches.

Exam Probability: **Medium**

36. *Answer choices:*

(see index for correct answer)

- a. surface-level diversity
- b. open system

- c. Disparagement
- d. imperative

Guidance: level 1

:: Business law ::

The term is used to designate a range of diverse, if often kindred, concepts. These have historically been addressed in a number of discrete disciplines, notably mathematics, physics, chemistry, ethics, aesthetics, ontology, and theology.

Exam Probability: **Medium**

37. *Answer choices:*

(see index for correct answer)

- a. Business.gov
- b. Voting trust
- c. Finance lease
- d. Contract failure

Guidance: level 1

:: Contract law ::

An _____ is a contract that has not yet been fully performed or fully executed. It is a contract in which both sides still have important performance remaining. However, an obligation to pay money, even if such obligation is material, does not usually make a contract executory. An obligation is material if a breach of contract would result from the failure to satisfy the obligation. A contract that has been fully performed by one party but not by the other party is not an _____ .

Exam Probability: **Medium**

38. *Answer choices:*

(see index for correct answer)

- a. Expectation damages
- b. Heads of loss
- c. Undue influence
- d. Piggy-back

Guidance: level 1

:: Fraud ::

The _____ refers to the requirement that certain kinds of contracts be memorialized in writing, signed by the party to be charged, with sufficient content to evidence the contract.

Exam Probability: **High**

39. *Answer choices:*

(see index for correct answer)

- a. Intrinsic fraud
- b. Sham marriage
- c. Welfare queen
- d. Identity theft

Guidance: level 1

:: Corporate finance ::

_____ is a contract law concept about the purchase of the release from a debt obligation. It is one of the methods by which parties to a contract may terminate their agreement. The release is completed by the transfer of valuable consideration that must not be the actual performance of the obligation itself. The accord is the agreement to discharge the obligation and the satisfaction is the legal "consideration" which binds the parties to the agreement. A valid accord does not discharge the prior contract; instead it suspends the right to enforce it in accordance with the terms of the accord contract, in which satisfaction, or performance of the contract will discharge both contracts . If the creditor breaches the accord, then the debtor will be able to bring up the existence of the accord in order to enjoin any action against him.

Exam Probability: **High**

40. *Answer choices:*

(see index for correct answer)

- a. Financial accelerator
- b. Commercial finance
- c. Thin capitalisation rules
- d. Accord and satisfaction

Guidance: level 1

:: ::

_____ is a judicial device in common law legal systems whereby a court may prevent, or "estop" a person from making assertions or from going back on his or her word; the person being sanctioned is "estopped". _____ may prevent someone from bringing a particular claim. Legal doctrines of _____ are based in both common law and equity.

Exam Probability: **Low**

41. *Answer choices:*

(see index for correct answer)

- a. imperative
- b. Estoppel
- c. empathy
- d. corporate values

Guidance: level 1

_____ is a concept of English common law and is a necessity for simple contracts but not for special contracts . The concept has been adopted by other common law jurisdictions, including the US.

Exam Probability: **Medium**

42. *Answer choices:*

(see index for correct answer)

- a. hierarchical
- b. Consideration
- c. similarity-attraction theory
- d. interpersonal communication

Guidance: level 1

:: Mereology ::

_____ , in the abstract, is what belongs to or with something, whether as an attribute or as a component of said thing. In the context of this article, it is one or more components , whether physical or incorporeal, of a person's estate; or so belonging to, as in being owned by, a person or jointly a group of people or a legal entity like a corporation or even a society. Depending on the nature of the _____ , an owner of _____ has the right to consume, alter, share, redefine, rent, mortgage, pawn, sell, exchange, transfer, give away or destroy it, or to exclude others from doing these things, as well as to perhaps abandon it; whereas regardless of the nature of the _____ , the owner thereof has the right to properly use it , or at the very least exclusively keep it.

Exam Probability: **Medium**

43. *Answer choices:*

(see index for correct answer)

- a. Mereotopology
- b. Meronomy
- c. Mereology
- d. Property

Guidance: level 1

:: Commerce ::

_____ relates to "the exchange of goods and services, especially on a large scale". It includes legal, economic, political, social, cultural and technological systems that operate in a country or in international trade.

44. *Answer choices:*

(see index for correct answer)

- a. Social gravity
- b. Commerce
- c. Linestanding
- d. Reseller

Guidance: level 1

:: ::

The Sherman Antitrust Act of 1890 was a United States antitrust law that regulates competition among enterprises, which was passed by Congress under the presidency of Benjamin Harrison.

Exam Probability: **Medium**

45. *Answer choices:*

(see index for correct answer)

- a. Sherman Act
- b. deep-level diversity
- c. empathy
- d. information systems assessment

:: Patent law ::

A _____ is generally any statement intended to specify or delimit the scope of rights and obligations that may be exercised and enforced by parties in a legally recognized relationship. In contrast to other terms for legally operative language, the term _____ usually implies situations that involve some level of uncertainty, waiver, or risk.

Exam Probability: **High**

46. *Answer choices:*

(see index for correct answer)

- a. Patentability
- b. Disclaimer
- c. Patent war
- d. Opposition proceeding

:: ::

An _____ is a contingent motivator. Traditional _____ s are extrinsic motivators which reward actions to yield a desired outcome. The effectiveness of traditional _____ s has changed as the needs of Western society have evolved. While the traditional _____ model is effective when there is a defined procedure and goal for a task, Western society started to require a higher volume of critical thinkers, so the traditional model became less effective. Institutions are now following a trend in implementing strategies that rely on intrinsic motivations rather than the extrinsic motivations that the traditional _____ s foster.

Exam Probability: **Low**

47. *Answer choices:*

(see index for correct answer)

- a. hierarchical
- b. corporate values
- c. Incentive
- d. similarity-attraction theory

Guidance: level 1

:: Criminal procedure ::

_____ is the adjudication process of the criminal law. While _____ differs dramatically by jurisdiction, the process generally begins with a formal criminal charge with the person on trial either being free on bail or incarcerated, and results in the conviction or acquittal of the defendant. _____ can be either in form of inquisitorial or adversarial _____ .

48. *Answer choices:*

(see index for correct answer)

- a. directed verdict
- b. Exoneration

Guidance: level 1

:: Contract law ::

An _____ —or acceleration covenant— in the law of contracts, is a term that fully matures the performance due from a party upon a breach of the contract. Such clauses are most prevalent in mortgages and similar contracts to purchase real estate in installments.

Exam Probability: **Medium**

49. *Answer choices:*

(see index for correct answer)

- a. Scots contract law
- b. Indian contract law
- c. Duress
- d. Acceleration clause

:: ::

_____ is a process whereby a person assumes the parenting of another, usually a child, from that person's biological or legal parent or parents.
Legal _____ s permanently transfers all rights and responsibilities, along with filiation, from the biological parent or parents.

Exam Probability: **Low**

50. *Answer choices:*
(see index for correct answer)

- a. Adoption
- b. process perspective
- c. functional perspective
- d. surface-level diversity

:: ::

A _____ is the party who initiates a lawsuit before a court. By doing so, the _____ seeks a legal remedy; if this search is successful, the court will issue judgment in favor of the _____ and make the appropriate court order . " _____ " is the term used in civil cases in most English-speaking jurisdictions, the notable exception being England and Wales, where a _____ has, since the introduction of the Civil Procedure Rules in 1999, been known as a "claimant", but that term also has other meanings. In criminal cases, the prosecutor brings the case against the defendant, but the key complaining party is often called the "complainant".

Exam Probability: **High**

51. *Answer choices:*

(see index for correct answer)

- a. levels of analysis
- b. Plaintiff
- c. imperative
- d. corporate values

Guidance: level 1

:: Industrial agreements ::

_____ is a process of negotiation between employers and a group of employees aimed at agreements to regulate working salaries, working conditions, benefits, and other aspects of workers' compensation and rights for workers. The interests of the employees are commonly presented by representatives of a trade union to which the employees belong. The collective agreements reached by these negotiations usually set out wage scales, working hours, training, health and safety, overtime, grievance mechanisms, and rights to participate in workplace or company affairs.

Exam Probability: **Low**

52. *Answer choices:*

(see index for correct answer)

- a. Collective bargaining
- b. Collaborative bargaining
- c. Bargaining unit
- d. Conciliation and Arbitration Act 1904

Guidance: level 1

:: Legal procedure ::

_____ , adjective law, or rules of court comprises the rules by which a court hears and determines what happens in civil, lawsuit, criminal or administrative proceedings. The rules are designed to ensure a fair and consistent application of due process or fundamental justice to all cases that come before a court.

53. *Answer choices:*

(see index for correct answer)

- a. Procedural law
- b. Closing argument
- c. Opening statement
- d. appellate

Guidance: level 1

:: Manufacturing ::

A _____ is a building for storing goods. _____ s are used by manufacturers, importers, exporters, wholesalers, transport businesses, customs, etc. They are usually large plain buildings in industrial parks on the outskirts of cities, towns or villages.

Exam Probability: **Low**

54. *Answer choices:*

(see index for correct answer)

- a. Process manufacturing
- b. Toolroom
- c. Factory tour

- d. Warehouse

Guidance: level 1

:: Consumer theory ::

A _____ is a technical term in psychology, economics and philosophy usually used in relation to choosing between alternatives. For example, someone prefers A over B if they would rather choose A than B.

Exam Probability: **Low**

55. *Answer choices:*

(see index for correct answer)

- a. Elasticity of intertemporal substitution
- b. Preference
- c. Hicksian demand function
- d. Consumer choice

Guidance: level 1

:: ::

A _____ is a person who trades in commodities produced by other people. Historically, a _____ is anyone who is involved in business or trade. _____ s have operated for as long as industry, commerce, and trade have existed. During the 16th-century, in Europe, two different terms for _____ s emerged: One term, meerseniers, described local traders such as bakers, grocers, etc.; while a new term, koopman (Dutch: koopman, described _____ s who operated on a global stage, importing and exporting goods over vast distances, and offering added-value services such as credit and finance.

Exam Probability: **Medium**

56. *Answer choices:*

(see index for correct answer)

- a. personal values
- b. Merchant
- c. open system
- d. hierarchical perspective

Guidance: level 1

:: Contract law ::

Generally, a _____ is a loan or a credit transaction in which the lender acquires a security interest in collateral owned by the borrower and is entitled to foreclose on or repossess the collateral in the event of the borrower's default. The terms of the relationship are governed by a contract, or security agreement. A common example would be a consumer who purchases a car on credit. If the consumer fails to make the payments on time, the lender will take the car and resell it, applying the proceeds of the sale toward the loan. Mortgages and deeds of trust are another example. In the United States, _____ s in personal property are governed by Article 9 of the Uniform Commercial Code .

Exam Probability: **Medium**

57. *Answer choices:*

(see index for correct answer)

- a. Secured transaction
- b. Shrink wrap contract
- c. Contingent contracts
- d. Fixed-price contract

Guidance: level 1

:: Insurance terms ::

A _____ in the broadest sense is a natural person or other legal entity who receives money or other benefits from a benefactor. For example, the _____ of a life insurance policy is the person who receives the payment of the amount of insurance after the death of the insured.

58. *Answer choices:*

(see index for correct answer)

- a. Self-revelation
- b. Split billing
- c. Beneficiary
- d. Certified marine insurance professional

Guidance: level 1

:: ::

Competition law is a law that promotes or seeks to maintain market competition by regulating anti-competitive conduct by companies. Competition law is implemented through public and private enforcement. Competition law is known as " _____ law" in the United States for historical reasons, and as "anti-monopoly law" in China and Russia. In previous years it has been known as trade practices law in the United Kingdom and Australia. In the European Union, it is referred to as both _____ and competition law.

59. *Answer choices:*

(see index for correct answer)

- a. cultural

- b. surface-level diversity
- c. imperative
- d. personal values

Guidance: level 1

Finance

Finance is a field that is concerned with the allocation (investment) of assets and liabilities over space and time, often under conditions of risk or uncertainty. Finance can also be defined as the science of money management. Participants in the market aim to price assets based on their risk level, fundamental value, and their expected rate of return. Finance can be split into three sub-categories: public finance, corporate finance and personal finance.

:: Mathematical finance ::

_____ is the value of an asset at a specific date. It measures the nominal future sum of money that a given sum of money is "worth" at a specified time in the future assuming a certain interest rate, or more generally, rate of return; it is the present value multiplied by the accumulation function. The value does not include corrections for inflation or other factors that affect the true value of money in the future. This is used in time value of money calculations.

Exam Probability: **Medium**

1. *Answer choices:*

(see index for correct answer)

- a. Convexity
- b. Present value
- c. Forward measure
- d. Future value

Guidance: level 1

:: Accounting systems ::

In bookkeeping, a _____ statement is a process that explains the difference on a specified date between the bank balance shown in an organization's bank statement, as supplied by the bank and the corresponding amount shown in the organization's own accounting records.

Exam Probability: **Low**

2. *Answer choices:*

(see index for correct answer)

- a. Convention of consistency
- b. Controlling account
- c. Off-balance sheet
- d. Waste book

Guidance: level 1

:: Bonds (finance) ::

A _____ is a fund established by an economic entity by setting aside revenue over a period of time to fund a future capital expense, or repayment of a long-term debt.

Exam Probability: **Low**

3. *Answer choices:*

(see index for correct answer)

- a. Global Country of World Peace
- b. Samurai bond
- c. Sinking fund
- d. Residential mortgage-backed security

Guidance: level 1

An _____ is a person that allocates capital with the expectation of a future financial return. Types of investments include: equity, debt securities, real estate, currency, commodity, token, derivatives such as put and call options, futures, forwards, etc. This definition makes no distinction between the _____ s in the primary and secondary markets. That is, someone who provides a business with capital and someone who buys a stock are both _____ s. An _____ who owns a stock is a shareholder.

Exam Probability: **Low**

4. *Answer choices:*

(see index for correct answer)

- a. imperative
- b. personal values
- c. hierarchical perspective
- d. information systems assessment

Guidance: level 1

:: Valuation (finance) ::

_____ refers to an assessment of the viability, stability, and profitability of a business, sub-business or project.

5. *Answer choices:*

(see index for correct answer)

- a. Value-in-use
- b. Appraisal Institute
- c. The Appraisal Foundation
- d. Dividend puzzle

Guidance: level 1

:: Fraud ::

In law, _____ is intentional deception to secure unfair or unlawful gain, or to deprive a victim of a legal right. _____ can violate civil law, a criminal law, or it may cause no loss of money, property or legal right but still be an element of another civil or criminal wrong. The purpose of _____ may be monetary gain or other benefits, for example by obtaining a passport, travel document, or driver's license, or mortgage _____, where the perpetrator may attempt to qualify for a mortgage by way of false statements.

Exam Probability: **Low**

6. *Answer choices:*

(see index for correct answer)

- a. Emil Rupp
- b. Double billing
- c. World Luxury Association
- d. Parcel mule scam

Guidance: level 1

:: Accounting terminology ::

_____ is money owed by a business to its suppliers shown as a liability on a company's balance sheet. It is distinct from notes payable liabilities, which are debts created by formal legal instrument documents.

Exam Probability: **High**

7. *Answer choices:*

(see index for correct answer)

- a. Impairment cost
- b. Record to report
- c. Accounts payable
- d. Capital expenditure

Guidance: level 1

:: Generally Accepted Accounting Principles ::

An _____ or profit and loss account is one of the financial statements of a company and shows the company's revenues and expenses during a particular period.

Exam Probability: **Low**

8. *Answer choices:*

(see index for correct answer)

- a. Statement of recommended practice
- b. Completed-contract method
- c. Net income
- d. Income statement

Guidance: level 1

:: Accounting terminology ::

In accounting/accountancy, _____ are journal entries usually made at the end of an accounting period to allocate income and expenditure to the period in which they actually occurred. The revenue recognition principle is the basis of making _____ that pertain to unearned and accrued revenues under accrual-basis accounting. They are sometimes called Balance Day adjustments because they are made on balance day.

Exam Probability: **Medium**

9. *Answer choices:*

(see index for correct answer)

- a. Accounts payable
- b. Adjusting entries
- c. Statement of financial position
- d. Chart of accounts

Guidance: level 1

:: Project management ::

Some scenarios associate "this kind of planning" with learning "life skills". _____ s are necessary, or at least useful, in situations where individuals need to know what time they must be at a specific location to receive a specific service, and where people need to accomplish a set of goals within a set time period.

Exam Probability: **High**

10. *Answer choices:*

(see index for correct answer)

- a. Goodwerp
- b. Pre-mortem
- c. Critical path drag
- d. LibrePlan

:: Accounting terminology ::

_____ is a legally enforceable claim for payment held by a business for goods supplied and/or services rendered that customers/clients have ordered but not paid for. These are generally in the form of invoices raised by a business and delivered to the customer for payment within an agreed time frame. _____ is shown in a balance sheet as an asset. It is one of a series of accounting transactions dealing with the billing of a customer for goods and services that the customer has ordered. These may be distinguished from notes receivable, which are debts created through formal legal instruments called promissory notes.

Exam Probability: **High**

11. *Answer choices:*

(see index for correct answer)

- a. Accounts receivable
- b. Checkoff
- c. Accrual
- d. Accounting equation

Guidance: level 1

:: Institutional investors ::

A _____ is an investment fund that pools capital from accredited investors or institutional investors and invests in a variety of assets, often with complex portfolio-construction and risk management techniques. It is administered by a professional investment management firm, and often structured as a limited partnership, limited liability company, or similar vehicle.

_____ s are generally distinct from mutual funds and regarded as alternative investments, as their use of leverage is not capped by regulators, and distinct from private equity funds, as the majority of _____ s invest in relatively liquid assets. However, funds which operate similarly to _____ s but are regulated similarly to mutual funds are available and known as liquid alternative investments.

Exam Probability: **High**

12. *Answer choices:*

(see index for correct answer)

- a. Capital Introduction
- b. Chartered Financial Analyst
- c. Gracy Title Company
- d. Admiral Administration

Guidance: level 1

:: ::

_____ involves decision making. It can include judging the merits of multiple options and selecting one or more of them. One can make a _____ between imagined options or between real options followed by the corresponding action. For example, a traveler might choose a route for a journey based on the preference of arriving at a given destination as soon as possible. The preferred route can then follow from information such as the length of each of the possible routes, traffic conditions, etc. The arrival at a _____ can include more complex motivators such as cognition, instinct, and feeling.

Exam Probability: **Low**

13. *Answer choices:*

(see index for correct answer)

- a. surface-level diversity
- b. Choice
- c. functional perspective
- d. hierarchical

Guidance: level 1

:: Financial risk ::

_____ is any of various types of risk associated with financing, including financial transactions that include company loans in risk of default. Often it is understood to include only downside risk, meaning the potential for financial loss and uncertainty about its extent.

14. *Answer choices:*

(see index for correct answer)

- a. Risk-free rate
- b. Financial risk
- c. Fixed bill
- d. ORRF Risk Research Forum

Guidance: level 1

:: Accounting terminology ::

Accounts are typically defined by an identifier and a caption or header and are coded by account type. In computerized accounting systems with computable quantity accounting, the accounts can have a quantity measure definition.

Exam Probability: **High**

15. *Answer choices:*

(see index for correct answer)

- a. Internal auditing
- b. Chart of accounts
- c. Record to report
- d. Fair value accounting

:: Stock market ::

_____ is a form of corporate equity ownership, a type of security. The terms voting share and ordinary share are also used frequently in other parts of the world; " _____ " being primarily used in the United States. They are known as Equity shares or Ordinary shares in the UK and other Commonwealth realms. This type of share gives the stockholder the right to share in the profits of the company, and to vote on matters of corporate policy and the composition of the members of the board of directors.

Exam Probability: **Medium**

16. *Answer choices:*

(see index for correct answer)

- a. Common stock
- b. No-par stock
- c. Chi-X Global
- d. Volume-weighted average price

:: ::

_____ is the collection of mechanisms, processes and relations by which corporations are controlled and operated. Governance structures and principles identify the distribution of rights and responsibilities among different participants in the corporation and include the rules and procedures for making decisions in corporate affairs. _____ is necessary because of the possibility of conflicts of interests between stakeholders, primarily between shareholders and upper management or among shareholders.

Exam Probability: **Medium**

17. *Answer choices:*

(see index for correct answer)

- a. corporate values
- b. imperative
- c. Corporate governance
- d. personal values

Guidance: level 1

:: Bonds (finance) ::

In finance, a _____ or convertible note or convertible debt is a type of bond that the holder can convert into a specified number of shares of common stock in the issuing company or cash of equal value. It is a hybrid security with debt- and equity-like features. It originated in the mid-19th century, and was used by early speculators such as Jacob Little and Daniel Drew to counter market cornering.

18. *Answer choices:*

(see index for correct answer)

- a. Collateralized debt obligation
- b. Kimchi bond
- c. General obligation bond
- d. Convertible bond

Guidance: level 1

:: ::

A shareholder is an individual or institution that legally owns one or more shares of stock in a public or private corporation. Shareholders may be referred to as members of a corporation. Legally, a person is not a shareholder in a corporation until their name and other details are entered in the corporation's register of shareholders or members.

Exam Probability: **High**

19. *Answer choices:*

(see index for correct answer)

- a. process perspective
- b. empathy

- c. functional perspective
- d. levels of analysis

Guidance: level 1

:: Business law ::

_____ is where a person's financial liability is limited to a fixed sum, most commonly the value of a person's investment in a company or partnership. If a company with _____ is sued, then the claimants are suing the company, not its owners or investors. A shareholder in a limited company is not personally liable for any of the debts of the company, other than for the amount already invested in the company and for any unpaid amount on the shares in the company, if any. The same is true for the members of a _____ partnership and the limited partners in a limited partnership. By contrast, sole proprietors and partners in general partnerships are each liable for all the debts of the business .

Exam Probability: **High**

20. *Answer choices:*

(see index for correct answer)

- a. Contract failure
- b. Limited liability
- c. Stick licensing
- d. Vehicle leasing

Guidance: level 1

_____ refers to a business or organization attempting to acquire goods or services to accomplish its goals. Although there are several organizations that attempt to set standards in the _____ process, processes can vary greatly between organizations. Typically the word " _____ " is not used interchangeably with the word "procurement", since procurement typically includes expediting, supplier quality, and transportation and logistics in addition to _____ .

Exam Probability: **Low**

21. *Answer choices:*

(see index for correct answer)

- a. imperative
- b. hierarchical
- c. Purchasing
- d. open system

Guidance: level 1

_____ is a marketing communication that employs an openly sponsored, non-personal message to promote or sell a product, service or idea. Sponsors of _____ are typically businesses wishing to promote their products or services. _____ is differentiated from public relations in that an advertiser pays for and has control over the message. It differs from personal selling in that the message is non-personal, i.e., not directed to a particular individual. _____ is communicated through various mass media, including traditional media such as newspapers, magazines, television, radio, outdoor _____ or direct mail; and new media such as search results, blogs, social media, websites or text messages. The actual presentation of the message in a medium is referred to as an advertisement, or "ad" or advert for short.

Exam Probability: **Medium**

22. *Answer choices:*

(see index for correct answer)

- a. Advertising
- b. process perspective
- c. surface-level diversity
- d. cultural

Guidance: level 1

:: Management accounting ::

_____ , or dollar contribution per unit, is the selling price per unit minus the variable cost per unit. "Contribution" represents the portion of sales revenue that is not consumed by variable costs and so contributes to the coverage of fixed costs. This concept is one of the key building blocks of break-even analysis.

Exam Probability: **Medium**

23. *Answer choices:*

(see index for correct answer)

- a. Dual overhead rate
- b. Target income sales
- c. Management accounting
- d. Total benefits of ownership

Guidance: level 1

:: Generally Accepted Accounting Principles ::

_____ , also referred to as the bottom line, net income, or net earnings is a measure of the profitability of a venture after accounting for all costs and taxes. It is the actual profit, and includes the operating expenses that are excluded from gross profit.

Exam Probability: **Medium**

24. *Answer choices:*

(see index for correct answer)

- a. Closing entries
- b. Earnings before interest and taxes
- c. Pro forma
- d. Expense

Guidance: level 1

:: ::

_____ is the collection of techniques, skills, methods, and processes used in the production of goods or services or in the accomplishment of objectives, such as scientific investigation. _____ can be the knowledge of techniques, processes, and the like, or it can be embedded in machines to allow for operation without detailed knowledge of their workings. Systems applying _____ by taking an input, changing it according to the system`s use, and then producing an outcome are referred to as _____ systems or technological systems.

Exam Probability: **High**

25. *Answer choices:*

(see index for correct answer)

- a. cultural
- b. deep-level diversity

- c. personal values
- d. open system

Guidance: level 1

:: Accounting journals and ledgers ::

_____ is a daybook or journal which is used to record transactions relating to adjustment entries, opening stock, accounting errors etc. The source documents of this prime entry book are journal voucher, copy of management reports and invoices.

Exam Probability: **Medium**

26. *Answer choices:*
(see index for correct answer)

- a. Sales journal
- b. Cash receipts journal
- c. Check register
- d. General journal

Guidance: level 1

:: Accounting in the United States ::

The _____ is a private-sector, nonprofit corporation created by the Sarbanes–Oxley Act of 2002 to oversee the audits of public companies and other issuers in order to protect the interests of investors and further the public interest in the preparation of informative, accurate and independent audit reports. The PCAOB also oversees the audits of broker-dealers, including compliance reports filed pursuant to federal securities laws, to promote investor protection. All PCAOB rules and standards must be approved by the U.S. Securities and Exchange Commission .

Exam Probability: **Medium**

27. *Answer choices:*

(see index for correct answer)

- a. Plug
- b. Institute of Internal Auditors
- c. Public Company Accounting Oversight Board
- d. Positive assurance

Guidance: level 1

:: Hazard analysis ::

Broadly speaking, a _____ is the combined effort of 1. identifying and analyzing potential events that may negatively impact individuals, assets, and/or the environment ; and 2. making judgments "on the tolerability of the risk on the basis of a risk analysis" while considering influencing factors . Put in simpler terms, a _____ analyzes what can go wrong, how likely it is to happen, what the potential consequences are, and how tolerable the identified risk is. As part of this process, the resulting determination of risk may be expressed in a quantitative or qualitative fashion. The _____ is an inherent part of an overall risk management strategy, which attempts to, after a _____ , "introduce control measures to eliminate or reduce" any potential risk-related consequences.

Exam Probability: **Low**

28. *Answer choices:*

(see index for correct answer)

- a. Swiss cheese model
- b. Risk assessment
- c. Hazard identification
- d. Hazardous Materials Identification System

Guidance: level 1

:: Accounting terminology ::

_____ or capital expense is the money a company spends to buy, maintain, or improve its fixed assets, such as buildings, vehicles, equipment, or land. It is considered a _____ when the asset is newly purchased or when money is used towards extending the useful life of an existing asset, such as repairing the roof.

Exam Probability: **High**

29. *Answer choices:*

(see index for correct answer)

- a. profit and loss statement
- b. Accounts receivable
- c. Capital expenditure
- d. outstanding balance

Guidance: level 1

:: Real estate valuation ::

_____ or OMV is the price at which an asset would trade in a competitive auction setting. _____ is often used interchangeably with open _____ , fair value or fair _____ , although these terms have distinct definitions in different standards, and may or may not differ in some circumstances.

Exam Probability: **Low**

30. *Answer choices:*

(see index for correct answer)

- a. Philip Michael Faraday
- b. Appraisal Standards Board
- c. Market value
- d. Real estate benchmarking

Guidance: level 1

:: Interest ::

In finance, _____ is the interest on a bond or loan that has accumulated since the principal investment, or since the previous coupon payment if there has been one already.

Exam Probability: **Medium**

31. *Answer choices:*

(see index for correct answer)

- a. Capital and Interest
- b. Penal interest
- c. Usury
- d. Accrued interest

Guidance: level 1

:: Financial regulatory authorities of the United States ::

The _____ is the revenue service of the United States federal government. The government agency is a bureau of the Department of the Treasury, and is under the immediate direction of the Commissioner of Internal Revenue, who is appointed to a five-year term by the President of the United States. The IRS is responsible for collecting taxes and administering the Internal Revenue Code, the main body of federal statutory tax law of the United States. The duties of the IRS include providing tax assistance to taxpayers and pursuing and resolving instances of erroneous or fraudulent tax filings. The IRS has also overseen various benefits programs, and enforces portions of the Affordable Care Act.

Exam Probability: **Low**

32. *Answer choices:*

(see index for correct answer)

- a. Office of Thrift Supervision
- b. Office of the Comptroller of the Currency
- c. Internal Revenue Service
- d. U.S. Securities and Exchange Commission

Guidance: level 1

:: Financial ratios ::

_____ is a measure of how revenue growth translates into growth in operating income. It is a measure of leverage, and of how risky, or volatile, a company's operating income is.

33. *Answer choices:*

(see index for correct answer)

- a. Fixed-asset turnover
- b. Operating leverage
- c. Greeks
- d. Return of capital

Guidance: level 1

:: ::

Business is the activity of making one's living or making money by producing or buying and selling products . Simply put, it is "any activity or enterprise entered into for profit. It does not mean it is a company, a corporation, partnership, or have any such formal organization, but it can range from a street peddler to General Motors."

34. *Answer choices:*

(see index for correct answer)

- a. personal values
- b. hierarchical perspective
- c. empathy
- d. Firm

Guidance: level 1

:: Generally Accepted Accounting Principles ::

A _____ is a reduction of the recognized value of something. In accounting, this is a recognition of the reduced or zero value of an asset. In income tax statements, this is a reduction of taxable income, as a recognition of certain expenses required to produce the income.

Exam Probability: **High**

35. *Answer choices:*
(see index for correct answer)

- a. Operating income before depreciation and amortization
- b. Liability
- c. Write-off
- d. Earnings before interest and taxes

Guidance: level 1

_____ is the process whereby a business sets the price at which it will sell its products and services, and may be part of the business's marketing plan. In setting prices, the business will take into account the price at which it could acquire the goods, the manufacturing cost, the market place, competition, market condition, brand, and quality of product.

Exam Probability: **Low**

36. *Answer choices:*

(see index for correct answer)

- a. hierarchical perspective
- b. Pricing
- c. functional perspective
- d. Character

Guidance: level 1

:: Financial risk ::

The _____ on a financial investment is the expected value of its return . It is a measure of the center of the distribution of the random variable that is the return.

Exam Probability: **Low**

37. *Answer choices:*

(see index for correct answer)

- a. Annualized loss expectancy
- b. Consistent pricing process
- c. Expected return
- d. Fuel price risk management

Guidance: level 1

:: Credit cards ::

A _____ is a payment card issued to users to enable the cardholder to pay a merchant for goods and services based on the cardholder's promise to the card issuer to pay them for the amounts plus the other agreed charges. The card issuer creates a revolving account and grants a line of credit to the cardholder, from which the cardholder can borrow money for payment to a merchant or as a cash advance.

Exam Probability: **Medium**

38. *Answer choices:*

(see index for correct answer)

- a. Credit CARD Act of 2009
- b. Bankcard

- c. Credit card
- d. Wireless identity theft

Guidance: level 1

:: Monopoly (economics) ::

A _____ is a form of intellectual property that gives its owner the legal right to exclude others from making, using, selling, and importing an invention for a limited period of years, in exchange for publishing an enabling public disclosure of the invention. In most countries _____ rights fall under civil law and the _____ holder needs to sue someone infringing the _____ in order to enforce his or her rights. In some industries _____ s are an essential form of competitive advantage; in others they are irrelevant.

Exam Probability: **High**

39. *Answer choices:*

(see index for correct answer)

- a. Trust
- b. Public utility
- c. State monopoly capitalism
- d. Monopsony

Guidance: level 1

:: ::

A _____ is an individual or institution that legally owns one or more shares of stock in a public or private corporation. _____ s may be referred to as members of a corporation. Legally, a person is not a _____ in a corporation until their name and other details are entered in the corporation's register of _____ s or members.

Exam Probability: **Medium**

40. *Answer choices:*

(see index for correct answer)

- a. similarity-attraction theory
- b. Shareholder
- c. process perspective
- d. interpersonal communication

Guidance: level 1

:: ::

An _____ , for United States federal income tax, is a closely held corporation that makes a valid election to be taxed under Subchapter S of Chapter 1 of the Internal Revenue Code. In general, _____ s do not pay any income taxes. Instead, the corporation's income or losses are divided among and passed through to its shareholders. The shareholders must then report the income or loss on their own individual income tax returns.

41. *Answer choices:*

(see index for correct answer)

- a. cultural
- b. functional perspective
- c. S corporation
- d. Sarbanes-Oxley act of 2002

Guidance: level 1

:: Financial economics ::

A _____ is defined to include property of any kind held by an assessee, whether connected with their business or profession or not connected with their business or profession. It includes all kinds of property, movable or immovable, tangible or intangible, fixed or circulating. Thus, land and building, plant and machinery, motorcar, furniture, jewellery, route permits, goodwill, tenancy rights, patents, trademarks, shares, debentures, securities, units, mutual funds, zero-coupon bonds etc. are _____ s.

Exam Probability: **Low**

42. *Answer choices:*

(see index for correct answer)

- a. Efficient-market hypothesis

- b. Interest rate parity
- c. Mid price
- d. Consumer leverage ratio

Guidance: level 1

:: Mereology ::

_____ , in the abstract, is what belongs to or with something, whether as an attribute or as a component of said thing. In the context of this article, it is one or more components , whether physical or incorporeal, of a person's estate; or so belonging to, as in being owned by, a person or jointly a group of people or a legal entity like a corporation or even a society. Depending on the nature of the _____ , an owner of _____ has the right to consume, alter, share, redefine, rent, mortgage, pawn, sell, exchange, transfer, give away or destroy it, or to exclude others from doing these things, as well as to perhaps abandon it; whereas regardless of the nature of the _____ , the owner thereof has the right to properly use it , or at the very least exclusively keep it.

Exam Probability: **Medium**

43. *Answer choices:*

(see index for correct answer)

- a. Property
- b. Mereotopology
- c. Mereological nihilism
- d. Mereology

:: Business law ::

A _____ , also known as the sole trader, individual entrepreneurship or proprietorship, is a type of enterprise that is owned and run by one person and in which there is no legal distinction between the owner and the business entity. A sole trader does not necessarily work `alone`—it is possible for the sole trader to employ other people.

Exam Probability: **Medium**

44. *Answer choices:*

(see index for correct answer)

- a. Unfair Commercial Practices Directive
- b. Partnership
- c. Court auction
- d. Sole proprietorship

:: ::

In marketing, a _____ is a ticket or document that can be redeemed for a financial discount or rebate when purchasing a product.

Exam Probability: **Medium**

45. *Answer choices:*

(see index for correct answer)

- a. Coupon
- b. corporate values
- c. Character
- d. open system

Guidance: level 1

:: ::

The U.S. _____ is an independent agency of the United States federal government. The SEC holds primary responsibility for enforcing the federal securities laws, proposing securities rules, and regulating the securities industry, the nation's stock and options exchanges, and other activities and organizations, including the electronic securities markets in the United States.

Exam Probability: **Medium**

46. *Answer choices:*

(see index for correct answer)

- a. Securities and Exchange Commission
- b. levels of analysis
- c. empathy
- d. deep-level diversity

Guidance: level 1

:: Business economics ::

In finance, _____ is the risk of losses caused by interest rate changes. The prices of most financial instruments, such as stocks and bonds move inversely with interest rates, so investors are subject to capital loss when rates rise.

Exam Probability: **Low**

47. *Answer choices:*

(see index for correct answer)

- a. Earnings before taxes
- b. Willingness to accept
- c. European embedded value
- d. Overnight cost

Guidance: level 1

:: Real estate ::

Amortisation is paying off an amount owed over time by making planned, incremental payments of principal and interest. To amortise a loan means "to kill it off". In accounting, amortisation refers to charging or writing off an intangible asset's cost as an operational expense over its estimated useful life to reduce a company's taxable income.

Exam Probability: **Low**

48. *Answer choices:*

(see index for correct answer)

- a. Burgage
- b. Studio apartment
- c. Insurability
- d. Amortization

Guidance: level 1

:: Currency ::

A _____ , in the most specific sense is money in any form when in use or circulation as a medium of exchange, especially circulating banknotes and coins. A more general definition is that a _____ is a system of money in common use, especially for people in a nation. Under this definition, US dollars , pounds sterling , Australian dollars , European euros , Russian rubles and Indian Rupees are examples of currencies. These various currencies are recognized as stores of value and are traded between nations in foreign exchange markets, which determine the relative values of the different currencies. Currencies in this sense are defined by governments, and each type has limited boundaries of acceptance.

Exam Probability: **High**

49. *Answer choices:*

(see index for correct answer)

- a. Donationcoin
- b. Unit of account
- c. Currency
- d. Currency money

Guidance: level 1

:: Manufacturing ::

_____ s are goods that have completed the manufacturing process but have not yet been sold or distributed to the end user.

50. *Answer choices:*

(see index for correct answer)

- a. Acheson process
- b. Parts book
- c. Toolroom
- d. Finished good

Guidance: level 1

:: ::

A _____ is the period used by governments for accounting and budget purposes, which varies between countries. It is also used for financial reporting by business and other organizations. Laws in many jurisdictions require company financial reports to be prepared and published on an annual basis, but generally do not require the reporting period to align with the calendar year . Taxation laws generally require accounting records to be maintained and taxes calculated on an annual basis, which usually corresponds to the _____ used for government purposes. The calculation of tax on an annual basis is especially relevant for direct taxation, such as income tax. Many annual government fees—such as Council rates, licence fees, etc.—are also levied on a _____ basis, while others are charged on an anniversary basis.

51. *Answer choices:*

(see index for correct answer)

- a. levels of analysis
- b. Fiscal year
- c. interpersonal communication
- d. hierarchical perspective

Guidance: level 1

:: ::

An _____ is an asset that lacks physical substance. It is defined in opposition to physical assets such as machinery and buildings. An _____ is usually very hard to evaluate. Patents, copyrights, franchises, goodwill, trademarks, and trade names. The general interpretation also includes software and other intangible computer based assets are all examples of _____ s. _____ s generally—though not necessarily—suffer from typical market failures of non-rivalry and non-excludability.

Exam Probability: **High**

52. *Answer choices:*

(see index for correct answer)

- a. open system
- b. hierarchical
- c. Intangible asset

- d. Sarbanes-Oxley act of 2002

Guidance: level 1

:: Consumer theory ::

A _____ is a technical term in psychology, economics and philosophy usually used in relation to choosing between alternatives. For example, someone prefers A over B if they would rather choose A than B.

Exam Probability: **Low**

53. *Answer choices:*

(see index for correct answer)

- a. Demand vacuum
- b. Hicksian demand function
- c. Demand set
- d. Permanent income hypothesis

Guidance: level 1

:: Inventory ::

It requires a detailed physical count, so that the company knows exactly how many of each goods brought on specific dates remained at year end inventory. When this information is found, the amount of goods are multiplied by their purchase cost at their purchase date, to get a number for the ending inventory cost.

Exam Probability: **Medium**

54. *Answer choices:*

(see index for correct answer)

- a. Perpetual inventory
- b. Order fulfillment
- c. Periodic inventory
- d. Specific identification

Guidance: level 1

:: Accounting terminology ::

A _____ contains all the accounts for recording transactions relating to a company's assets, liabilities, owners' equity, revenue, and expenses. In modern accounting software or ERP, the _____ works as a central repository for accounting data transferred from all subledgers or modules like accounts payable, accounts receivable, cash management, fixed assets, purchasing and projects. The _____ is the backbone of any accounting system which holds financial and non-financial data for an organization. The collection of all accounts is known as the _____. Each account is known as a ledger account. In a manual or non-computerized system this may be a large book. The statement of financial position and the statement of income and comprehensive income are both derived from the _____. Each account in the _____ consists of one or more pages. The _____ is where posting to the accounts occurs. Posting is the process of recording amounts as credits, and amounts as debits, in the pages of the _____. Additional columns to the right hold a running activity total.

Exam Probability: **High**

55. *Answer choices:*

(see index for correct answer)

- a. Mark-to-market
- b. General ledger
- c. Basis of accounting
- d. revenue recognition principle

Guidance: level 1

:: Government bonds ::

A _____ or sovereign bond is a bond issued by a national government, generally with a promise to pay periodic interest payments called coupon payments and to repay the face value on the maturity date. The aim of a _____ is to support government spending. _____ s are usually denominated in the country's own currency, in which case the government cannot be forced to default, although it may choose to do so. If a government is close to default on its debt the media often refer to this as a sovereign debt crisis.

Exam Probability: **Low**

56. *Answer choices:*

(see index for correct answer)

- a. Eurobonds
- b. Government bond
- c. South Carolina v. Baker
- d. Sovereign bond

Guidance: level 1

:: Money ::

Cash and _____ s are the most liquid current assets found on a business's balance sheet. _____ s are short-term commitments "with temporarily idle cash and easily convertible into a known cash amount". An investment normally counts to be a _____ when it has a short maturity period of 90 days or less, and can be included in the cash and _____ s balance from the date of acquisition when it carries an insignificant risk of changes in the asset value; with more than 90 days maturity, the asset is not considered as cash and _____ s. Equity investments mostly are excluded from _____ s, unless they are essentially _____ s, for instance, if the preferred shares acquired within a short maturity period and with specified recovery date.

Exam Probability: **Low**

57. *Answer choices:*

(see index for correct answer)

- a. Real de alerce
- b. Allowance
- c. Key money
- d. Cash equivalent

Guidance: level 1

:: ::

_____ is a political and social philosophy promoting traditional social institutions in the context of culture and civilization. The central tenets of _____ include tradition, human imperfection, organic society, hierarchy, authority, and property rights. Conservatives seek to preserve a range of institutions such as religion, parliamentary government, and property rights, with the aim of emphasizing social stability and continuity. The more traditional elements—reactionaries—oppose modernism and seek a return to "the way things were".

Exam Probability: **High**

58. *Answer choices:*

(see index for correct answer)

- a. Conservatism
- b. empathy
- c. co-culture
- d. hierarchical

Guidance: level 1

:: Income taxes ::

An _____ is a tax imposed on individuals or entities that varies with respective income or profits . _____ generally is computed as the product of a tax rate times taxable income. Taxation rates may vary by type or characteristics of the taxpayer.

59. *Answer choices:*

(see index for correct answer)

- a. Hall income tax
- b. Individual income tax in Singapore
- c. Shome Panel
- d. Income tax

Guidance: level 1

Human resource management

Human resource (HR) management is the strategic approach to the effective management of organization workers so that they help the business gain a competitive advantage. It is designed to maximize employee performance in service of an employer's strategic objectives. HR is primarily concerned with the management of people within organizations, focusing on policies and on systems. HR departments are responsible for overseeing employee-benefits design, employee recruitment, training and development, performance appraisal, and rewarding (e.g., managing pay and benefit systems). HR also concerns itself with organizational change and industrial relations, that is, the balancing of organizational practices with requirements arising from collective bargaining and from governmental laws.

:: Recruitment ::

_____ is a tool companies and organizations use as a way to communicate the good and the bad characteristics of the job during the hiring process of new employees, or as a tool to reestablish job specificity for existing employees. _____ s should provide the individuals with a well-rounded description that details what obligations the individual can expect to perform while working for that specific company. Descriptions may include, but are not limited to, work environment, expectations, and Company policies .

Exam Probability: **High**

1. *Answer choices:*

(see index for correct answer)

- a. The Select Family of Staffing Companies
- b. Candidate submittal
- c. Structured interview
- d. Realistic job preview

Guidance: level 1

:: Business models ::

A _____ is a diagram that is used to document the primary strategic goals being pursued by an organization or management team. It is an element of the documentation associated with the Balanced Scorecard, and in particular is characteristic of the second generation of Balanced Scorecard designs that first appeared during the mid-1990s. The first diagrams of this type appeared in the early 1990s, and the idea of using this type of diagram to help document Balanced Scorecard was discussed in a paper by Drs. Robert S. Kaplan and David P. Norton in 1996.

Exam Probability: **Medium**

2. *Answer choices:*

(see index for correct answer)

- a. Strategy map
- b. Sailing Ship Effect
- c. Business-agile enterprise
- d. Business Model Canvas

Guidance: level 1

:: ::

_____ is a labor union representing almost 1.9 million workers in over 100 occupations in the United States and Canada. SEIU is focused on organizing workers in three sectors: health care , including hospital, home care and nursing home workers; public services ; and property services .

3. *Answer choices:*

(see index for correct answer)

- a. Service Employees International Union
- b. imperative
- c. functional perspective
- d. personal values

Guidance: level 1

:: Organizational behavior ::

_____ is the state or fact of exclusive rights and control over property, which may be an object, land/real estate or intellectual property. _____ involves multiple rights, collectively referred to as title, which may be separated and held by different parties.

4. *Answer choices:*

(see index for correct answer)

- a. Boreout
- b. Ownership
- c. Nut Island effect

- d. Organizational behavior management

Guidance: level 1

:: Employment compensation ::

Compensation and benefits is a sub-discipline of human resources, focused on employee compensation and benefits policy-making. While compensation and benefits are tangible, there are intangible rewards such as recognition, work-life and development. Combined, these are referred to as _____ s . The term "compensation and benefits" refers to the discipline as well as the rewards themselves.

Exam Probability: **Low**

5. *Answer choices:*
(see index for correct answer)

- a. Broodfonds
- b. Reservation wage
- c. Maximum wage
- d. Pay Bands

Guidance: level 1

:: Hazard analysis ::

A _____ is an agent which has the potential to cause harm to a vulnerable target. The terms " _____ " and "risk" are often used interchangeably. However, in terms of risk assessment, they are two very distinct terms. A _____ is any agent that can cause harm or damage to humans, property, or the environment. Risk is defined as the probability that exposure to a _____ will lead to a negative consequence, or more simply, a _____ poses no risk if there is no exposure to that _____ .

Exam Probability: **Medium**

6. *Answer choices:*

(see index for correct answer)

- a. Risk assessment
- b. Hazard identification
- c. Swiss cheese model
- d. Hazardous Materials Identification System

Guidance: level 1

:: Asset ::

In financial accounting, an _____ is any resource owned by the business. Anything tangible or intangible that can be owned or controlled to produce value and that is held by a company to produce positive economic value is an _____ . Simply stated, _____ s represent value of ownership that can be converted into cash . The balance sheet of a firm records the monetary value of the _____ s owned by that firm. It covers money and other valuables belonging to an individual or to a business.

7. *Answer choices:*

(see index for correct answer)

- a. Current asset
- b. Asset

Guidance: level 1

:: Production and manufacturing ::

_____ is a set of techniques and tools for process improvement. Though as a shortened form it may be found written as 6S, it should not be confused with the methodology known as 6S .

8. *Answer choices:*

(see index for correct answer)

- a. Fieldbus
- b. Joint product
- c. Six Sigma
- d. Business Planning and Control System

Guidance: level 1

An _____ is a process where candidates are examined to determine their suitability for specific types of employment, especially management or military command. The candidates' personality and aptitudes are determined by techniques including interviews, group exercises, presentations, examinations and psychometric testing.

Exam Probability: **Medium**

9. *Answer choices:*

(see index for correct answer)

- a. levels of analysis
- b. personal values
- c. corporate values
- d. Assessment center

Guidance: level 1

:: Network theory ::

A _____ is a social structure made up of a set of social actors , sets of dyadic ties, and other social interactions between actors. The _____ perspective provides a set of methods for analyzing the structure of whole social entities as well as a variety of theories explaining the patterns observed in these structures. The study of these structures uses _____ analysis to identify local and global patterns, locate influential entities, and examine network dynamics.

Exam Probability: **Low**

10. *Answer choices:*

(see index for correct answer)

- a. Network formation
- b. Social network
- c. Degree distribution
- d. Weighted network

Guidance: level 1

:: ::

A _____ is the ability to carry out a task with determined results often within a given amount of time, energy, or both. _____ s can often be divided into domain-general and domain-specific _____ s. For example, in the domain of work, some general _____ s would include time management, teamwork and leadership, self-motivation and others, whereas domain-specific _____ s would be used only for a certain job. _____ usually requires certain environmental stimuli and situations to assess the level of _____ being shown and used.

Exam Probability: **High**

11. *Answer choices:*

(see index for correct answer)

- a. empathy
- b. similarity-attraction theory
- c. Skill
- d. Sarbanes-Oxley act of 2002

Guidance: level 1

:: Socialism ::

In sociology, _____ is the process of internalizing the norms and ideologies of society. _____ encompasses both learning and teaching and is thus "the means by which social and cultural continuity are attained".

Exam Probability: **Low**

12. *Answer choices:*

(see index for correct answer)

- a. Post-capitalism
- b. Socialist feminism
- c. Socialization
- d. Gucci socialist

Guidance: level 1

:: Evaluation methods ::

In social psychology, _____ is the process of looking at oneself in order to assess aspects that are important to one's identity. It is one of the motives that drive self-evaluation, along with self-verification and self-enhancement. Sedikides suggests that the _____ motive will prompt people to seek information to confirm their uncertain self-concept rather than their certain self-concept and at the same time people use _____ to enhance their certainty of their own self-knowledge. However, the _____ motive could be seen as quite different from the other two self-evaluation motives. Unlike the other two motives through _____ people are interested in the accuracy of their current self view, rather than improving their self-view. This makes _____ the only self-evaluative motive that may cause a person's self-esteem to be damaged.

Exam Probability: **Low**

13. *Answer choices:*

(see index for correct answer)

- a. Self-assessment
- b. Moral statistics
- c. quasi-experimental
- d. Pick chart

Guidance: level 1

:: Behaviorism ::

In behavioral psychology, _____ is a consequence applied that will strengthen an organism's future behavior whenever that behavior is preceded by a specific antecedent stimulus. This strengthening effect may be measured as a higher frequency of behavior , longer duration , greater magnitude , or shorter latency . There are two types of _____ , known as positive _____ and negative _____ ; positive is where by a reward is offered on expression of the wanted behaviour and negative is taking away an undesirable element in the persons environment whenever the desired behaviour is achieved.

Exam Probability: **Medium**

14. *Answer choices:*

(see index for correct answer)

- a. Reinforcement
- b. contingency management
- c. social facilitation
- d. Matching Law

:: Trade union legislation ::

The _____ is the name for several legislative bills on US labor law which have been proposed and sometimes introduced into one or both chambers of the U.S. Congress.

Exam Probability: **High**

15. *Answer choices:*

(see index for correct answer)

- a. Labor Management Relations Act of 1947
- b. Employee Free Choice Act
- c. Trade Union Act 1984
- d. Employment Act 1982

:: ::

A _____ is a technical analysis of a biological specimen, for example urine, hair, blood, breath, sweat, and/or oral fluid/saliva—to determine the presence or absence of specified parent drugs or their metabolites. Major applications of _____ ing include detection of the presence of performance enhancing steroids in sport, employers and parole/probation officers screening for drugs prohibited by law and police officers testing for the presence and concentration of alcohol in the blood commonly referred to as BAC . BAC tests are typically administered via a breathalyzer while urinalysis is used for the vast majority of _____ ing in sports and the workplace. Numerous other methods with varying degrees of accuracy, sensitivity , and detection periods exist.

Exam Probability: **Low**

16. *Answer choices:*

(see index for correct answer)

- a. empathy
- b. Drug test
- c. Character
- d. information systems assessment

Guidance: level 1

___

:: Management ::

_____ is a technique used by some employers to rotate their employees' assigned jobs throughout their employment. Employers practice this technique for a number of reasons. It was designed to promote flexibility of employees and to keep employees interested into staying with the company/organization which employs them. There is also research that shows how _____ s help relieve the stress of employees who work in a job that requires manual labor.

Exam Probability: **High**

17. *Answer choices:*

(see index for correct answer)

- a. Corporate transparency
- b. Hierarchical organization
- c. Interim management
- d. Job rotation

Guidance: level 1

:: ::

A _____ contract is a form of employment that carries fewer hours per week than a full-time job. They work in shifts. The shifts are often rotational. Workers are considered to be _____ if they commonly work fewer than 30 hours per week. According to the International Labour Organization, the number of _____ workers has increased from one-fourth to a half in the past 20 years in most developed countries, excluding the United States. There are many reasons for working _____ , including the desire to do so, having one's hours cut back by an employer and being unable to find a full-time job. The International Labour Organisation Convention 175 requires that _____ workers be treated no less favourably than full-time workers.

Exam Probability: **High**

18. *Answer choices:*

(see index for correct answer)

- a. Part-time
- b. information systems assessment
- c. interpersonal communication
- d. surface-level diversity

Guidance: level 1

:: Human resource management ::

A _____ is a form of payment from an employer to an employee, which may be specified in an employment contract. It is contrasted with piece wages, where each job, hour or other unit is paid separately, rather than on a periodic basis. From the point of view of running a business, _____ can also be viewed as the cost of acquiring and retaining human resources for running operations, and is then termed personnel expense or _____ expense. In accounting, salaries are recorded in payroll accounts.

Exam Probability: **Low**

19. *Answer choices:*

(see index for correct answer)

- a. Human resources
- b. Adaptive performance
- c. Labour is not a commodity
- d. Pay in lieu of notice

Guidance: level 1

:: Human resource management ::

_____ means increasing the scope of a job through extending the range of its job duties and responsibilities generally within the same level and periphery. _____ involves combining various activities at the same level in the organization and adding them to the existing job. It is also called the horizontal expansion of job activities. This contradicts the principles of specialisation and the division of labour whereby work is divided into small units, each of which is performed repetitively by an individual worker and the responsibilities are always clear. Some motivational theories suggest that the boredom and alienation caused by the division of labour can actually cause efficiency to fall. Thus, _____ seeks to motivate workers through reversing the process of specialisation. A typical approach might be to replace assembly lines with modular work; instead of an employee repeating the same step on each product, they perform several tasks on a single item. In order for employees to be provided with _____ they will need to be retrained in new fields to understand how each field works.

Exam Probability: **High**

20. *Answer choices:*

(see index for correct answer)

- a. ABC Consultants
- b. Job enlargement
- c. Focal Point Review
- d. Management development

Guidance: level 1

:: Human resource management ::

_____ are the people who make up the workforce of an organization, business sector, or economy. "Human capital" is sometimes used synonymously with " _____ ", although human capital typically refers to a narrower effect . Likewise, other terms sometimes used include manpower, talent, labor, personnel, or simply people.

Exam Probability: **Low**

21. *Answer choices:*

(see index for correct answer)

- a. Vendor management system
- b. war for talent
- c. Human resources
- d. Workplace mentoring

Guidance: level 1

:: Financial statements ::

In financial accounting, a _____ or statement of financial position or statement of financial condition is a summary of the financial balances of an individual or organization, whether it be a sole proprietorship, a business partnership, a corporation, private limited company or other organization such as Government or not-for-profit entity. Assets, liabilities and ownership equity are listed as of a specific date, such as the end of its financial year. A _____ is often described as a "snapshot of a company's financial condition". Of the four basic financial statements, the _____ is the only statement which applies to a single point in time of a business' calendar year.

Exam Probability: **High**

22. *Answer choices:*

(see index for correct answer)

- a. Balance sheet
- b. Statement on Auditing Standards No. 70: Service Organizations
- c. Government financial statements
- d. Emphasis of matter

Guidance: level 1

:: Labour relations ::

_____ is a form of protest in which people congregate outside a place of work or location where an event is taking place. Often, this is done in an attempt to dissuade others from going in , but it can also be done to draw public attention to a cause. Picketers normally endeavor to be non-violent. It can have a number of aims, but is generally to put pressure on the party targeted to meet particular demands or cease operations. This pressure is achieved by harming the business through loss of customers and negative publicity, or by discouraging or preventing workers or customers from entering the site and thereby preventing the business from operating normally.

Exam Probability: **High**

23. *Answer choices:*

(see index for correct answer)

- a. Lockout
- b. Jesse Simons
- c. Disciplinary counseling
- d. Union shop

Guidance: level 1

:: Validity (statistics) ::

In psychometrics, criterion or concrete validity is the extent to which a measure is related to an outcome. _____ is often divided into concurrent and predictive validity. Concurrent validity refers to a comparison between the measure in question and an outcome assessed at the same time. In Standards for Educational & Psychological Tests, it states, "concurrent validity reflects only the status quo at a particular time." Predictive validity, on the other hand, compares the measure in question with an outcome assessed at a later time. Although concurrent and predictive validity are similar, it is cautioned to keep the terms and findings separated. "Concurrent validity should not be used as a substitute for predictive validity without an appropriate supporting rationale."

Exam Probability: **High**

24. *Answer choices:*

(see index for correct answer)

- a. Construct validity
- b. Face validity
- c. Criterion validity
- d. External validity

Guidance: level 1

:: Employment ::

The _____ is an individual's metaphorical "journey" through learning, work and other aspects of life. There are a number of ways to define _____ and the term is used in a variety of ways.

25. *Answer choices:*

(see index for correct answer)

- a. Job shadow
- b. Proven
- c. Iron rice bowl
- d. Working parent

Guidance: level 1

:: Organizational theory ::

_____ is the process of creating, retaining, and transferring knowledge within an organization. An organization improves over time as it gains experience. From this experience, it is able to create knowledge. This knowledge is broad, covering any topic that could better an organization. Examples may include ways to increase production efficiency or to develop beneficial investor relations. Knowledge is created at four different units: individual, group, organizational, and inter organizational.

Exam Probability: **Medium**

26. *Answer choices:*

(see index for correct answer)

- a. Organizational learning

- b. Smart city
- c. High reliability organization
- d. Solid line reporting

Guidance: level 1

:: Recruitment ::

A _____ or background investigation is the process of looking up and compiling criminal records, commercial records, and financial records of an individual or an organization. The frequency, purpose, and legitimacy of _____ s varies between countries, industries, and individuals. A variety of methods are used to complete such a check, from comprehensive data base search to personal references.

Exam Probability: **Medium**

27. *Answer choices:*

(see index for correct answer)

- a. Multiple mini interview
- b. Probation
- c. Background check
- d. Riviera Partners

Guidance: level 1

:: Industrial engineering ::

_____ is the formal process that sits alongside Requirements analysis and focuses on the human elements of the requirements.

Exam Probability: **High**

28. *Answer choices:*

(see index for correct answer)

- a. Systematic layout planning
- b. Needs analysis
- c. Pilot plant
- d. Work Measurement

Guidance: level 1

:: Occupational safety and health ::

Note: Parts of this article are written from the perspective of aircraft safety analysis techniques and definitions; these may not represent current best practice and the article needs to be updated to represent a more generic description of _____ and discussion of more modern standards and techniques.

Exam Probability: **Medium**

29. *Answer choices:*

(see index for correct answer)

- a. CANOSH
- b. Health and safety law
- c. National Fire Fighter Near-Miss Reporting System
- d. Hazard analysis

Guidance: level 1

:: Human resource management ::

_____ is the application of information technology for both networking and supporting at least two individual or collective actors in their shared performing of HR activities.

Exam Probability: **High**

30. *Answer choices:*

(see index for correct answer)

- a. Expense management
- b. Joint Personnel Administration
- c. Herrmann Brain Dominance Instrument
- d. E-HRM

Guidance: level 1

:: Human resource management ::

_____ are transactions in which the ownership of companies, other business organizations, or their operating units are transferred or consolidated with other entities. As an aspect of strategic management, M&A can allow enterprises to grow or downsize, and change the nature of their business or competitive position.

Exam Probability: **High**

31. *Answer choices:*

(see index for correct answer)

- a. Mentorship
- b. Diversity Icebreaker
- c. Mergers and acquisitions
- d. Person specification

Guidance: level 1

:: Recruitment ::

A _____ is a quantitative research method commonly employed in survey research. The aim of this approach is to ensure that each interview is presented with exactly the same questions in the same order. This ensures that answers can be reliably aggregated and that comparisons can be made with confidence between sample subgroups or between different survey periods.

Exam Probability: **High**

32. *Answer choices:*

(see index for correct answer)

- a. Common Recruitment Examination
- b. Riviera Partners
- c. Employability
- d. Railway Recruitment Control Board

Guidance: level 1

:: Business ethics ::

In United States labor law, a _____ exists when one's behavior within a workplace creates an environment that is difficult or uncomfortable for another person to work in, due to discrimination. Common complaints in sexual harassment lawsuits include fondling, suggestive remarks, sexually-suggestive photos displayed in the workplace, use of sexual language, or off-color jokes. Small matters, annoyances, and isolated incidents are usually not considered to be statutory violations of the discrimination laws. For a violation to impose liability, the conduct must create a work environment that would be intimidating, hostile, or offensive to a reasonable person. An employer can be held liable for failing to prevent these workplace conditions, unless it can prove that it attempted to prevent the harassment and that the employee failed to take advantage of existing harassment counter-measures or tools provided by the employer.

Exam Probability: **High**

33. *Answer choices:*

(see index for correct answer)

- a. Unfree labour
- b. Walmarting
- c. Altruistic corporate social responsibility
- d. Hostile work environment

Guidance: level 1

:: ::

Refresher/ _____ is the process of learning a new or the same old skill or trade for the same group of personnel. Refresher/ _____ is required to be provided on regular basis to avoid personnel obsolescence due to technological changes & the individuals memory capacity. This short term instruction course shall serve to re-acquaint personnel with skills previously learnt or to bring one's knowledge or skills up-to-date so that skills stay sharp. This kind of training could be provided annually or more frequently as maybe required, based on the importance of consistency of the task of which the skill is involved. Examples of refreshers are cGMP, GDP, HSE trainings.

_____ shall also be conducted for an employee, when the employee is rated as 'not qualified' for a skill or knowledge, as determined based on the assessment of answers in the training questionnaire of the employee.

Exam Probability: **High**

34. *Answer choices:*

(see index for correct answer)

- a. empathy
- b. hierarchical perspective
- c. cultural
- d. Retraining

Guidance: level 1

:: Ethically disputed business practices ::

An _____ in US labor law refers to certain actions taken by employers or unions that violate the National Labor Relations Act of 1935 29 U.S.C. § 151–169 and other legislation. Such acts are investigated by the National Labor Relations Board .

Exam Probability: **High**

35. *Answer choices:*

(see index for correct answer)

- a. Wrongful dismissal
- b. Error account
- c. Tobashi scheme
- d. Unfair labor practice

Guidance: level 1

:: United Kingdom labour law ::

The _____ was a series of programs, public work projects, financial reforms, and regulations enacted by President Franklin D. Roosevelt in the United States between 1933 and 1936. It responded to needs for relief, reform, and recovery from the Great Depression. Major federal programs included the Civilian Conservation Corps , the Civil Works Administration , the Farm Security Administration , the National Industrial Recovery Act of 1933 and the Social Security Administration . They provided support for farmers, the unemployed, youth and the elderly. The _____ included new constraints and safeguards on the banking industry and efforts to re-inflate the economy after prices had fallen sharply. _____ programs included both laws passed by Congress as well as presidential executive orders during the first term of the presidency of Franklin D. Roosevelt.

Exam Probability: **High**

36. *Answer choices:*

(see index for correct answer)

- a. Paternity and Adoption Leave Regulations 2002
- b. Employers and Workmen Act 1875
- c. Collective laissez faire
- d. New Deal

Guidance: level 1

:: Options (finance) ::

_____ is a contractual agreement between a corporation and recipients of phantom shares that bestow upon the grantee the right to a cash payment at a designated time or in association with a designated event in the future, which payment is to be in an amount tied to the market value of an equivalent number of shares of the corporation's stock. Thus, the amount of the payout will increase as the stock price rises, and decrease if the stock falls, but without the recipient actually receiving any stock. Like other forms of stock-based compensation plans, _____ broadly serves to align the interests of recipients and shareholders, incent contribution to share value, and encourage the retention or continued participation of contributors. Recipients are typically employees, but may also be directors, third-party vendors, or others.

Exam Probability: **Medium**

37. *Answer choices:*

(see index for correct answer)

- a. Chicago Options Associates
- b. Greenspan put
- c. LEAPS
- d. Naked put

Guidance: level 1

:: Behavior ::

_____ refers to behavior-change procedures that were employed during the 1970s and early 1980s. Based on methodological behaviorism, overt behavior was modified with presumed consequences, including artificial positive and negative reinforcement contingencies to increase desirable behavior, or administering positive and negative punishment and/or extinction to reduce problematic behavior. For the treatment of phobias, habituation and punishment were the basic principles used in flooding, a subcategory of desensitization.

Exam Probability: **High**

38. *Answer choices:*

(see index for correct answer)

- a. Behavior modification
- b. theory of reasoned action

Guidance: level 1

:: Business ethics ::

_____ is a pejorative term for a workplace that has very poor, socially unacceptable working conditions. The work may be difficult, dangerous, climatically challenged or underpaid. Workers in _____ s may work long hours with low pay, regardless of laws mandating overtime pay or a minimum wage; child labor laws may also be violated. The Fair Labor Association's "2006 Annual Public Report" inspected factories for FLA compliance in 18 countries including Bangladesh, El Salvador, Colombia, Guatemala, Malaysia, Thailand, Tunisia, Turkey, China, India, Vietnam, Honduras, Indonesia, Brazil, Mexico, and the US. The U.S. Department of Labor's "2015 Findings on the Worst Forms of Child Labor" found that "18 countries did not meet the International Labour Organization's recommendation for an adequate number of inspectors."

Exam Probability: **Low**

39. *Answer choices:*

(see index for correct answer)

- a. Sweatshop
- b. Employee raiding
- c. Integrity management
- d. Burson-Marsteller

Guidance: level 1

:: Personal finance ::

_____ is an arrangement in which a portion of an employee's income is paid out at a later date after which the income was earned. Examples of _____ include pensions, retirement plans, and employee stock options. The primary benefit of most _____ is the deferral of tax to the date at which the employee receives the income.

Exam Probability: **High**

40. *Answer choices:*

(see index for correct answer)

- a. Deferred compensation
- b. Prestige Bulletin
- c. West One Bridging Index
- d. The Money Tracker

Guidance: level 1

:: ::

_____ is the administration of an organization, whether it is a business, a not-for-profit organization, or government body. _____ includes the activities of setting the strategy of an organization and coordinating the efforts of its employees to accomplish its objectives through the application of available resources, such as financial, natural, technological, and human resources. The term "_____" may also refer to those people who manage an organization.

41. *Answer choices:*

(see index for correct answer)

- a. hierarchical
- b. levels of analysis
- c. deep-level diversity
- d. Management

Guidance: level 1

:: Psychometrics ::

Electronic assessment, also known as e-assessment, _____ , computer assisted/mediated assessment and computer-based assessment, is the use of information technology in various forms of assessment such as educational assessment, health assessment, psychiatric assessment, and psychological assessment. This may utilize an online computer connected to a network. This definition embraces a wide range of student activity ranging from the use of a word processor to on-screen testing. Specific types of e-assessment include multiple choice, online/electronic submission, computerized adaptive testing and computerized classification testing.

Exam Probability: **High**

42. *Answer choices:*

(see index for correct answer)

- a. Online assessment
- b. Multitrait-multimethod matrix
- c. Sten scores
- d. Adaptive comparative judgement

Guidance: level 1

:: Occupational safety and health ::

A safety data sheet , _____ , or product safety data sheet is a document that lists information relating to occupational safety and health for the use of various substances and products. SDSs are a widely used system for cataloging information on chemicals, chemical compounds, and chemical mixtures. SDS information may include instructions for the safe use and potential hazards associated with a particular material or product, along with spill-handling procedures. SDS formats can vary from source to source within a country depending on national requirements.

Exam Probability: **Low**

43. *Answer choices:*

(see index for correct answer)

- a. Falling
- b. Donald Hunter
- c. Manganese
- d. Material safety data sheet

:: Employment compensation ::

A _____ is a type of employee benefit plan offered in the United States pursuant to Section 125 of the Internal Revenue Code. Its name comes from the earliest such plans that allowed employees to choose between different types of benefits, similar to the ability of a customer to choose among available items in a cafeteria. Qualified _____ s are excluded from gross income. To qualify, a _____ must allow employees to choose from two or more benefits consisting of cash or qualified benefit plans. The Internal Revenue Code explicitly excludes deferred compensation plans from qualifying as a _____ subject to a gross income exemption. Section 125 also provides two exceptions.

Exam Probability: **Medium**

44. *Answer choices:*

(see index for correct answer)

- a. salary sacrifice
- b. Medical Care and Sickness Benefits Convention, 1969
- c. Stock appreciation right
- d. Salary calculator

:: Organizational theory ::

Decentralisation is the process by which the activities of an organization, particularly those regarding planning and decision making, are distributed or delegated away from a central, authoritative location or group. Concepts of _____ have been applied to group dynamics and management science in private businesses and organizations, political science, law and public administration, economics, money and technology.

Exam Probability: **High**

45. *Answer choices:*

(see index for correct answer)

- a. Battlefield promotion
- b. Decentralization
- c. Organizational performance
- d. Staff augmentation

Guidance: level 1

:: Labor terms ::

_____ , often called DI or disability income insurance, or income protection, is a form of insurance that insures the beneficiary's earned income against the risk that a disability creates a barrier for a worker to complete the core functions of their work. For example, the worker may suffer from an inability to maintain composure in the case of psychological disorders or an injury, illness or condition that causes physical impairment or incapacity to work. It encompasses paid sick leave, short-term disability benefits , and long-term disability benefits . Statistics show that in the US a disabling accident occurs, on average, once every second. In fact, nearly 18.5% of Americans are currently living with a disability, and 1 out of every 4 persons in the US workforce will suffer a disabling injury before retirement.

Exam Probability: **Low**

46. *Answer choices:*

(see index for correct answer)

- a. Strike action
- b. Capital services
- c. All other occupational illnesses
- d. Disability insurance

Guidance: level 1

:: Cognitive biases ::

In personality psychology, _____ is the degree to which people believe that they have control over the outcome of events in their lives, as opposed to external forces beyond their control. Understanding of the concept was developed by Julian B. Rotter in 1954, and has since become an aspect of personality studies. A person's "locus" is conceptualized as internal or external .

Exam Probability: **High**

47. *Answer choices:*

(see index for correct answer)

- a. Group attribution error
- b. Availability heuristic
- c. Locus of control
- d. Wishful thinking

Guidance: level 1

:: Belief ::

_____ is an umbrella term of influence. _____ can attempt to influence a person's beliefs, attitudes, intentions, motivations, or behaviors. In business, _____ is a process aimed at changing a person's attitude or behavior toward some event, idea, object, or other person, by using written, spoken words or visual tools to convey information, feelings, or reasoning, or a combination thereof. _____ is also an often used tool in the pursuit of personal gain, such as election campaigning, giving a sales pitch, or in trial advocacy. _____ can also be interpreted as using one's personal or positional resources to change people's behaviors or attitudes. Systematic _____ is the process through which attitudes or beliefs are leveraged by appeals to logic and reason. Heuristic _____ on the other hand is the process through which attitudes or beliefs are leveraged by appeals to habit or emotion.

Exam Probability: **Low**

48. *Answer choices:*

(see index for correct answer)

- a. Persuasion
- b. Ethics of belief
- c. Sententia certa
- d. Doxa

Guidance: level 1

:: ::

In business strategy, _____ is establishing a competitive advantage by having the lowest cost of operation in the industry. _____ is often driven by company efficiency, size, scale, scope and cumulative experience .A _____ strategy aims to exploit scale of production, well-defined scope and other economies , producing highly standardized products, using advanced technology.In recent years, more and more companies have chosen a strategic mix to achieve market leadership. These patterns consist of simultaneous _____ , superior customer service and product leadership. Walmart has succeeded across the world due to its _____ strategy. The company has cut down on exesses at every point of production and thus are able to provide the consumers with quality products at low prices.

Exam Probability: **Low**

49. *Answer choices:*

(see index for correct answer)

- a. Cost leadership
- b. functional perspective
- c. deep-level diversity
- d. Character

Guidance: level 1

:: Management ::

_____ is the kind of knowledge that is difficult to transfer to another person by means of writing it down or verbalizing it. For example, that London is in the United Kingdom is a piece of explicit knowledge that can be written down, transmitted, and understood by a recipient. However, the ability to speak a language, ride a bicycle, knead dough, play a musical instrument, or design and use complex equipment requires all sorts of knowledge that is not always known explicitly, even by expert practitioners, and which is difficult or impossible to explicitly transfer to other people.

Exam Probability: **High**

50. *Answer choices:*

(see index for correct answer)

- a. Tacit knowledge
- b. Managerial Psychology
- c. Quick response manufacturing
- d. Gemba

Guidance: level 1

:: Employee relations ::

_____ is a fundamental concept in the effort to understand and describe, both qualitatively and quantitatively, the nature of the relationship between an organization and its employees. An "engaged employee" is defined as one who is fully absorbed by and enthusiastic about their work and so takes positive action to further the organization's reputation and interests. An engaged employee has a positive attitude towards the organization and its values. In contrast, a disengaged employee may range from someone doing the bare minimum at work, up to an employee who is actively damaging the company's work output and reputation.

Exam Probability: **High**

51. *Answer choices:*

(see index for correct answer)

- a. Employee engagement
- b. Employee handbook
- c. Fringe benefit
- d. employee stock ownership

Guidance: level 1

:: Employment ::

_____ is measuring the output of a particular business process or procedure, then modifying the process or procedure to increase the output, increase efficiency, or increase the effectiveness of the process or procedure. _____ can be applied to either individual performance such as an athlete or organizational performance such as a racing team or a commercial business.

52. *Answer choices:*

(see index for correct answer)

- a. Participatory ergonomics
- b. Make-work job
- c. Contingent employment
- d. Illicit work

Guidance: level 1

:: Validity (statistics) ::

In psychometrics, _____ refers to the extent to which a measure represents all facets of a given construct. For example, a depression scale may lack _____ if it only assesses the affective dimension of depression but fails to take into account the behavioral dimension. An element of subjectivity exists in relation to determining _____ , which requires a degree of agreement about what a particular personality trait such as extraversion represents. A disagreement about a personality trait will prevent the gain of a high _____ .

Exam Probability: **High**

53. *Answer choices:*

(see index for correct answer)

- a. Verification and validation
- b. Test validity
- c. Statistical conclusion
- d. Content validity

Guidance: level 1

:: Offshoring ::

A _____ is the temporary suspension or permanent termination of employment of an employee or, more commonly, a group of employees for business reasons, such as personnel management or downsizing an organization. Originally, _____ referred exclusively to a temporary interruption in work, or employment but this has evolved to a permanent elimination of a position in both British and US English, requiring the addition of "temporary" to specify the original meaning of the word. A _____ is not to be confused with wrongful termination. Laid off workers or displaced workers are workers who have lost or left their jobs because their employer has closed or moved, there was insufficient work for them to do, or their position or shift was abolished . Downsizing in a company is defined to involve the reduction of employees in a workforce. Downsizing in companies became a popular practice in the 1980s and early 1990s as it was seen as a way to deliver better shareholder value as it helps to reduce the costs of employers . Indeed, recent research on downsizing in the U.S., UK, and Japan suggests that downsizing is being regarded by management as one of the preferred routes to help declining organizations, cutting unnecessary costs, and improve organizational performance. Usually a _____ occurs as a cost cutting measure.

Exam Probability: **High**

54. *Answer choices:*

(see index for correct answer)

- a. Antex
- b. Sourcing advisory
- c. Offshore outsourcing
- d. Layoff

Guidance: level 1

:: Management ::

In business, a _____ is the attribute that allows an organization to outperform its competitors. A _____ may include access to natural resources, such as high-grade ores or a low-cost power source, highly skilled labor, geographic location, high entry barriers, and access to new technology.

Exam Probability: **Medium**

55. *Answer choices:*

(see index for correct answer)

- a. Product life-cycle management
- b. Community-based management
- c. Competitive advantage
- d. Planning

Guidance: level 1

:: Problem solving ::

A _____ is a unit or formation established to work on a single defined task or activity. Originally introduced by the United States Navy, the term has now caught on for general usage and is a standard part of NATO terminology. Many non-military organizations now create " _____ s" or task groups for temporary activities that might have once been performed by ad hoc committees.

Exam Probability: **High**

56. *Answer choices:*

(see index for correct answer)

- a. Task force
- b. Creative Education Foundation
- c. Cognitive acceleration
- d. Trial and error

Guidance: level 1

:: Employment compensation ::

A _____ is pay and benefits employees receive when they leave employment at a company unwillfully. In addition to their remaining regular pay, it may include some of the following.

57. *Answer choices:*

(see index for correct answer)

- a. Equal pay for equal work
- b. Fiduciary management
- c. Severance package
- d. Salary calculator

Guidance: level 1

:: Validity (statistics) ::

In psychometrics, _____ is the extent to which a score on a scale or test predicts scores on some criterion measure.

58. *Answer choices:*

(see index for correct answer)

- a. Criterion validity
- b. Internal validity
- c. Statistical conclusion
- d. Predictive validity

:: Employment compensation ::

_____ is a notional derivative of a Health Reimbursement Arrangement , a type of US employer-funded health benefit plan that reimburses employees for out-of-pocket medical expenses and, in limited cases, to pay for health insurance plan premiums.

Exam Probability: **High**

59. *Answer choices:*

(see index for correct answer)

- a. Severance package
- b. Fringe benefits tax
- c. Health Reimbursement Account
- d. Corporate child care

Information systems

Information systems (IS) are formal, sociotechnical, organizational systems designed to collect, process, store, and distribute information. In a sociotechnical perspective Information Systems are composed by four components: technology, process, people and organizational structure.

:: Data management ::

_____ is a form of intellectual property that grants the creator of an original creative work an exclusive legal right to determine whether and under what conditions this original work may be copied and used by others, usually for a limited term of years. The exclusive rights are not absolute but limited by limitations and exceptions to _____ law, including fair use. A major limitation on _____ on ideas is that _____ protects only the original expression of ideas, and not the underlying ideas themselves.

Exam Probability: **Medium**

1. *Answer choices:*

(see index for correct answer)

- a. Content migration
- b. Copyright
- c. Data field
- d. Control break

Guidance: level 1

:: ::

Sustainability is the process of people maintaining change in a balanced environment, in which the exploitation of resources, the direction of investments, the orientation of technological development and institutional change are all in harmony and enhance both current and future potential to meet human needs and aspirations. For many in the field, sustainability is defined through the following interconnected domains or pillars: environment, economic and social, which according to Fritjof Capra is based on the principles of Systems Thinking. Sub-domains of _____ development have been considered also: cultural, technological and political. While _____ development may be the organizing principle for sustainability for some, for others, the two terms are paradoxical . _____ development is the development that meets the needs of the present without compromising the ability of future generations to meet their own needs. Brundtland Report for the World Commission on Environment and Development introduced the term of _____ development.

Exam Probability: **Low**

2. *Answer choices:*

(see index for correct answer)

- a. imperative
- b. surface-level diversity
- c. Sustainable
- d. Character

Guidance: level 1

:: ::

_____ are electronic transfer of money from one bank account to another, either within a single financial institution or across multiple institutions, via computer-based systems, without the direct intervention of bank staff.

Exam Probability: **High**

3. *Answer choices:*

(see index for correct answer)

- a. Electronic funds transfer
- b. co-culture
- c. functional perspective
- d. levels of analysis

Guidance: level 1

:: Management ::

The _____ is a strategy performance management tool – a semi-standard structured report, that can be used by managers to keep track of the execution of activities by the staff within their control and to monitor the consequences arising from these actions.

Exam Probability: **Low**

4. *Answer choices:*

- a. Risk management
- b. Balanced scorecard
- c. Business process improvement
- d. Relevance paradox

Guidance: level 1

:: Payment systems ::

_____ s are part of a payment system issued by financial institutions, such as a bank, to a customer that enables its owner to access the funds in the customer's designated bank accounts, or through a credit account and make payments by electronic funds transfer and access automated teller machines . Such cards are known by a variety of names including bank cards, ATM cards, MAC , client cards, key cards or cash cards.

Exam Probability: **Low**

5. *Answer choices:*

- a. Payment card
- b. Demand draft
- c. Mobile purchasing
- d. Check 21 Act

:: Computer memory ::

_____ is an electronic non-volatile computer storage medium that can be electrically erased and reprogrammed.

Exam Probability: **Medium**

6. *Answer choices:*

(see index for correct answer)

- a. Flash memory
- b. NCache
- c. EPROM
- d. PLEDM

:: Online companies ::

_____ is a business directory service and crowd-sourced review forum, and a public company of the same name that is headquartered in San Francisco, California. The company develops, hosts and markets the _____ .com website and the _____ mobile app, which publish crowd-sourced reviews about businesses. It also operates an online reservation service called _____ Reservations.

Exam Probability: **High**

7. *Answer choices:*

(see index for correct answer)

- a. Teledesic
- b. DailyBooth
- c. Yelp
- d. Direct Ferries

Guidance: level 1

:: E-commerce ::

_____ , and its now-deprecated predecessor, Secure Sockets Layer , are cryptographic protocols designed to provide communications security over a computer network. Several versions of the protocols find widespread use in applications such as web browsing, email, instant messaging, and voice over IP . Websites can use TLS to secure all communications between their servers and web browsers.

8. *Answer choices:*

- a. Computer reservations system
- b. Transport Layer Security
- c. Storefront
- d. AbleCommerce

Guidance: level 1

:: Statistical laws ::

In statistics and business, a _____ of some distributions of numbers is the portion of the distribution having a large number of occurrences far from the "head" or central part of the distribution. The distribution could involve popularities, random numbers of occurrences of events with various probabilities, etc. The term is often used loosely, with no definition or arbitrary definition, but precise definitions are possible.

Exam Probability: **Medium**

9. *Answer choices:*

- a. Law of the unconscious statistician
- b. Safety in numbers

- c. Law of averages
- d. Long tail

Guidance: level 1

:: Information systems ::

A _____ is an information system that supports business or organizational decision-making activities. DSSs serve the management, operations and planning levels of an organization and help people make decisions about problems that may be rapidly changing and not easily specified in advance—i.e. unstructured and semi-structured decision problems. _____ s can be either fully computerized or human-powered, or a combination of both.

Exam Probability: **High**

10. *Answer choices:*

(see index for correct answer)

- a. TOPS
- b. Policy appliances
- c. Process development execution system
- d. FAO GM Foods Platform

Guidance: level 1

:: ::

A _____ is a published declaration of the intentions, motives, or views of the issuer, be it an individual, group, political party or government. A _____ usually accepts a previously published opinion or public consensus or promotes a new idea with prescriptive notions for carrying out changes the author believes should be made. It often is political or artistic in nature, but may present an individual's life stance. _____ s relating to religious belief are generally referred to as creeds.

Exam Probability: **High**

11. *Answer choices:*

(see index for correct answer)

- a. interpersonal communication
- b. information systems assessment
- c. levels of analysis
- d. Manifesto

Guidance: level 1

:: Data analysis ::

_____ , also referred to as text data mining, roughly equivalent to text analytics, is the process of deriving high-quality information from text. High-quality information is typically derived through the devising of patterns and trends through means such as statistical pattern learning. _____ usually involves the process of structuring the input text , deriving patterns within the structured data, and finally evaluation and interpretation of the output. 'High quality' in _____ usually refers to some combination of relevance, novelty, and interest. Typical _____ tasks include text categorization, text clustering, concept/entity extraction, production of granular taxonomies, sentiment analysis, document summarization, and entity relation modeling .

Exam Probability: **High**

12. *Answer choices:*

(see index for correct answer)

- a. LISREL
- b. Text mining
- c. Synqera
- d. Exponential smoothing

Guidance: level 1

:: Web security exploits ::

A _____ is a baked or cooked food that is small, flat and sweet. It usually contains flour, sugar and some type of oil or fat. It may include other ingredients such as raisins, oats, chocolate chips, nuts, etc.

13. *Answer choices:*

(see index for correct answer)

- a. PLA Unit 61398
- b. Referer spoofing
- c. Cookie
- d. HTTP header injection

Guidance: level 1

:: Ubiquitous computing ::

A _____ , chip card, or integrated circuit card is a physical electronic authorization device, used to control access to a resource. It is typically a plastic credit card sized card with an embedded integrated circuit. Many _____ s include a pattern of metal contacts to electrically connect to the internal chip. Others are contactless, and some are both. _____ s can provide personal identification, authentication, data storage, and application processing. Applications include identification, financial, mobile phones , public transit, computer security, schools, and healthcare.

_____ s may provide strong security authentication for single sign-on within organizations. Several nations have deployed _____ s throughout their populations.

Exam Probability: **Low**

14. *Answer choices:*

(see index for correct answer)

- a. Wireless lock
- b. Smart card
- c. Contactless smart card
- d. Intelligent street

Guidance: level 1

:: Information technology management ::

The term _____ is used to refer to periods when a system is unavailable. _____ or outage duration refers to a period of time that a system fails to provide or perform its primary function. Reliability, availability, recovery, and unavailability are related concepts. The unavailability is the proportion of a time-span that a system is unavailable or offline. This is usually a result of the system failing to function because of an unplanned event, or because of routine maintenance .

Exam Probability: **Low**

15. *Answer choices:*
(see index for correct answer)

- a. Mobile document access
- b. NetIQ
- c. Business Information Services Library
- d. Downtime

:: Geographic information systems ::

_____ is the computational process of transforming a physical address description to a location on the Earth's surface . Reverse _____ , on the other hand, converts geographic coordinates to a description of a location, usually the name of a place or an addressable location. _____ relies on a computer representation of address points, the street / road network, together with postal and administrative boundaries.

Exam Probability: **High**

16. *Answer choices:*

(see index for correct answer)

- a. Buffer
- b. Interlis
- c. AM/FM/GIS
- d. Geocoding

:: Confidence tricks ::

_____ is the fraudulent attempt to obtain sensitive information such as usernames, passwords and credit card details by disguising oneself as a trustworthy entity in an electronic communication. Typically carried out by email spoofing or instant messaging, it often directs users to enter personal information at a fake website which matches the look and feel of the legitimate site.

Exam Probability: **Low**

17. *Answer choices:*

(see index for correct answer)

- a. Fortune telling fraud
- b. The switch
- c. Scams in intellectual property
- d. Sucker list

Guidance: level 1

:: Management ::

In business, a _____ is the attribute that allows an organization to outperform its competitors. A _____ may include access to natural resources, such as high-grade ores or a low-cost power source, highly skilled labor, geographic location, high entry barriers, and access to new technology.

Exam Probability: **High**

18. *Answer choices:*

(see index for correct answer)

- a. Certified Project Management Professional
- b. Sales outsourcing
- c. Managerial economics
- d. Competitive advantage

Guidance: level 1

:: ::

Collaborative software or _____ is application software designed to help people involved in a common task to achieve their goals. One of the earliest definitions of collaborative software is "intentional group processes plus software to support them".

Exam Probability: **Medium**

19. *Answer choices:*

(see index for correct answer)

- a. open system
- b. process perspective
- c. Groupware
- d. functional perspective

:: Data security ::

In information technology, a _____ , or data _____ , or the process of backing up, refers to the copying into an archive file of computer data that is already in secondary storage—so that it may be used to restore the original after a data loss event. The verb form is "back up" , whereas the noun and adjective form is " _____ ".

Exam Probability: **Medium**

20. *Answer choices:*

(see index for correct answer)

- a. Backup
- b. Administrative share
- c. Information security management system
- d. Security controls

:: Payment systems ::

An _____ is an electronic telecommunications device that enables customers of financial institutions to perform financial transactions, such as cash withdrawals, deposits, transfer funds, or obtaining account information, at any time and without the need for direct interaction with bank staff.

Exam Probability: **Medium**

21. *Answer choices:*

(see index for correct answer)

- a. Automated teller machine
- b. Invoicera
- c. Amazon Coin
- d. Betalingsservice

Guidance: level 1

:: Marketing ::

_____ is a business model in which consumers create value and businesses consume that value. For example, when a consumer writes reviews or when a consumer gives a useful idea for new product development then that consumer is creating value for the business if the business adopts the input. In the C2B model, a reverse auction or demand collection model, enables buyers to name or demand their own price, which is often binding, for a specific good or service. Inside of a consumer to business market the roles involved in the transaction must be established and the consumer must offer something of value to the business.

22. *Answer choices:*

(see index for correct answer)

- a. Consumer-to-business
- b. One Town One Product
- c. Leverage
- d. Gambling advertising

Guidance: level 1

:: Search engine optimization ::

_____ is an algorithm used by Google Search to rank web pages in their search engine results. _____ was named after Larry Page, one of the founders of Google. _____ is a way of measuring the importance of website pages. According to Google.

Exam Probability: **Low**

23. *Answer choices:*

(see index for correct answer)

- a. Sitemap index
- b. PageRank
- c. Moz

- d. Highervisibility

Guidance: level 1

:: Security compliance ::

_____ refers to the inability to withstand the effects of a hostile environment. A window of _____ is a time frame within which defensive measures are diminished, compromised or lacking.

Exam Probability: **High**

24. *Answer choices:*

(see index for correct answer)

- a. Nikto Web Scanner
- b. Vulnerability
- c. Federal Information Security Management Act of 2002
- d. Information assurance vulnerability alert

Guidance: level 1

:: Distribution, retailing, and wholesaling ::

_____ measures the performance of a system. Certain goals are defined and the _____ gives the percentage to which those goals should be achieved. Fill rate is different from _____ .

Exam Probability: **High**

25. *Answer choices:*

(see index for correct answer)

- a. Wholesale list
- b. Service level
- c. Open Payment Initiative
- d. Pacific Comics

Guidance: level 1

:: Management ::

A _____ describes the rationale of how an organization creates, delivers, and captures value, in economic, social, cultural or other contexts. The process of _____ construction and modification is also called _____ innovation and forms a part of business strategy.

Exam Probability: **Medium**

26. *Answer choices:*

(see index for correct answer)

- a. Business model
- b. Empowerment
- c. Libertarian management
- d. Event chain methodology

Guidance: level 1

:: Metadata ::

_____ s usage can be discovered by inspection of software applications or application data files through a process of manual or automated Application Discovery and Understanding. Once _____ s are discovered they can be registered in a metadata registry.

Exam Probability: **Medium**

27. *Answer choices:*
(see index for correct answer)

- a. Preservation Metadata: Implementation Strategies
- b. Filename extension
- c. Metatable
- d. Data element

Guidance: level 1

_____ LLC is an American multinational technology company that specializes in Internet-related services and products, which include online advertising technologies, search engine, cloud computing, software, and hardware. It is considered one of the Big Four technology companies, alongside Amazon, Apple and Facebook.

Exam Probability: **High**

28. *Answer choices:*
(see index for correct answer)

- a. functional perspective
- b. Google
- c. empathy
- d. similarity-attraction theory

Guidance: level 1

:: Strategic management ::

_____ is a management term for an element that is necessary for an organization or project to achieve its mission. Alternative terms are key result area and key success factor .

Exam Probability: **Medium**

29. *Answer choices:*

(see index for correct answer)

- a. Strategic control
- b. Operational responsiveness
- c. Talent portfolio management
- d. Critical success factor

Guidance: level 1

:: Data transmission ::

In telecommunications and computing, _____ is the number of bits that are conveyed or processed per unit of time.

Exam Probability: **Medium**

30. *Answer choices:*

(see index for correct answer)

- a. Shaping codes
- b. Transmission time
- c. Buffer underrun
- d. Bit rate

Guidance: level 1

:: Data ::

_____ is a branch of mathematics working with data collection, organization, analysis, interpretation and presentation. In applying _____ to, for example, a scientific, industrial, or social problem, it is conventional to begin with a statistical population or a statistical model process to be studied. Populations can be diverse topics such as "all people living in a country" or "every atom composing a crystal". _____ deals with every aspect of data, including the planning of data collection in terms of the design of surveys and experiments. See glossary of probability and _____ .

Exam Probability: **High**

31. *Answer choices:*

(see index for correct answer)

- a. Data acquisition
- b. Statistics
- c. Serial concatenated convolutional codes
- d. Synthetic data

Guidance: level 1

:: Data management ::

In business, _____ is a method used to define and manage the critical data of an organization to provide, with data integration, a single point of reference. The data that is mastered may include reference data- the set of permissible values, and the analytical data that supports decision making.

Exam Probability: **Medium**

32. *Answer choices:*

(see index for correct answer)

- a. datum
- b. Rainbow Storage
- c. IMS VDEX
- d. Computer-aided software engineering

Guidance: level 1

:: E-commerce ::

Electronic governance or e-governance is the application of information and communication technology for delivering government services, exchange of information, communication transactions, integration of various stand-alone systems and services between _____ , government-to-business , government-to-government , government-to-employees as well as back-office processes and interactions within the entire government framework. Through e-governance, government services are made available to citizens in a convenient, efficient, and transparent manner. The three main target groups that can be distinguished in governance concepts are government, citizens, andbusinesses/interest groups. In e-governance, there are no distinct boundaries.

Exam Probability: **High**

33. *Answer choices:*

(see index for correct answer)

- a. SIE
- b. AsiaPay
- c. Government-to-citizen
- d. BuildDirect

Guidance: level 1

:: Finance ::

_____ is a financial estimate intended to help buyers and owners determine the direct and indirect costs of a product or system. It is a management accounting concept that can be used in full cost accounting or even ecological economics where it includes social costs.

Exam Probability: **Medium**

34. *Answer choices:*

(see index for correct answer)

- a. Present value of revenues auction
- b. Mutual fund separation theorem
- c. Total cost of ownership
- d. Lead auditor

Guidance: level 1

:: Data management ::

_____ is a set of processes and technologies that supports the collection, managing, and publishing of information in any form or medium. When stored and accessed via computers, this information may be more specifically referred to as digital content, or simply as content.

Exam Probability: **Low**

35. *Answer choices:*

(see index for correct answer)

- a. Tuple
- b. Enterprise Data Planning
- c. Content management
- d. Cognos ReportNet

Guidance: level 1

:: Business planning ::

_____ is an organization's process of defining its strategy, or direction, and making decisions on allocating its resources to pursue this strategy. It may also extend to control mechanisms for guiding the implementation of the strategy. _____ became prominent in corporations during the 1960s and remains an important aspect of strategic management. It is executed by strategic planners or strategists, who involve many parties and research sources in their analysis of the organization and its relationship to the environment in which it competes.

Exam Probability: **Medium**

36. *Answer choices:*
(see index for correct answer)

- a. operational planning
- b. Community Futures
- c. Exit planning

- d. Strategic planning

Guidance: level 1

:: Data management ::

In computing, a _____ , also known as an enterprise _____ , is a system used for reporting and data analysis, and is considered a core component of business intelligence. DWs are central repositories of integrated data from one or more disparate sources. They store current and historical data in one single place that are used for creating analytical reports for workers throughout the enterprise.

Exam Probability: **High**

37. *Answer choices:*

(see index for correct answer)

- a. Head/tail Breaks
- b. Super column
- c. Data storage device
- d. Query language

Guidance: level 1

:: Computer access control protocols ::

An _____ is a type of computer communications protocol or cryptographic protocol specifically designed for transfer of authentication data between two entities. It allows the receiving entity to authenticate the connecting entity as well as authenticate itself to the connecting entity by declaring the type of information needed for authentication as well as syntax. It is the most important layer of protection needed for secure communication within computer networks.

Exam Probability: **High**

38. *Answer choices:*

(see index for correct answer)

- a. CRAM-MD5
- b. Yahalom
- c. IEEE 802.1X
- d. NTLMSSP

Guidance: level 1

:: Computing input devices ::

In computing, an _____ is a piece of computer hardware equipment used to provide data and control signals to an information processing system such as a computer or information appliance. Examples of _____ s include keyboards, mouse, scanners, digital cameras and joysticks. Audio _____ s may be used for purposes including speech recognition. Many companies are utilizing speech recognition to help assist users to use their device.

39. *Answer choices:*

(see index for correct answer)

- a. Griffin PowerMate
- b. Input device
- c. Doxie
- d. TREVENTUS

Guidance: level 1

:: Network performance ::

_____ is a distributed computing paradigm which brings computer data storage closer to the location where it is needed. Computation is largely or completely performed on distributed device nodes. _____ pushes applications, data and computing power away from centralized points to locations closer to the user. The target of _____ is any application or general functionality needing to be closer to the source of the action where distributed systems technology interacts with the physical world. _____ does not need contact with any centralized cloud, although it may interact with one. In contrast to cloud computing, _____ refers to decentralized data processing at the edge of the network.

Exam Probability: **Low**

40. *Answer choices:*

(see index for correct answer)

- a. Bandwidth guaranteed polling
- b. Robust random early detection
- c. Aryaka
- d. Iperf

Guidance: level 1

:: Infographics ::

A _____ is a graphical representation of data, in which "the data is represented by symbols, such as bars in a bar _____ , lines in a line _____ , or slices in a pie _____ ". A _____ can represent tabular numeric data, functions or some kinds of qualitative structure and provides different info.

Exam Probability: **High**

41. *Answer choices:*

(see index for correct answer)

- a. Chart
- b. Signage systems
- c. Energy Systems Language
- d. Storyboard

Guidance: level 1

:: ::

_____ is an American video-sharing website headquartered in San Bruno, California. Three former PayPal employees—Chad Hurley, Steve Chen, and Jawed Karim—created the service in February 2005. Google bought the site in November 2006 for US$1.65 billion; _____ now operates as one of Google's subsidiaries.

Exam Probability: **Low**

42. *Answer choices:*

(see index for correct answer)

- a. imperative
- b. functional perspective
- c. co-culture
- d. YouTube

Guidance: level 1

:: Fraud ::

In law, _____ is intentional deception to secure unfair or unlawful gain, or to deprive a victim of a legal right. _____ can violate civil law , a criminal law , or it may cause no loss of money, property or legal right but still be an element of another civil or criminal wrong. The purpose of _____ may be monetary gain or other benefits, for example by obtaining a passport, travel document, or driver's license, or mortgage _____ , where the perpetrator may attempt to qualify for a mortgage by way of false statements.

Exam Probability: **Low**

43. *Answer choices:*

(see index for correct answer)

- a. Senior Medicare Patrols
- b. Fraud
- c. Accreditation mill
- d. Mussolini diaries

Guidance: level 1

:: Management ::

Porter's Five Forces Framework is a tool for analyzing competition of a business. It draws from industrial organization economics to derive five forces that determine the competitive intensity and, therefore, the attractiveness of an industry in terms of its profitability. An "unattractive" industry is one in which the effect of these five forces reduces overall profitability. The most unattractive industry would be one approaching "pure competition", in which available profits for all firms are driven to normal profit levels. The five-forces perspective is associated with its originator, Michael E. Porter of Harvard University. This framework was first published in Harvard Business Review in 1979.

Exam Probability: **Low**

44. *Answer choices:*

(see index for correct answer)

- a. Court of Assistants
- b. Shamrock Organization
- c. Porter five forces analysis
- d. Discovery-driven planning

Guidance: level 1

:: ::

A _____ is a control panel usually located directly ahead of a vehicle's driver, displaying instrumentation and controls for the vehicle's operation.

45. *Answer choices:*

(see index for correct answer)

- a. surface-level diversity
- b. hierarchical perspective
- c. Character
- d. open system

Guidance: level 1

:: Internet marketing ::

_____ is the measurement, collection, analysis and reporting of web data for purposes of understanding and optimizing web usage. However, _____ is not just a process for measuring web traffic but can be used as a tool for business and market research, and to assess and improve the effectiveness of a website. _____ applications can also help companies measure the results of traditional print or broadcast advertising campaigns. It helps one to estimate how traffic to a website changes after the launch of a new advertising campaign. _____ provides information about the number of visitors to a website and the number of page views. It helps gauge traffic and popularity trends which is useful for market research.

46. *Answer choices:*

(see index for correct answer)

- a. Micro content
- b. Pay per click
- c. Web analytics
- d. Internet presence management

Guidance: level 1

:: Internet advertising ::

_____ , according to the United States federal law known as the Anti _____ Consumer Protection Act, is registering, trafficking in, or using an Internet domain name with bad faith intent to profit from the goodwill of a trademark belonging to someone else. The cybersquatter then offers to sell the domain to the person or company who owns a trademark contained within the name at an inflated price.

Exam Probability: **Low**

47. *Answer choices:*

(see index for correct answer)

- a. Online advertising in China
- b. Behavioral retargeting
- c. DoubleClick for Publishers by Google
- d. Initiative for a Competitive Online Marketplace

Guidance: level 1

:: Outsourcing ::

A service-level agreement is a commitment between a service provider and a client. Particular aspects of the service – quality, availability, responsibilities – are agreed between the service provider and the service user. The most common component of SLA is that the services should be provided to the customer as agreed upon in the contract. As an example, Internet service providers and telcos will commonly include _____ s within the terms of their contracts with customers to define the level of service being sold in plain language terms. In this case the SLA will typically have a technical definition in mean time between failures , mean time to repair or mean time to recovery ; identifying which party is responsible for reporting faults or paying fees; responsibility for various data rates; throughput; jitter; or similar measurable details.

Exam Probability: **High**

48. *Answer choices:*

(see index for correct answer)

- a. Print and mail outsourcing
- b. Chinggis Technologies
- c. Divestiture
- d. Harvey Nash

Guidance: level 1

:: ::

A _____ is a telecommunications network that extends over a large geographical distance for the primary purpose of computer networking. _____ s are often established with leased telecommunication circuits.

49. *Answer choices:*

(see index for correct answer)

- a. Wide Area Network
- b. imperative
- c. empathy
- d. information systems assessment

Guidance: level 1

:: Satellite navigation systems ::

_____ Galilei was an Italian astronomer, physicist and engineer, sometimes described as a polymath. _____ has been called the "father of observational astronomy", the "father of modern physics", the "father of the scientific method", and the "father of modern science".

50. *Answer choices:*

(see index for correct answer)

- a. Galileo
- b. Regional Positioning and Timing System
- c. Vehicle tracking system
- d. X-ray pulsar-based navigation

Guidance: level 1

:: Telecommunication theory ::

In reliability theory and reliability engineering, the term _____ has the following meanings.

Exam Probability: **High**

51. *Answer choices:*

(see index for correct answer)

- a. Routing and wavelength assignment
- b. Net gain
- c. Availability
- d. Phase perturbation

Guidance: level 1

:: ::

A _____ is a research instrument consisting of a series of questions for the purpose of gathering information from respondents. The _____ was invented by the Statistical Society of London in 1838.

Exam Probability: **Low**

52. *Answer choices:*

(see index for correct answer)

- a. Sarbanes-Oxley act of 2002
- b. Questionnaire
- c. similarity-attraction theory
- d. empathy

Guidance: level 1

:: Data management ::

_____ is a data management concept concerning the capability that enables an organization to ensure that high data quality exists throughout the complete lifecycle of the data. The key focus areas of _____ include availability, usability, consistency, data integrity and data security and includes establishing processes to ensure effective data management throughout the enterprise such as accountability for the adverse effects of poor data quality and ensuring that the data which an enterprise has can be used by the entire organization.

Exam Probability: **High**

53. *Answer choices:*

(see index for correct answer)

- a. Client-side persistent data
- b. Data governance
- c. Commitment ordering
- d. Data integration

Guidance: level 1

:: Networking hardware ::

A network interface controller is a computer hardware component that connects a computer to a computer network.

Exam Probability: **High**

54. *Answer choices:*

(see index for correct answer)

- a. Console server
- b. Network interface card
- c. bridging

:: Google services ::

_____ is a web mapping service developed by Google. It offers satellite imagery, aerial photography, street maps, 360° panoramic views of streets , real-time traffic conditions, and route planning for traveling by foot, car, bicycle and air , or public transportation.

Exam Probability: **Low**

55. *Answer choices:*

(see index for correct answer)

- a. Google Maps
- b. A Google A Day
- c. Google Public DNS
- d. Google Alerts

:: Fraud ::

_____ is the deliberate use of someone else's identity, usually as a method to gain a financial advantage or obtain credit and other benefits in the other person's name, and perhaps to the other person's disadvantage or loss. The person whose identity has been assumed may suffer adverse consequences, especially if they are held responsible for the perpetrator's actions.

_____ occurs when someone uses another's personally identifying information, like their name, identifying number, or credit card number, without their permission, to commit fraud or other crimes. The term _____ was coined in 1964. Since that time, the definition of _____ has been statutorily prescribed throughout both the U.K. and the United States as the theft of personally identifying information, generally including a person's name, date of birth, social security number, driver's license number, bank account or credit card numbers, PIN numbers, electronic signatures, fingerprints, passwords, or any other information that can be used to access a person's financial resources.

Exam Probability: **Medium**

56. *Answer choices:*

(see index for correct answer)

- a. Missing trader fraud
- b. Pharma fraud
- c. Identity theft
- d. Regummed stamp

Guidance: level 1

:: Data management ::

_____ is "data [information] that provides information about other data". Many distinct types of _____ exist, among these descriptive _____ , structural _____ , administrative _____ , reference _____ and statistical _____ .

Exam Probability: **High**

57. *Answer choices:*

- a. Edge data integration
- b. Head/tail Breaks
- c. Online complex processing
- d. Data Transformation Services

Guidance: level 1

:: Commercial item transport and distribution ::

In commerce, supply-chain management , the management of the flow of goods and services, involves the movement and storage of raw materials, of work-in-process inventory, and of finished goods from point of origin to point of consumption. Interconnected or interlinked networks, channels and node businesses combine in the provision of products and services required by end customers in a supply chain. Supply-chain management has been defined as the "design, planning, execution, control, and monitoring of supply-chain activities with the objective of creating net value, building a competitive infrastructure, leveraging worldwide logistics, synchronizing supply with demand and measuring performance globally."SCM practice draws heavily from the areas of industrial engineering, systems engineering, operations management, logistics, procurement, information technology, and marketing and strives for an integrated approach. Marketing channels play an important role in supply-chain management. Current research in supply-chain management is concerned with topics related to sustainability and risk management, among others. Some suggest that the "people dimension" of SCM, ethical issues, internal integration, transparency/visibility, and human capital/talent management are topics that have, so far, been underrepresented on the research agenda.

Exam Probability: **Low**

58. *Answer choices:*

(see index for correct answer)

- a. Yacht transport
- b. Bulk cargo
- c. Freight interline system
- d. Cross-docking

Guidance: level 1

:: Computer memory ::

_____ is a type of non-volatile memory used in computers and other electronic devices. Data stored in ROM can only be modified slowly, with difficulty, or not at all, so it is mainly used to store firmware or application software in plug-in cartridges.

Exam Probability: **High**

59. *Answer choices:*

(see index for correct answer)

- a. Rambus
- b. Mellon optical memory
- c. Write-only memory
- d. Read-only memory

Guidance: level 1

Marketing

Marketing is the study and management of exchange relationships. Marketing is the business process of creating relationships with and satisfying customers. With its focus on the customer, marketing is one of the premier components of business management.

Marketing is defined by the American Marketing Association as "the activity, set of institutions, and processes for creating, communicating, delivering, and exchanging offerings that have value for customers, clients, partners, and society at large."

:: ::

In the broadest sense, _____ is any practice which contributes to the sale of products to a retail consumer. At a retail in-store level, _____ refers to the variety of products available for sale and the display of those products in such a way that it stimulates interest and entices customers to make a purchase.

Exam Probability: **Medium**

1. *Answer choices:*

(see index for correct answer)

- a. Merchandising
- b. corporate values
- c. surface-level diversity
- d. interpersonal communication

Guidance: level 1

:: Social psychology ::

_____ s is a qualitative methodology used to describe consumers on psychological attributes. _____ s have been applied to the study of personality, values, opinions, attitudes, interests, and lifestyles. While _____ s are often equated with lifestyle research, it has been argued that _____ s should apply to the study of cognitive attributes such as attitudes, interests, opinions, and beliefs while lifestyle should apply to the study of overt behavior . Because this area of research focuses on activities, interests, and opinions, _____ factors are sometimes abbreviated to `AIO variables`.

2. *Answer choices:*

(see index for correct answer)

- a. sociometer
- b. acculturation
- c. self-disclosure
- d. Psychographic

Guidance: level 1

:: ::

Distribution is one of the four elements of the marketing mix. Distribution is the process of making a product or service available for the consumer or business user who needs it. This can be done directly by the producer or service provider, or using indirect channels with distributors or intermediaries. The other three elements of the marketing mix are product, pricing, and promotion.

Exam Probability: **High**

3. *Answer choices:*

(see index for correct answer)

- a. hierarchical
- b. Distribution channel

- c. process perspective
- d. information systems assessment

Guidance: level 1

:: Decision theory ::

Within economics the concept of _____ is used to model worth or value, but its usage has evolved significantly over time. The term was introduced initially as a measure of pleasure or satisfaction within the theory of utilitarianism by moral philosophers such as Jeremy Bentham and John Stuart Mill. But the term has been adapted and reapplied within neoclassical economics, which dominates modern economic theory, as a _____ function that represents a consumer's preference ordering over a choice set. As such, it is devoid of its original interpretation as a measurement of the pleasure or satisfaction obtained by the consumer from that choice.

Exam Probability: **Low**

4. *Answer choices:*

(see index for correct answer)

- a. Emotional bias
- b. Secretary problem
- c. Shared decision-making
- d. Utility

Guidance: level 1

:: Basic financial concepts ::

_____ is a sustained increase in the general price level of goods and services in an economy over a period of time. When the general price level rises, each unit of currency buys fewer goods and services; consequently, _____ reflects a reduction in the purchasing power per unit of money a loss of real value in the medium of exchange and unit of account within the economy. The measure of _____ is the _____ rate, the annualized percentage change in a general price index, usually the consumer price index, over time. The opposite of _____ is deflation.

Exam Probability: **Low**

5. *Answer choices:*

(see index for correct answer)

- a. Maturity date
- b. Inflation
- c. Eurodollar
- d. Present value of costs

Guidance: level 1

:: ::

_____ is the process of gathering and measuring information on targeted variables in an established system, which then enables one to answer relevant questions and evaluate outcomes. _____ is a component of research in all fields of study including physical and social sciences, humanities, and business. While methods vary by discipline, the emphasis on ensuring accurate and honest collection remains the same. The goal for all _____ is to capture quality evidence that allows analysis to lead to the formulation of convincing and credible answers to the questions that have been posed.

Exam Probability: **Medium**

6. *Answer choices:*

(see index for correct answer)

- a. hierarchical perspective
- b. similarity-attraction theory
- c. co-culture
- d. surface-level diversity

Guidance: level 1

:: ::

A _____ is a discussion or informational website published on the World Wide Web consisting of discrete, often informal diary-style text entries . Posts are typically displayed in reverse chronological order, so that the most recent post appears first, at the top of the web page. Until 2009, _____ s were usually the work of a single individual, occasionally of a small group, and often covered a single subject or topic. In the 2010s, "multi-author _____ s" emerged, featuring the writing of multiple authors and sometimes professionally edited. MABs from newspapers, other media outlets, universities, think tanks, advocacy groups, and similar institutions account for an increasing quantity of _____ traffic. The rise of Twitter and other "micro _____ ging" systems helps integrate MABs and single-author _____ s into the news media. _____ can also be used as a verb, meaning to maintain or add content to a _____ .

Exam Probability: **Medium**

7. *Answer choices:*

(see index for correct answer)

- a. functional perspective
- b. Blog
- c. surface-level diversity
- d. process perspective

Guidance: level 1

:: ::

_____ is a marketing communication that employs an openly sponsored, non-personal message to promote or sell a product, service or idea. Sponsors of _____ are typically businesses wishing to promote their products or services. _____ is differentiated from public relations in that an advertiser pays for and has control over the message. It differs from personal selling in that the message is non-personal, i.e., not directed to a particular individual. _____ is communicated through various mass media, including traditional media such as newspapers, magazines, television, radio, outdoor _____ or direct mail; and new media such as search results, blogs, social media, websites or text messages. The actual presentation of the message in a medium is referred to as an advertisement, or "ad" or advert for short.

Exam Probability: **High**

8. *Answer choices:*

(see index for correct answer)

- a. Character
- b. functional perspective
- c. personal values
- d. Advertising

Guidance: level 1

:: ::

An _____ is an area of the production, distribution, or trade, and consumption of goods and services by different agents. Understood in its broadest sense, `The _____ is defined as a social domain that emphasize the practices, discourses, and material expressions associated with the production, use, and management of resources`. Economic agents can be individuals, businesses, organizations, or governments. Economic transactions occur when two parties agree to the value or price of the transacted good or service, commonly expressed in a certain currency. However, monetary transactions only account for a small part of the economic domain.

Exam Probability: **Medium**

9. *Answer choices:*

(see index for correct answer)

- a. deep-level diversity
- b. information systems assessment
- c. hierarchical perspective
- d. personal values

Guidance: level 1

:: ::

_____ , in general use, is a devotion and faithfulness to a nation, cause, philosophy, country, group, or person. Philosophers disagree on what can be an object of _____ , as some argue that _____ is strictly interpersonal and only another human being can be the object of _____ . The definition of _____ in law and political science is the fidelity of an individual to a nation, either one's nation of birth, or one's declared home nation by oath .

Exam Probability: **Low**

10. *Answer choices:*

(see index for correct answer)

- a. open system
- b. levels of analysis
- c. surface-level diversity
- d. corporate values

Guidance: level 1

:: Data management ::

_____ is a form of intellectual property that grants the creator of an original creative work an exclusive legal right to determine whether and under what conditions this original work may be copied and used by others, usually for a limited term of years. The exclusive rights are not absolute but limited by limitations and exceptions to _____ law, including fair use. A major limitation on _____ on ideas is that _____ protects only the original expression of ideas, and not the underlying ideas themselves.

11. *Answer choices:*

(see index for correct answer)

- a. Asset Description Metadata Schema
- b. Association rule learning
- c. Data independence
- d. Copyright

Guidance: level 1

:: Credit cards ::

The _____ Company, also known as Amex, is an American multinational financial services corporation headquartered in Three World Financial Center in New York City. The company was founded in 1850 and is one of the 30 components of the Dow Jones Industrial Average. The company is best known for its charge card, credit card, and traveler's cheque businesses.

Exam Probability: **Low**

12. *Answer choices:*

(see index for correct answer)

- a. EnRoute
- b. Wirecard

- c. American Express
- d. Accolades Card

Guidance: level 1

:: Market research ::

An _____ or lighthouse customer is an early customer of a given company, product, or technology. The term originates from Everett M. Rogers' Diffusion of Innovations .

Exam Probability: **High**

13. *Answer choices:*

(see index for correct answer)

- a. Online panel
- b. AQH Share
- c. Competitor analysis
- d. Gerson Lehrman Group

Guidance: level 1

:: Marketing ::

_____ is the marketing of products that are presumed to be environmentally safe. It incorporates a broad range of activities, including product modification, changes to the production process, sustainable packaging, as well as modifying advertising. Yet defining _____ is not a simple task where several meanings intersect and contradict each other; an example of this will be the existence of varying social, environmental and retail definitions attached to this term. Other similar terms used are environmental marketing and ecological marketing.

Exam Probability: **Medium**

14. *Answer choices:*

(see index for correct answer)

- a. Double bottom line
- b. DirectIndustry
- c. Marchitecture
- d. Green marketing

Guidance: level 1

:: Management occupations ::

_____ ship is the process of designing, launching and running a new business, which is often initially a small business. The people who create these businesses are called _____ s.

Exam Probability: **High**

15. *Answer choices:*

(see index for correct answer)

- a. Arts administration
- b. Entrepreneur
- c. Financial secretary
- d. Adjutant general

Guidance: level 1

:: Business models ::

_____ es are privately owned corporations, partnerships, or sole proprietorships that have fewer employees and/or less annual revenue than a regular-sized business or corporation. Businesses are defined as "small" in terms of being able to apply for government support and qualify for preferential tax policy varies depending on the country and industry. _____ es range from fifteen employees under the Australian Fair Work Act 2009, fifty employees according to the definition used by the European Union, and fewer than five hundred employees to qualify for many U.S. _____ Administration programs. While _____ es can also be classified according to other methods, such as annual revenues, shipments, sales, assets, or by annual gross or net revenue or net profits, the number of employees is one of the most widely used measures.

Exam Probability: **High**

16. *Answer choices:*

(see index for correct answer)

- a. Small business
- b. Collective business system
- c. Meta learning
- d. Premium business model

Guidance: level 1

:: Advertising ::

A _____ is a document used by creative professionals and agencies to develop creative deliverables: visual design, copy, advertising, web sites, etc. The document is usually developed by the requestor and approved by the creative team of designers, writers, and project managers. In some cases, the project's _____ may need creative director approval before work will commence.

Exam Probability: **High**

17. *Answer choices:*

(see index for correct answer)

- a. Tradio
- b. Cidade Limpa
- c. Advertising exchange
- d. Advertising to children

Guidance: level 1

:: Manufacturing ::

A _____ is a building for storing goods. _____ s are used by manufacturers, importers, exporters, wholesalers, transport businesses, customs, etc. They are usually large plain buildings in industrial parks on the outskirts of cities, towns or villages.

Exam Probability: **Low**

18. *Answer choices:*

(see index for correct answer)

- a. Greatpac
- b. Warehouse
- c. Acheson process
- d. Guitar manufacturing

Guidance: level 1

:: Commercial item transport and distribution ::

In commerce, supply-chain management , the management of the flow of goods and services, involves the movement and storage of raw materials, of work-in-process inventory, and of finished goods from point of origin to point of consumption. Interconnected or interlinked networks, channels and node businesses combine in the provision of products and services required by end customers in a supply chain. Supply-chain management has been defined as the "design, planning, execution, control, and monitoring of supply-chain activities with the objective of creating net value, building a competitive infrastructure, leveraging worldwide logistics, synchronizing supply with demand and measuring performance globally."SCM practice draws heavily from the areas of industrial engineering, systems engineering, operations management, logistics, procurement, information technology, and marketing and strives for an integrated approach. Marketing channels play an important role in supply-chain management. Current research in supply-chain management is concerned with topics related to sustainability and risk management, among others. Some suggest that the "people dimension" of SCM, ethical issues, internal integration, transparency/visibility, and human capital/talent management are topics that have, so far, been underrepresented on the research agenda.

Exam Probability: **Medium**

19. *Answer choices:*

(see index for correct answer)

- a. Common carrier
- b. Mid-stream operation
- c. Semi-trailer truck
- d. Warehouse receipt

Guidance: level 1

:: ::

_____ consists of using generic or ad hoc methods in an orderly manner to find solutions to problems. Some of the problem-solving techniques developed and used in philosophy, artificial intelligence, computer science, engineering, mathematics, or medicine are related to mental problem-solving techniques studied in psychology.

Exam Probability: **Medium**

20. *Answer choices:*

(see index for correct answer)

- a. interpersonal communication
- b. open system
- c. surface-level diversity
- d. Problem Solving

Guidance: level 1

:: Stock market ::

The _____ of a corporation is all of the shares into which ownership of the corporation is divided. In American English, the shares are commonly known as "_____ s". A single share of the _____ represents fractional ownership of the corporation in proportion to the total number of shares. This typically entitles the _____ holder to that fraction of the company's earnings, proceeds from liquidation of assets , or voting power, often dividing these up in proportion to the amount of money each _____ holder has invested. Not all _____ is necessarily equal, as certain classes of _____ may be issued for example without voting rights, with enhanced voting rights, or with a certain priority to receive profits or liquidation proceeds before or after other classes of shareholders.

Exam Probability: **Medium**

21. *Answer choices:*

(see index for correct answer)

- a. American Depositary Share
- b. Stock
- c. Qualified institutional placement
- d. French auction

Guidance: level 1

:: Supply chain management ::

The _____ is a barcode symbology that is widely used in the United States, Canada, United Kingdom, Australia, New Zealand, in Europe and other countries for tracking trade items in stores.

22. *Answer choices:*

- a. Calculating demand forecast accuracy
- b. Chain of responsibility
- c. Supply chain management software
- d. ThoughtSpeed Corporation

Guidance: level 1

:: Behaviorism ::

In behavioral psychology, _____ is a consequence applied that will strengthen an organism's future behavior whenever that behavior is preceded by a specific antecedent stimulus. This strengthening effect may be measured as a higher frequency of behavior , longer duration , greater magnitude , or shorter latency . There are two types of _____ , known as positive _____ and negative _____ ; positive is where by a reward is offered on expression of the wanted behaviour and negative is taking away an undesirable element in the persons environment whenever the desired behaviour is achieved.

23. *Answer choices:*

- a. Matching Law
- b. contingency management
- c. Reinforcement
- d. chaining

Guidance: level 1

:: ::

_____ is the collection of techniques, skills, methods, and processes used in the production of goods or services or in the accomplishment of objectives, such as scientific investigation. _____ can be the knowledge of techniques, processes, and the like, or it can be embedded in machines to allow for operation without detailed knowledge of their workings. Systems applying _____ by taking an input, changing it according to the system's use, and then producing an outcome are referred to as _____ systems or technological systems.

Exam Probability: **Low**

24. *Answer choices:*

(see index for correct answer)

- a. imperative
- b. Character
- c. deep-level diversity
- d. co-culture

:: Market research ::

_____ is an organized effort to gather information about target markets or customers. It is a very important component of business strategy. The term is commonly interchanged with marketing research; however, expert practitioners may wish to draw a distinction, in that marketing research is concerned specifically about marketing processes, while _____ is concerned specifically with markets.

Exam Probability: **High**

25. *Answer choices:*

(see index for correct answer)

- a. Market research
- b. Cluster sampling
- c. 6-3-5 Brainwriting
- d. LRMR

:: Contract law ::

A _____ is a legally-binding agreement which recognises and governs the rights and duties of the parties to the agreement. A _____ is legally enforceable because it meets the requirements and approval of the law. An agreement typically involves the exchange of goods, services, money, or promises of any of those. In the event of breach of _____ , the law awards the injured party access to legal remedies such as damages and cancellation.

Exam Probability: **High**

26. *Answer choices:*

(see index for correct answer)

- a. Seal
- b. Reciprocal obligation
- c. Parent company guarantee
- d. Contract

Guidance: level 1

:: Decision theory ::

A _____ is a deliberate system of principles to guide decisions and achieve rational outcomes. A _____ is a statement of intent, and is implemented as a procedure or protocol. Policies are generally adopted by a governance body within an organization. Policies can assist in both subjective and objective decision making. Policies to assist in subjective decision making usually assist senior management with decisions that must be based on the relative merits of a number of factors, and as a result are often hard to test objectively, e.g. work-life balance _____ . In contrast policies to assist in objective decision making are usually operational in nature and can be objectively tested, e.g. password _____ .

Exam Probability: **Medium**

27. *Answer choices:*

(see index for correct answer)

- a. Risk compensation
- b. Analysis paralysis
- c. Trade study
- d. Policy

Guidance: level 1

:: Marketing ::

_____ , sometimes called trigger-based or event-driven marketing, is a marketing strategy that uses two-way communication channels to allow consumers to connect with a company directly. Although this exchange can take place in person, in the last decade it has increasingly taken place almost exclusively online through email, social media, and blogs.

Exam Probability: **Medium**

28. *Answer choices:*

(see index for correct answer)

- a. Interactive marketing
- b. Postmodern communication
- c. Counteradvertising
- d. European Information Technology Observatory

Guidance: level 1

:: Brokered programming ::

An _____ is a form of television commercial, which generally includes a toll-free telephone number or website. Most often used as a form of direct response television , long-form _____ s are typically 28:30 or 58:30 minutes in length. _____ s are also known as paid programming . This phenomenon started in the United States, where _____ s were typically shown overnight , outside peak prime time hours for commercial broadcasters. Some television stations chose to air _____ s as an alternative to the former practice of signing off. Some channels air _____ s 24 hours. Some stations also choose to air _____ s during the daytime hours mostly on weekends to fill in for unscheduled network or syndicated programming. By 2009, most _____ spending in the U.S. occurred during the early morning, daytime and evening hours, or in the afternoon. Stations in most countries around the world have instituted similar media structures. The _____ industry is worth over $200 billion.

Exam Probability: **High**

29. *Answer choices:*

(see index for correct answer)

- a. One Magnificent Morning
- b. Brokered programming
- c. Toonzai
- d. Leased access

Guidance: level 1

:: Management ::

_____ is the organizational discipline which focuses on the practical application of marketing orientation, techniques and methods inside enterprises and organizations and on the management of a firm`s marketing resources and activities.

Exam Probability: **Medium**

30. *Answer choices:*

(see index for correct answer)

- a. Submission management
- b. Clean-sheet review
- c. Management fad
- d. Marketing management

Guidance: level 1

:: Data analysis ::

_____ is a process of inspecting, cleansing, transforming, and modeling data with the goal of discovering useful information, informing conclusions, and supporting decision-making. _____ has multiple facets and approaches, encompassing diverse techniques under a variety of names, and is used in different business, science, and social science domains. In today`s business world, _____ plays a role in making decisions more scientific and helping businesses operate more effectively.

Exam Probability: **Medium**

31. *Answer choices:*

(see index for correct answer)

- a. Random mapping
- b. Data analysis
- c. Principal geodesic analysis
- d. Aggregative Contingent Estimation

Guidance: level 1

:: Business planning ::

_____ is an organization's process of defining its strategy, or direction, and making decisions on allocating its resources to pursue this strategy. It may also extend to control mechanisms for guiding the implementation of the strategy. _____ became prominent in corporations during the 1960s and remains an important aspect of strategic management. It is executed by strategic planners or strategists, who involve many parties and research sources in their analysis of the organization and its relationship to the environment in which it competes.

Exam Probability: **Medium**

32. *Answer choices:*

(see index for correct answer)

- a. Gap analysis
- b. Exit planning

- c. Stakeholder management
- d. Strategic planning

Guidance: level 1

:: ::

Management is the administration of an organization, whether it is a
business, a not-for-profit organization, or government body. Management
includes the activities of setting the strategy of an organization and
coordinating the efforts of its employees to accomplish its objectives through
the application of available resources, such as financial, natural,
technological, and human resources. The term "management" may also refer to
those people who manage an organization.

Exam Probability: **Low**

33. *Answer choices:*

(see index for correct answer)

- a. functional perspective
- b. corporate values
- c. Manager
- d. information systems assessment

Guidance: level 1

:: Sales ::

_____ is a business discipline which is focused on the practical application of sales techniques and the management of a firm's sales operations. It is an important business function as net sales through the sale of products and services and resulting profit drive most commercial business. These are also typically the goals and performance indicators of _____ .

Exam Probability: **High**

34. *Answer choices:*

(see index for correct answer)

- a. Patent cliff
- b. Closed-end leasing
- c. System sales
- d. Sale and rent back

Guidance: level 1

:: ::

_____ is a term frequently used in marketing. It is a measure of how products and services supplied by a company meet or surpass customer expectation. _____ is defined as "the number of customers, or percentage of total customers, whose reported experience with a firm, its products, or its services exceeds specified satisfaction goals."

35. *Answer choices:*

(see index for correct answer)

- a. levels of analysis
- b. functional perspective
- c. open system
- d. hierarchical

Guidance: level 1

:: Cognitive dissonance ::

In the field of psychology, _____ is the mental discomfort experienced by a person who holds two or more contradictory beliefs, ideas, or values. This discomfort is triggered by a situation in which a person's belief clashes with new evidence perceived by the person. When confronted with facts that contradict beliefs, ideals, and values, people will try to find a way to resolve the contradiction to reduce their discomfort.

36. *Answer choices:*

(see index for correct answer)

- a. Self-refuting idea
- b. Doublethink

- c. Cognitive dissonance
- d. The Fox and the Grapes

Guidance: level 1

:: Product management ::

A _____ , trade mark, or trade-mark is a recognizable sign, design, or expression which identifies products or services of a particular source from those of others, although _____ s used to identify services are usually called service marks. The _____ owner can be an individual, business organization, or any legal entity. A _____ may be located on a package, a label, a voucher, or on the product itself. For the sake of corporate identity, _____ s are often displayed on company buildings. It is legally recognized as a type of intellectual property.

Exam Probability: **Low**

37. *Answer choices:*
(see index for correct answer)

- a. Promise Index
- b. Trademark
- c. Product family engineering
- d. Product information management

Guidance: level 1

:: Commerce ::

_____ relates to "the exchange of goods and services, especially on a large scale". It includes legal, economic, political, social, cultural and technological systems that operate in a country or in international trade.

Exam Probability: **Medium**

38. *Answer choices:*

(see index for correct answer)

- a. Bargaining power
- b. Commerce
- c. GT Nexus
- d. Country commercial guides

Guidance: level 1

:: Market research ::

_____ refers to a collection of methods that managers use to analyze an organization's internal and external environment to understand the organization's capabilities, customers, and business environment. The _____ consists of several methods of analysis: The 5Cs Analysis, SWOT analysis and Porter five forces analysis. A Marketing Plan is created to guide businesses on how to communicate the benefits of their products to the needs of potential customer. The _____ is the second step in the marketing plan and is a critical step in establishing a long term relationship with customers.

39. *Answer choices:*

(see index for correct answer)

- a. CoolBrands
- b. Shanghai Metals Market
- c. Computer-assisted web interviewing
- d. Situation analysis

Guidance: level 1

:: ::

_____ s uses different marketing channels and tools in combination: _____ channels focus on any way a business communicates a message to its desired market, or the market in general. A _____ tool can be anything from: advertising, personal selling, direct marketing, sponsorship, communication, and promotion to public relations.

40. *Answer choices:*

(see index for correct answer)

- a. co-culture
- b. information systems assessment

- c. Marketing communication
- d. surface-level diversity

Guidance: level 1

:: Services management and marketing ::

_____ is a specialised branch of marketing. _____ emerged as a separate field of study in the early 1980s, following the recognition that the unique characteristics of services required different strategies compared with the marketing of physical goods.

Exam Probability: **High**

41. *Answer choices:*

(see index for correct answer)

- a. Service design
- b. Services marketing
- c. Night service
- d. Viable systems approach

Guidance: level 1

:: Progressive Era in the United States ::

The Clayton Antitrust Act of 1914 , was a part of United States antitrust law with the goal of adding further substance to the U.S. antitrust law regime; the _____ sought to prevent anticompetitive practices in their incipiency. That regime started with the Sherman Antitrust Act of 1890, the first Federal law outlawing practices considered harmful to consumers . The _____ specified particular prohibited conduct, the three-level enforcement scheme, the exemptions, and the remedial measures.

Exam Probability: **Low**

42. *Answer choices:*

(see index for correct answer)

- a. Mann Act
- b. pragmatism
- c. Clayton Antitrust Act

Guidance: level 1

:: Television commercials ::

_____ is a characteristic that distinguishes physical entities that have biological processes, such as signaling and self-sustaining processes, from those that do not, either because such functions have ceased , or because they never had such functions and are classified as inanimate. Various forms of _____ exist, such as plants, animals, fungi, protists, archaea, and bacteria. The criteria can at times be ambiguous and may or may not define viruses, viroids, or potential synthetic _____ as "living". Biology is the science concerned with the study of _____ .

43. *Answer choices:*

(see index for correct answer)

- a. Grrr
- b. Fridge
- c. The Force
- d. Life

Guidance: level 1

:: Auctioneering ::

An _____ is a process of buying and selling goods or services by offering them up for bid, taking bids, and then selling the item to the highest bidder. The open ascending price _____ is arguably the most common form of _____ in use today. Participants bid openly against one another, with each subsequent bid required to be higher than the previous bid. An _____ eer may announce prices, bidders may call out their bids themselves , or bids may be submitted electronically with the highest current bid publicly displayed. In a Dutch _____ , the _____ eer begins with a high asking price for some quantity of like items; the price is lowered until a participant is willing to accept the _____ eer's price for some quantity of the goods in the lot or until the seller's reserve price is met. While _____ s are most associated in the public imagination with the sale of antiques, paintings, rare collectibles and expensive wines, _____ s are also used for commodities, livestock, radio spectrum and used cars. In economic theory, an _____ may refer to any mechanism or set of trading rules for exchange.

44. *Answer choices:*

(see index for correct answer)

- a. Bidding fee auction
- b. Vehicle impoundment
- c. National Auctioneers Association
- d. Chinese auction

Guidance: level 1

:: Competition (economics) ::

_____ arises whenever at least two parties strive for a goal which cannot be shared: where one's gain is the other's loss .

45. *Answer choices:*

(see index for correct answer)

- a. Level playing field
- b. Economic forces
- c. Competition
- d. Transfer pricing

:: ::

_____ is a process whereby a person assumes the parenting of another, usually a child, from that person's biological or legal parent or parents. Legal _____ s permanently transfers all rights and responsibilities, along with filiation, from the biological parent or parents.

Exam Probability: **High**

46. *Answer choices:*

(see index for correct answer)

- a. Adoption
- b. empathy
- c. interpersonal communication
- d. hierarchical perspective

:: Summary statistics ::

_____ is the number of occurrences of a repeating event per unit of time. It is also referred to as temporal _____ , which emphasizes the contrast to spatial _____ and angular _____ . The period is the duration of time of one cycle in a repeating event, so the period is the reciprocal of the _____ . For example: if a newborn baby's heart beats at a _____ of 120 times a minute, its period—the time interval between beats—is half a second . _____ is an important parameter used in science and engineering to specify the rate of oscillatory and vibratory phenomena, such as mechanical vibrations, audio signals , radio waves, and light.

Exam Probability: **Medium**

47. *Answer choices:*

(see index for correct answer)

- a. Pareto index
- b. Frequency
- c. Robin Hood index
- d. Higher-order statistics

Guidance: level 1

:: ::

An _____ is the production of goods or related services within an economy. The major source of revenue of a group or company is the indicator of its relevant _____ . When a large group has multiple sources of revenue generation, it is considered to be working in different industries. Manufacturing _____ became a key sector of production and labour in European and North American countries during the Industrial Revolution, upsetting previous mercantile and feudal economies. This came through many successive rapid advances in technology, such as the production of steel and coal.

Exam Probability: **High**

48. *Answer choices:*

(see index for correct answer)

- a. Industry
- b. Sarbanes-Oxley act of 2002
- c. Character
- d. hierarchical perspective

Guidance: level 1

:: ::

The _____ is an agreement signed by Canada, Mexico, and the United States, creating a trilateral trade bloc in North America. The agreement came into force on January 1, 1994, and superseded the 1988 Canada–United States Free Trade Agreement between the United States and Canada. The NAFTA trade bloc is one of the largest trade blocs in the world by gross domestic product.

Exam Probability: **Low**

49. *Answer choices:*

(see index for correct answer)

- a. corporate values
- b. North American Free Trade Agreement
- c. hierarchical perspective
- d. deep-level diversity

Guidance: level 1

:: Legal terms ::

A _____ is a person who is called upon to issue a response to a communication made by another. The term is used in legal contexts, in survey methodology, and in psychological conditioning.

Exam Probability: **Medium**

50. *Answer choices:*

(see index for correct answer)

- a. Pain and suffering
- b. Medical advice
- c. Parole
- d. Respondent

:: Marketing ::

_____ s are structured marketing strategies designed by merchants to encourage customers to continue to shop at or use the services of businesses associated with each program. These programs exist covering most types of commerce, each one having varying features and rewards-schemes.

Exam Probability: **Low**

51. *Answer choices:*

(see index for correct answer)

- a. Kronos Effect
- b. Advertising media selection
- c. Customer interaction tracker
- d. Loyalty program

:: International trade ::

_____ or globalisation is the process of interaction and integration among people, companies, and governments worldwide. As a complex and multifaceted phenomenon, _____ is considered by some as a form of capitalist expansion which entails the integration of local and national economies into a global, unregulated market economy. _____ has grown due to advances in transportation and communication technology. With the increased global interactions comes the growth of international trade, ideas, and culture. _____ is primarily an economic process of interaction and integration that's associated with social and cultural aspects. However, conflicts and diplomacy are also large parts of the history of _____ , and modern _____ .

Exam Probability: **Medium**

52. *Answer choices:*

(see index for correct answer)

- a. Rybczynski theorem
- b. State trading enterprises
- c. Trade mission
- d. Balanced trade

Guidance: level 1

:: Product development ::

_____ is the understanding of the dynamics of the product in order to showcase the best qualities and maximum features of the product. Marketers spend a lot of time and research in order to target their attended audience. Marketers will look into a _____ before marketing a product towards their customers.

Exam Probability: **Medium**

53. *Answer choices:*

(see index for correct answer)

- a. Walter Heidenfels
- b. Virtual prototyping
- c. Collaborative product development
- d. Product concept

Guidance: level 1

:: Production economics ::

In microeconomics, _____ are the cost advantages that enterprises obtain due to their scale of operation , with cost per unit of output decreasing with increasing scale.

Exam Probability: **High**

54. *Answer choices:*

- a. Learning-by-doing
- b. Economies of scale
- c. Post-Fordism
- d. Factor price

Guidance: level 1

:: Advertising ::

_____ is the behavioral and cognitive process of selectively concentrating on a discrete aspect of information, whether deemed subjective or objective, while ignoring other perceivable information. It is a state of arousal. It is the taking possession by the mind in clear and vivid form of one out of what seem several simultaneous objects or trains of thought. Focalization, the concentration of consciousness, is of its essence. _____ has also been described as the allocation of limited cognitive processing resources.

Exam Probability: **High**

55. *Answer choices:*

- a. Barker channel
- b. Thetextpage
- c. Attention

- d. Time-compressed speech

Guidance: level 1

:: Business law ::

A _____ is an arrangement where parties, known as partners, agree to cooperate to advance their mutual interests. The partners in a _____ may be individuals, businesses, interest-based organizations, schools, governments or combinations. Organizations may partner to increase the likelihood of each achieving their mission and to amplify their reach. A _____ may result in issuing and holding equity or may be only governed by a contract.

Exam Probability: **Low**

56. *Answer choices:*
(see index for correct answer)

- a. Subordination
- b. Apparent authority
- c. Partnership
- d. Leave of absence

Guidance: level 1

:: ::

In _____ relations and communication science, _____ s are groups of individual people, and the _____ is the totality of such groupings. This is a different concept to the sociological concept of the Öffentlichkeit or _____ sphere. The concept of a _____ has also been defined in political science, psychology, marketing, and advertising. In _____ relations and communication science, it is one of the more ambiguous concepts in the field. Although it has definitions in the theory of the field that have been formulated from the early 20th century onwards, it has suffered in more recent years from being blurred, as a result of conflation of the idea of a _____ with the notions of audience, market segment, community, constituency, and stakeholder.

Exam Probability: **Medium**

57. *Answer choices:*

(see index for correct answer)

- a. Character
- b. similarity-attraction theory
- c. hierarchical perspective
- d. Public

Guidance: level 1

:: ::

_____ or accountancy is the measurement, processing, and communication of financial information about economic entities such as businesses and corporations. The modern field was established by the Italian mathematician Luca Pacioli in 1494. _____ , which has been called the "language of business", measures the results of an organization's economic activities and conveys this information to a variety of users, including investors, creditors, management, and regulators. Practitioners of _____ are known as accountants. The terms " _____ " and "financial reporting" are often used as synonyms.

Exam Probability: **High**

58. *Answer choices:*

(see index for correct answer)

- a. similarity-attraction theory
- b. cultural
- c. co-culture
- d. Accounting

Guidance: level 1

:: Advertising techniques ::

In promotion and of advertising, a _____ or show consists of a person`s written or spoken statement extolling the virtue of a product. The term " _____ " most commonly applies to the sales-pitches attributed to ordinary citizens, whereas the word "endorsement" usually applies to pitches by celebrities. _____ s can be part of communal marketing. Sometimes, the cartoon character can be a _____ in a commercial.

Exam Probability: **High**

59. *Answer choices:*

(see index for correct answer)

- a. Dolly Dimples
- b. Incomplete comparison
- c. Testimonial
- d. Media clip

Guidance: level 1

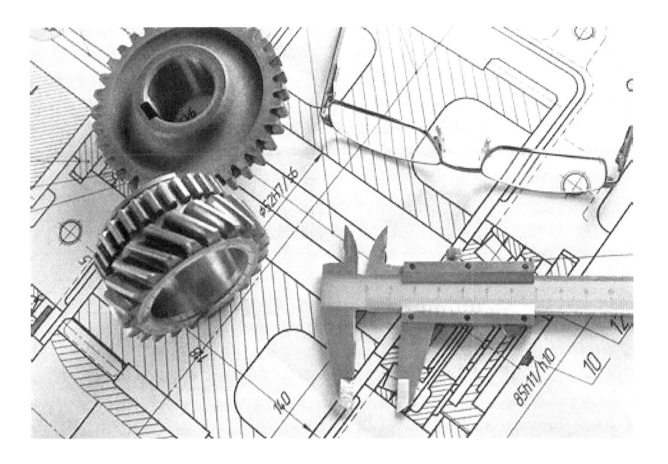

Manufacturing

Manufacturing is the production of merchandise for use or sale using labor and machines, tools, chemical and biological processing, or formulation. The term may refer to a range of human activity, from handicraft to high tech, but is most commonly applied to industrial design , in which raw materials are transformed into finished goods on a large scale. Such finished goods may be sold to other manufacturers for the production of other, more complex products, such as aircraft, household appliances, furniture, sports equipment or automobiles, or sold to wholesalers, who in turn sell them to retailers, who then sell them to end users and consumers.

:: Packaging materials ::

_____ is a non-crystalline, amorphous solid that is often transparent and has widespread practical, technological, and decorative uses in, for example, window panes, tableware, and optoelectronics. The most familiar, and historically the oldest, types of manufactured _____ are "silicate _____ es" based on the chemical compound silica , the primary constituent of sand. The term _____ , in popular usage, is often used to refer only to this type of material, which is familiar from use as window _____ and in _____ bottles. Of the many silica-based _____ es that exist, ordinary glazing and container _____ is formed from a specific type called soda-lime _____ , composed of approximately 75% silicon dioxide , sodium oxide from sodium carbonate , calcium oxide , also called lime, and several minor additives.

Exam Probability: **Low**

1. *Answer choices:*

(see index for correct answer)

- a. Polymethylpentene
- b. Medium-density polyethylene
- c. Saran
- d. Glass

Guidance: level 1

:: Product management ::

_____ is the state of being which occurs when an object, service, or practice is no longer wanted even though it may still be in good working order; however, the international standard EN62402 _____ Management - Application Guide defines _____ as being the "transition from availability of products by the original manufacturer or supplier to unavailability". _____ frequently occurs because a replacement has become available that has, in sum, more advantages compared to the disadvantages incurred by maintaining or repairing the original. Obsolete also refers to something that is already disused or discarded, or antiquated. Typically, _____ is preceded by a gradual decline in popularity.

Exam Probability: **High**

2. *Answer choices:*

(see index for correct answer)

- a. Rapid prototyping
- b. Electronic registration mark
- c. Coolanol
- d. Obsolescence

Guidance: level 1

:: Project management ::

Contemporary business and science treat as a _____ any undertaking, carried out individually or collaboratively and possibly involving research or design, that is carefully planned to achieve a particular aim.

3. *Answer choices:*

(see index for correct answer)

- a. Gregory T. Haugan
- b. Punch list
- c. Point of total assumption
- d. Participatory impact pathways analysis

Guidance: level 1

:: Quality ::

A _____ is an initiating cause of either a condition or a causal chain that leads to an outcome or effect of interest. The term denotes the earliest, most basic, `deepest`, cause for a given behavior; most often a fault. The idea is that you can only see an error by its manifest signs. Those signs can be widespread, multitudinous, and convoluted, whereas the _____ leading to them often is a lot simpler.

Exam Probability: **High**

4. *Answer choices:*

(see index for correct answer)

- a. Ringtest
- b. Customer Service Excellence

- c. Root cause
- d. Robustification

Guidance: level 1

:: Production and manufacturing ::

_____ is a comprehensive and rigorous industrial process by which a previously sold, leased, used, worn or non-functional product or part is returned to a 'like-new' or 'better-than-new' condition, from both a quality and performance perspective, through a controlled, reproducible and sustainable process.

Exam Probability: **Medium**

5. *Answer choices:*

(see index for correct answer)

- a. IBM RFID Information Center
- b. First pass yield
- c. Detailed division of labor
- d. Remanufacturing

Guidance: level 1

:: Management ::

_____ is a term used in business and Information Technology to describe the in-depth process of capturing customer's expectations, preferences and aversions. Specifically, the _____ is a market research technique that produces a detailed set of customer wants and needs, organized into a hierarchical structure, and then prioritized in terms of relative importance and satisfaction with current alternatives. _____ studies typically consist of both qualitative and quantitative research steps. They are generally conducted at the start of any new product, process, or service design initiative in order to better understand the customer's wants and needs, and as the key input for new product definition, Quality Function Deployment , and the setting of detailed design specifications.

Exam Probability: **Medium**

6. *Answer choices:*

(see index for correct answer)

- a. Voice of the customer
- b. Product differentiation
- c. Fredmund Malik
- d. Mobile sales enablement

Guidance: level 1

:: Management ::

_____ is an iterative four-step management method used in business for the control and continuous improvement of processes and products. It is also known as the Deming circle/cycle/wheel, the Shewhart cycle, the control circle/cycle, or plan–do–study–act . Another version of this _____ cycle is O _____ . The added "O" stands for observation or as some versions say: "Observe the current condition." This emphasis on observation and current condition has currency with the literature on lean manufacturing and the Toyota Production System. The _____ cycle, with Ishikawa's changes, can be traced back to S. Mizuno of the Tokyo Institute of Technology in 1959.

Exam Probability: **Medium**

7. *Answer choices:*

(see index for correct answer)

- a. Work breakdown structure
- b. Line of business
- c. Extended enterprise
- d. Discovery-driven planning

Guidance: level 1

:: Information technology management ::

_____ is a collective term for all approaches to prepare , support and help individuals, teams, and organizations in making organizational change. The most common change drivers include: technological evolution, process reviews, crisis, and consumer habit changes; pressure from new business entrants, acquisitions, mergers, and organizational restructuring. It includes methods that redirect or redefine the use of resources, business process, budget allocations, or other modes of operation that significantly change a company or organization. Organizational _____ considers the full organization and what needs to change, while _____ may be used solely to refer to how people and teams are affected by such organizational transition. It deals with many different disciplines, from behavioral and social sciences to information technology and business solutions.

Exam Probability: **Medium**

8. *Answer choices:*

(see index for correct answer)

- a. Business Information Services Library
- b. Change management
- c. Lean IT
- d. Service Measurement Index

Guidance: level 1

:: Supply chain management ::

A _____ is a type of auction in which the traditional roles of buyer and seller are reversed. Thus, there is one buyer and many potential sellers. In an ordinary auction , buyers compete to obtain goods or services by offering increasingly higher prices. In contrast, in a _____ , the sellers compete to obtain business from the buyer and prices will typically decrease as the sellers underbid each other.

Exam Probability: **High**

9. *Answer choices:*

(see index for correct answer)

- a. Application service provider
- b. RevPAR
- c. Procurement
- d. Gideon Hillman Consulting

Guidance: level 1

:: Occupational safety and health ::

_____ is a chemical element with symbol Pb and atomic number 82. It is a heavy metal that is denser than most common materials. _____ is soft and malleable, and also has a relatively low melting point. When freshly cut, _____ is silvery with a hint of blue; it tarnishes to a dull gray color when exposed to air. _____ has the highest atomic number of any stable element and three of its isotopes are endpoints of major nuclear decay chains of heavier elements.

10. *Answer choices:*

(see index for correct answer)

- a. Thermal work limit
- b. Risk Information Exchange
- c. Donald Hunter
- d. CLP Regulation

Guidance: level 1

:: Production and manufacturing ::

_____ is the production under license of technology developed elsewhere. It is an especially prominent commercial practice in developing nations, which often approach _____ as a starting point for indigenous industrial development.

Exam Probability: **High**

11. *Answer choices:*

(see index for correct answer)

- a. Manufacturing process management
- b. Fieldbus Foundation
- c. Rolled throughput yield

- d. Licensed production

Guidance: level 1

:: Infographics ::

The _____ is a form used to collect data in real time at the location where the data is generated. The data it captures can be quantitative or qualitative. When the information is quantitative, the _____ is sometimes called a tally sheet.

Exam Probability: **High**

12. *Answer choices:*

(see index for correct answer)

- a. Archaeological illustration
- b. Table
- c. Check sheet
- d. Wigmore chart

Guidance: level 1

:: Project management ::

In general usage, a _____ is a comprehensive evaluation of an individual's current pay and future financial state by using current known variables to predict future income, asset values and withdrawal plans. This often includes a budget which organizes an individual's finances and sometimes includes a series of steps or specific goals for spending and saving in the future. This plan allocates future income to various types of expenses, such as rent or utilities, and also reserves some income for short-term and long-term savings. A _____ is sometimes referred to as an investment plan, but in personal finance a _____ can focus on other specific areas such as risk management, estates, college, or retirement.

Exam Probability: **Medium**

13. *Answer choices:*

(see index for correct answer)

- a. Effective Development Group
- b. Cone of Uncertainty
- c. Project anatomy
- d. Master of Science in Project Management

Guidance: level 1

:: Project management ::

In economics, _____ is the assignment of available resources to various uses. In the context of an entire economy, resources can be allocated by various means, such as markets or central planning.

14. *Answer choices:*

(see index for correct answer)

- a. Hammock activity
- b. RationalPlan
- c. Virtual design and construction
- d. The Practice Standard for Scheduling

Guidance: level 1

:: Materials ::

A _____ , also known as a feedstock, unprocessed material, or primary commodity, is a basic material that is used to produce goods, finished products, energy, or intermediate materials which are feedstock for future finished products. As feedstock, the term connotes these materials are bottleneck assets and are highly important with regard to producing other products. An example of this is crude oil, which is a _____ and a feedstock used in the production of industrial chemicals, fuels, plastics, and pharmaceutical goods; lumber is a _____ used to produce a variety of products including all types of furniture. The term " _____ " denotes materials in minimally processed or unprocessed in states; e.g., raw latex, crude oil, cotton, coal, raw biomass, iron ore, air, logs, or water i.e. "...any product of agriculture, forestry, fishing and any other mineral that is in its natural form or which has undergone the transformation required to prepare it for internationally marketing in substantial volumes."

15. *Answer choices:*

(see index for correct answer)

- a. Materials World
- b. Propolis
- c. Drawdown chart
- d. Putty

Guidance: level 1

:: Industrial processes ::

A _____ is a device used for high-temperature heating. The name derives from Latin word fornax, which means oven. The heat energy to fuel a _____ may be supplied directly by fuel combustion, by electricity such as the electric arc _____ , or through induction heating in induction _____ s.

Exam Probability: **Medium**

16. *Answer choices:*

(see index for correct answer)

- a. Hot isostatic pressing
- b. Borax method
- c. Furnace
- d. Magnetorheological finishing

:: Teams ::

A _____ usually refers to a group of individuals who work together from different geographic locations and rely on communication technology such as email, FAX, and video or voice conferencing services in order to collaborate. The term can also refer to groups or teams that work together asynchronously or across organizational levels. Powell, Piccoli and Ives define _____ s as "groups of geographically, organizationally and/or time dispersed workers brought together by information and telecommunication technologies to accomplish one or more organizational tasks." According to Ale Ebrahim et. al. , _____ s can also be defined as "small temporary groups of geographically, organizationally and/or time dispersed knowledge workers who coordinate their work predominantly with electronic information and communication technologies in order to accomplish one or more organization tasks."

Exam Probability: **Low**

17. *Answer choices:*

(see index for correct answer)

- a. Virtual team
- b. Team-building

:: Management ::

_____ is a category of business activity made possible by software tools that aim to provide customers with both independence from vendors and better means for engaging with vendors. These same tools can also apply to individuals' relations with other institutions and organizations.

Exam Probability: **Low**

18. *Answer choices:*

(see index for correct answer)

- a. Toxic leader
- b. Vendor relationship management
- c. Modes of leadership
- d. Integrative thinking

Guidance: level 1

:: Business process ::

A committee is a body of one or more persons that is subordinate to a deliberative assembly. Usually, the assembly sends matters into a committee as a way to explore them more fully than would be possible if the assembly itself were considering them. Committees may have different functions and their type of work differ depending on the type of the organization and its needs.

Exam Probability: **Medium**

19. *Answer choices:*

(see index for correct answer)

- a. IBM Blueworks Live
- b. Intention mining
- c. Steering committee
- d. Software Ideas Modeler

Guidance: level 1

:: Costs ::

In economics, _____ is the total economic cost of production and is made up of variable cost, which varies according to the quantity of a good produced and includes inputs such as labour and raw materials, plus fixed cost, which is independent of the quantity of a good produced and includes inputs that cannot be varied in the short term: fixed costs such as buildings and machinery, including sunk costs if any. Since cost is measured per unit of time, it is a flow variable.

Exam Probability: **Low**

20. *Answer choices:*

(see index for correct answer)

- a. Total cost
- b. Quality costs
- c. Cost overrun

- d. Travel and subsistence

Guidance: level 1

:: Information systems ::

_____ is the process of creating, sharing, using and managing the knowledge and information of an organisation. It refers to a multidisciplinary approach to achieving organisational objectives by making the best use of knowledge.

Exam Probability: **Low**

21. *Answer choices:*

(see index for correct answer)

- a. Manufacturing execution system
- b. Knowledge management
- c. Strategic information system
- d. Data flow diagram

Guidance: level 1

:: ::

_____ refers to the confirmation of certain characteristics of an object, person, or organization. This confirmation is often, but not always, provided by some form of external review, education, assessment, or audit. Accreditation is a specific organization's process of _____ . According to the National Council on Measurement in Education, a _____ test is a credentialing test used to determine whether individuals are knowledgeable enough in a given occupational area to be labeled "competent to practice" in that area.

Exam Probability: **Low**

22. *Answer choices:*

(see index for correct answer)

- a. imperative
- b. hierarchical perspective
- c. open system
- d. empathy

Guidance: level 1

:: Production and manufacturing ::

A BOM can define products as they are designed , as they are ordered , as they are built , or as they are maintained . The different types of BOMs depend on the business need and use for which they are intended. In process industries, the BOM is also known as the formula, recipe, or ingredients list. The phrase "bill of material" is frequently used by engineers as an adjective to refer not to the literal bill, but to the current production configuration of a product, to distinguish it from modified or improved versions under study or in test.

Exam Probability: **Medium**

23. *Answer choices:*

(see index for correct answer)

- a. Digital materialization
- b. Bill of materials
- c. Virtual manufacturing network
- d. International Automotive Task Force

Guidance: level 1

:: Lean manufacturing ::

_____ is the Sino-Japanese word for "improvement". In business, _____ refers to activities that continuously improve all functions and involve all employees from the CEO to the assembly line workers. It also applies to processes, such as purchasing and logistics, that cross organizational boundaries into the supply chain. It has been applied in healthcare, psychotherapy, life-coaching, government, and banking.

24. *Answer choices:*

(see index for correct answer)

- a. Frequent deliveries
- b. Failure mode and effects analysis
- c. Andon
- d. Lean CFP driven

Guidance: level 1

:: Quality ::

The _____ , formerly the _____ Control , is a knowledge-based global community of quality professionals, with nearly 80,000 members dedicated to promoting and advancing quality tools, principles, and practices in their workplaces and communities.

Exam Probability: **Low**

25. *Answer choices:*

(see index for correct answer)

- a. Robustification
- b. Secure Stations Scheme
- c. European Organization for Quality

- d. American Society for Quality

Guidance: level 1

:: Software testing ::

_____ 1 was the first artificial Earth satellite. The Soviet Union launched it into an elliptical low Earth orbit on 4 October 1957, orbiting for three weeks before its batteries died, then silently for two more months before falling back into the atmosphere. It was a 58 cm diameter polished metal sphere, with four external radio antennas to broadcast radio pulses. Its radio signal was easily detectable even by radio amateurs, and the 65° inclination and duration of its orbit made its flight path cover virtually the entire inhabited Earth. This surprise success precipitated the American _____ crisis and triggered the Space Race, a part of the Cold War. The launch was the beginning of a new era of political, military, technological, and scientific developments.

Exam Probability: **High**

26. *Answer choices:*

(see index for correct answer)

- a. Test data generation
- b. Dynamic testing
- c. Sputnik
- d. Recovery testing

Guidance: level 1

:: Management ::

_____ is the process of thinking about the activities required to achieve a desired goal. It is the first and foremost activity to achieve desired results. It involves the creation and maintenance of a plan, such as psychological aspects that require conceptual skills. There are even a couple of tests to measure someone's capability of _____ well. As such, _____ is a fundamental property of intelligent behavior. An important further meaning, often just called " _____ " is the legal context of permitted building developments.

Exam Probability: **Low**

27. *Answer choices:*

- a. Organizational space
- b. Middle management
- c. Crisis plan
- d. Director

Guidance: level 1

:: Project management ::

In economics and business decision-making, a sunk cost is a cost that has already been incurred and cannot be recovered.

Exam Probability: **High**

28. *Answer choices:*

(see index for correct answer)

- a. Gold plating
- b. Association for Project Management
- c. Sunk costs
- d. Project blog

Guidance: level 1

:: Project management ::

Some scenarios associate "this kind of planning" with learning "life skills". _____ s are necessary, or at least useful, in situations where individuals need to know what time they must be at a specific location to receive a specific service, and where people need to accomplish a set of goals within a set time period.

Exam Probability: **Low**

29. *Answer choices:*

(see index for correct answer)

- a. 10,000ft
- b. Starmad
- c. Schedule
- d. Australian Institute of Project Management

Guidance: level 1

:: ::

_____ is a kind of action that occur as two or more objects have an effect upon one another. The idea of a two-way effect is essential in the concept of _____ , as opposed to a one-way causal effect. A closely related term is interconnectivity, which deals with the _____ s of _____ s within systems: combinations of many simple _____ s can lead to surprising emergent phenomena. _____ has different tailored meanings in various sciences. Changes can also involve _____ .

Exam Probability: **High**

30. *Answer choices:*

(see index for correct answer)

- a. open system
- b. Interaction
- c. hierarchical
- d. surface-level diversity

:: Process management ::

When used in the context of communication networks, such as Ethernet or packet radio, _____ or network _____ is the rate of successful message delivery over a communication channel. The data these messages belong to may be delivered over a physical or logical link, or it can pass through a certain network node. _____ is usually measured in bits per second , and sometimes in data packets per second or data packets per time slot.

Exam Probability: **High**

31. *Answer choices:*

(see index for correct answer)

- a. Business process network
- b. Process consultant
- c. Value grid
- d. Throughput

:: Distribution, retailing, and wholesaling ::

_____ measures the performance of a system. Certain goals are defined and the _____ gives the percentage to which those goals should be achieved. Fill rate is different from _____ .

Exam Probability: **Low**

32. *Answer choices:*

(see index for correct answer)

- a. Service level
- b. 350 West Mart Center
- c. Hypermarket
- d. Sales variance

Guidance: level 1

:: Mereology ::

_____ , in the abstract, is what belongs to or with something, whether as an attribute or as a component of said thing. In the context of this article, it is one or more components , whether physical or incorporeal, of a person's estate; or so belonging to, as in being owned by, a person or jointly a group of people or a legal entity like a corporation or even a society. Depending on the nature of the _____ , an owner of _____ has the right to consume, alter, share, redefine, rent, mortgage, pawn, sell, exchange, transfer, give away or destroy it, or to exclude others from doing these things, as well as to perhaps abandon it; whereas regardless of the nature of the _____ , the owner thereof has the right to properly use it , or at the very least exclusively keep it.

33. *Answer choices:*

(see index for correct answer)

- a. Mereology
- b. Non-wellfounded mereology
- c. Mereotopology
- d. Simple

Guidance: level 1

:: Production and manufacturing ::

_____ is a concept in purchasing and project management for securing the quality and timely delivery of goods and components.

34. *Answer choices:*

(see index for correct answer)

- a. Expediting
- b. Follow-the-sun
- c. Dynamic simulation
- d. Beltweigher

:: Management ::

An _____ is a loosely coupled, self-organizing network of firms that combine their economic output to provide products and services offerings to the market. Firms in the _____ may operate independently, for example, through market mechanisms, or cooperatively through agreements and contracts. They provide value added service or product to the OEM .

Exam Probability: **High**

35. *Answer choices:*

(see index for correct answer)

- a. Production flow analysis
- b. Resource breakdown structure
- c. Managerial economics
- d. Extended enterprise

:: Metals ::

A _____ is a material that, when freshly prepared, polished, or fractured, shows a lustrous appearance, and conducts electricity and heat relatively well. _____ s are typically malleable or ductile . A _____ may be a chemical element such as iron, or an alloy such as stainless steel.

Exam Probability: **Low**

36. *Answer choices:*

(see index for correct answer)

- a. Half-metal
- b. Metal
- c. Metal powder
- d. Alonizing

Guidance: level 1

:: Sensitivity analysis ::

_____ is the study of how the uncertainty in the output of a mathematical model or system can be divided and allocated to different sources of uncertainty in its inputs. A related practice is uncertainty analysis, which has a greater focus on uncertainty quantification and propagation of uncertainty; ideally, uncertainty and _____ should be run in tandem.

Exam Probability: **Medium**

37. *Answer choices:*

- a. Elementary effects method
- b. Variance-based sensitivity analysis
- c. Fourier amplitude sensitivity testing
- d. Tornado diagram

Guidance: level 1

:: Information technology management ::

_____ concerns a cycle of organizational activity: the acquisition of information from one or more sources, the custodianship and the distribution of that information to those who need it, and its ultimate disposition through archiving or deletion.

Exam Probability: **Low**

38. *Answer choices:*

- a. Digital Fuel
- b. Global Information Governance Day
- c. Information technology operations
- d. Bachelor in Information Management

:: ::

_____ is the process of making predictions of the future based on past and present data and most commonly by analysis of trends. A commonplace example might be estimation of some variable of interest at some specified future date. Prediction is a similar, but more general term. Both might refer to formal statistical methods employing time series, cross-sectional or longitudinal data, or alternatively to less formal judgmental methods. Usage can differ between areas of application: for example, in hydrology the terms "forecast" and "_____" are sometimes reserved for estimates of values at certain specific future times, while the term "prediction" is used for more general estimates, such as the number of times floods will occur over a long period.

Exam Probability: **High**

39. *Answer choices:*

(see index for correct answer)

- a. Character
- b. functional perspective
- c. surface-level diversity
- d. Forecasting

:: Project management ::

A _____ is a team whose members usually belong to different groups, functions and are assigned to activities for the same project. A team can be divided into sub-teams according to need. Usually _____ s are only used for a defined period of time. They are disbanded after the project is deemed complete. Due to the nature of the specific formation and disbandment, _____ s are usually in organizations.

Exam Probability: **Medium**

40. *Answer choices:*

(see index for correct answer)

- a. Project team
- b. Rapid Results
- c. Transfer of Burden
- d. System anatomy

Guidance: level 1

:: Management ::

Business _____ is a discipline in operations management in which people use various methods to discover, model, analyze, measure, improve, optimize, and automate business processes. BPM focuses on improving corporate performance by managing business processes. Any combination of methods used to manage a company's business processes is BPM. Processes can be structured and repeatable or unstructured and variable. Though not required, enabling technologies are often used with BPM.

41. *Answer choices:*

(see index for correct answer)

- a. Process management
- b. Complementary assets
- c. Personal offshoring
- d. Product Development and Systems Engineering Consortium

Guidance: level 1

:: Direct marketing ::

_____ Inc. is an American privately owned multi-level marketing company. According to Direct Selling News, _____ was the sixth largest network marketing company in the world in 2018, with a wholesale volume of US$3.25 billion. _____ is based in Addison, Texas, outside Dallas. The company was founded by _____ Ash in 1963. Richard Rogers, _____ `s son, is the chairman, and David Holl is president and was named CEO in 2006.

42. *Answer choices:*

(see index for correct answer)

- a. Robinson list
- b. Cold calling

- c. Guthy-Renker
- d. Mary Kay

:: Promotion and marketing communications ::

The _____ of American Manufacturers, now ThomasNet, is an online platform for supplier discovery and product sourcing in the US and Canada. It was once known as the "big green books" and "Thomas Registry", and was a multi-volume directory of industrial product information covering 650,000 distributors, manufacturers and service companies within 67,000-plus industrial categories that is now published on ThomasNet.

Exam Probability: **High**

43. *Answer choices:*

(see index for correct answer)

- a. Sales promotion
- b. Thomas Register
- c. Press kit
- d. Worthy Book

:: Project management ::

_____ is a work methodology emphasizing the parallelisation of tasks , which is sometimes called simultaneous engineering or integrated product development using an integrated product team approach. It refers to an approach used in product development in which functions of design engineering, manufacturing engineering, and other functions are integrated to reduce the time required to bring a new product to market.

Exam Probability: **Low**

44. *Answer choices:*

(see index for correct answer)

- a. Project risk management
- b. Master of Science in Project Management
- c. Concurrent engineering
- d. Case competition

Guidance: level 1

:: Supply chain management ::

_____ is a core supply chain function and includes supply chain planning and supply chain execution capabilities. Specifically, _____ is the capability firms use to plan total material requirements. The material requirements are communicated to procurement and other functions for sourcing. _____ is also responsible for determining the amount of material to be deployed at each stocking location across the supply chain, establishing material replenishment plans, determining inventory levels to hold for each type of inventory , and communicating information regarding material needs throughout the extended supply chain.

Exam Probability: **Medium**

45. *Answer choices:*

(see index for correct answer)

- a. competitive bidding
- b. Service parts pricing
- c. Mobile asset management
- d. Supply chain management software

Guidance: level 1

:: Production and manufacturing ::

In industry, _____ is a system of maintaining and improving the integrity of production and quality systems through the machines, equipment, processes, and employees that add business value to an organization.

46. *Answer choices:*

(see index for correct answer)

- a. Mockup
- b. Total productive maintenance
- c. Economic region of production
- d. Profibus

Guidance: level 1

:: Evaluation ::

_____ is a way of preventing mistakes and defects in manufactured products and avoiding problems when delivering products or services to customers; which ISO 9000 defines as "part of quality management focused on providing confidence that quality requirements will be fulfilled". This defect prevention in _____ differs subtly from defect detection and rejection in quality control and has been referred to as a shift left since it focuses on quality earlier in the process .

Exam Probability: **Low**

47. *Answer choices:*

(see index for correct answer)

- a. Technology assessment

- b. Quality assurance
- c. Educational assessment
- d. Problem

Guidance: level 1

:: Management ::

In organizational studies, _____ is the efficient and effective development of an organization's resources when they are needed. Such resources may include financial resources, inventory, human skills, production resources, or information technology and natural resources.

Exam Probability: **Low**

48. *Answer choices:*

(see index for correct answer)

- a. Dynamic enterprise modeling
- b. Office management
- c. Mobile sales enablement
- d. Main Street Manager

Guidance: level 1

:: Production and manufacturing ::

_____ is a systematic method to improve the "value" of goods or products and services by using an examination of function. Value, as defined, is the ratio of function to cost. Value can therefore be manipulated by either improving the function or reducing the cost. It is a primary tenet of _____ that basic functions be preserved and not be reduced as a consequence of pursuing value improvements.

Exam Probability: **Medium**

49. *Answer choices:*

(see index for correct answer)

- a. Economic region of production
- b. Citect
- c. Value engineering
- d. Job shop

Guidance: level 1

:: Information technology management ::

_____ is the discipline of engineering concerned with the principles and practice of product and service quality assurance and control. In the software development, it is the management, development, operation and maintenance of IT systems and enterprise architectures with a high quality standard.

Exam Probability: **Medium**

50. *Answer choices:*

(see index for correct answer)

- a. EDIFACT
- b. Quality Engineering
- c. Information Services Procurement Library
- d. Campustours

Guidance: level 1

:: Supply chain management ::

_____ is the process of finding and agreeing to terms, and acquiring goods, services, or works from an external source, often via a tendering or competitive bidding process. _____ is used to ensure the buyer receives goods, services, or works at the best possible price when aspects such as quality, quantity, time, and location are compared. Corporations and public bodies often define processes intended to promote fair and open competition for their business while minimizing risks such as exposure to fraud and collusion.

Exam Probability: **Low**

51. *Answer choices:*

(see index for correct answer)

- a. Strategic material
- b. Pharmacode
- c. National Centre for Cold-chain Development

- d. Procurement

Guidance: level 1

:: Industrial organization ::

In economics, specifically general equilibrium theory, a perfect market is defined by several idealizing conditions, collectively called _____ . In theoretical models where conditions of _____ hold, it has been theoretically demonstrated that a market will reach an equilibrium in which the quantity supplied for every product or service, including labor, equals the quantity demanded at the current price. This equilibrium would be a Pareto optimum.

Exam Probability: **Low**

52. *Answer choices:*

(see index for correct answer)

- a. Switching cost
- b. Hold-up problem
- c. Limit price
- d. Path dependence

Guidance: level 1

:: ::

_____ refers to a business or organization attempting to acquire goods or services to accomplish its goals. Although there are several organizations that attempt to set standards in the _____ process, processes can vary greatly between organizations. Typically the word " _____ " is not used interchangeably with the word "procurement", since procurement typically includes expediting, supplier quality, and transportation and logistics in addition to _____ .

Exam Probability: **High**

53. *Answer choices:*

(see index for correct answer)

- a. Purchasing
- b. Character
- c. deep-level diversity
- d. hierarchical perspective

Guidance: level 1

:: Industrial design ::

In physics and mathematics, the _____ of a mathematical space is informally defined as the minimum number of coordinates needed to specify any point within it. Thus a line has a _____ of one because only one coordinate is needed to specify a point on it for example, the point at 5 on a number line. A surface such as a plane or the surface of a cylinder or sphere has a _____ of two because two coordinates are needed to specify a point on it for example, both a latitude and longitude are required to locate a point on the surface of a sphere. The inside of a cube, a cylinder or a sphere is three- _____ al because three coordinates are needed to locate a point within these spaces.

Exam Probability: **Medium**

54. *Answer choices:*

(see index for correct answer)

- a. Dimension
- b. Process simulation
- c. Slow design
- d. Objectified

Guidance: level 1

:: Insulators ::

A _____ is a piece of soft cloth large enough either to cover or to enfold a great portion of the user's body, usually when sleeping or otherwise at rest, thereby trapping radiant bodily heat that otherwise would be lost through convection, and so keeping the body warm.

55. *Answer choices:*

(see index for correct answer)

- a. Mechanical insulation
- b. Multi-layer insulation
- c. Blanket
- d. Vacuum insulated panel

Guidance: level 1

:: Natural materials ::

_____ is a finely-grained natural rock or soil material that combines one or more _____ minerals with possible traces of quartz , metal oxides and organic matter. Geologic _____ deposits are mostly composed of phyllosilicate minerals containing variable amounts of water trapped in the mineral structure. _____ s are plastic due to particle size and geometry as well as water content, and become hard, brittle and non–plastic upon drying or firing. Depending on the soil's content in which it is found, _____ can appear in various colours from white to dull grey or brown to deep orange-red.

Exam Probability: **Low**

56. *Answer choices:*

(see index for correct answer)

- a. Natural material
- b. Clay
- c. Crushed stone
- d. Alternative natural materials

Guidance: level 1

:: ::

In production, research, retail, and accounting, a _____ is the value of money that has been used up to produce something or deliver a service, and hence is not available for use anymore. In business, the _____ may be one of acquisition, in which case the amount of money expended to acquire it is counted as _____ . In this case, money is the input that is gone in order to acquire the thing. This acquisition _____ may be the sum of the _____ of production as incurred by the original producer, and further _____ s of transaction as incurred by the acquirer over and above the price paid to the producer. Usually, the price also includes a mark-up for profit over the _____ of production.

Exam Probability: **High**

57. *Answer choices:*

(see index for correct answer)

- a. Cost
- b. levels of analysis
- c. similarity-attraction theory
- d. information systems assessment

:: Procurement ::

A _____ is a standard business process whose purpose is to invite suppliers into a bidding process to bid on specific products or services. RfQ generally means the same thing as Call for bids and Invitation for bid .

Exam Probability: **Low**

58. *Answer choices:*

(see index for correct answer)

- a. Bid and proposal
- b. Best value procurement
- c. Request for quotation
- d. Purchasing process

:: Sampling (statistics) ::

_____ uses statistical sampling to determine whether to accept or reject a production lot of material. It has been a common quality control technique used in industry. It is usually done as products leaves the factory, or in some cases even within the factory. Most often a producer supplies a consumer a number of items and a decision to accept or reject the items is made by determining the number of defective items in a sample from the lot. The lot is accepted if the number of defects falls below where the acceptance number or otherwise the lot is rejected.

Exam Probability: **Low**

59. *Answer choices:*

(see index for correct answer)

- a. Balanced repeated replication
- b. Expander walk sampling
- c. Imperfect induction
- d. Stratified sampling

Guidance: level 1

Commerce

Commerce relates to "the exchange of goods and services, especially on a large scale." It includes legal, economic, political, social, cultural and technological systems that operate in any country or internationally.

:: ::

In marketing jargon, product lining is offering several related products for sale individually. Unlike product bundling, where several products are combined into one group, which is then offered for sale as a units, product lining involves offering the products for sale separately. A line can comprise related products of various sizes, types, colors, qualities, or prices. Line depth refers to the number of subcategories a category has. Line consistency refers to how closely related the products that make up the line are. Line vulnerability refers to the percentage of sales or profits that are derived from only a few products in the line.

Exam Probability: **Low**

1. *Answer choices:*

(see index for correct answer)

- a. Product mix
- b. similarity-attraction theory
- c. hierarchical perspective
- d. empathy

Guidance: level 1

:: ::

An _____ in international trade is a good or service produced in one country that is bought by someone in another country. The seller of such goods and services is an _____ er; the foreign buyer is an importer.

2. *Answer choices:*

(see index for correct answer)

- a. cultural
- b. hierarchical perspective
- c. Export
- d. levels of analysis

Guidance: level 1

:: Quality management ::

_____ ensures that an organization, product or service is consistent. It has four main components: quality planning, quality assurance, quality control and quality improvement. _____ is focused not only on product and service quality, but also on the means to achieve it. _____ , therefore, uses quality assurance and control of processes as well as products to achieve more consistent quality. What a customer wants and is willing to pay for it determines quality. It is written or unwritten commitment to a known or unknown consumer in the market . Thus, quality can be defined as fitness for intended use or, in other words, how well the product performs its intended function

3. *Answer choices:*

(see index for correct answer)

- a. QC Reporting
- b. Det Norske Veritas
- c. Quality policy
- d. External quality assessment

Guidance: level 1

:: ::

_____ is the collaborative effort of a team to achieve a common goal or to complete a task in the most effective and efficient way. This concept is seen within the greater framework of a team, which is a group of interdependent individuals who work together towards a common goal. Basic requirements for effective _____ are an adequate team size, available resources for the team to make use of, and clearly defined roles within the team in order for everyone to have a clear purpose. _____ is present in any context where a group of people are working together to achieve a common goal. These contexts include an industrial organization, athletics, a school, and the healthcare system. In each of these settings, the level of _____ and interdependence can vary from low, to intermediate, to high, depending on the amount of communication, interaction, and collaboration present between team members.

Exam Probability: **Medium**

4. *Answer choices:*

(see index for correct answer)

- a. Teamwork
- b. functional perspective

- c. surface-level diversity
- d. interpersonal communication

Guidance: level 1

:: Confidence tricks ::

_____ is the fraudulent attempt to obtain sensitive information such as usernames, passwords and credit card details by disguising oneself as a trustworthy entity in an electronic communication. Typically carried out by email spoofing or instant messaging, it often directs users to enter personal information at a fake website which matches the look and feel of the legitimate site.

Exam Probability: **Medium**

5. *Answer choices:*

(see index for correct answer)

- a. Phishing
- b. Thai tailor scam
- c. Email fraud
- d. Great Reality TV Swindle

Guidance: level 1

:: Commerce ::

A _____ is an employee within a company, business or other organization who is responsible at some level for buying or approving the acquisition of goods and services needed by the company. Responsible for buying the best quality products, goods and services for their company at the most competitive prices, _____ s work in a wide range of sectors for many different organizations. The position responsibilities may be the same as that of a buyer or purchasing agent, or may include wider supervisory or managerial responsibilities. A _____ may oversee the acquisition of materials needed for production, general supplies for offices and facilities, equipment, or construction contracts. A _____ often supervises purchasing agents and buyers, but in small companies the _____ may also be the purchasing agent or buyer. The _____ position may also carry the title "Procurement Manager" or in the public sector, "Procurement Officer". He or she can come from both an Engineering or Economics background.

Exam Probability: **High**

6. *Answer choices:*

(see index for correct answer)

- a. Purchasing manager
- b. Sales quote
- c. Country commercial guides
- d. Requisition

Guidance: level 1

:: Payment systems ::

_____ s are part of a payment system issued by financial institutions, such as a bank, to a customer that enables its owner to access the funds in the customer's designated bank accounts, or through a credit account and make payments by electronic funds transfer and access automated teller machines . Such cards are known by a variety of names including bank cards, ATM cards, MAC , client cards, key cards or cash cards.

Exam Probability: **High**

7. *Answer choices:*

(see index for correct answer)

- a. Wire transfer
- b. Certified Payment-Card Industry Security Implementer
- c. Payment card
- d. CHAPS

Guidance: level 1

:: Hospitality industry ::

_____ refers to the relationship between a guest and a host, wherein the host receives the guest with goodwill, including the reception and entertainment of guests, visitors, or strangers. Louis, chevalier de Jaucourt describes _____ in the Encyclopédie as the virtue of a great soul that cares for the whole universe through the ties of humanity.

Exam Probability: **Low**

8. *Answer choices:*

(see index for correct answer)

- a. Hospitality
- b. Hospitality industry
- c. Cover charge
- d. Travel insurance

Guidance: level 1

:: Dot-com bubble ::

_____ , Inc., is a web search engine and web portal established in 1994, spun out of Carnegie Mellon University. _____ also encompasses a network of email, webhosting, social networking, and entertainment websites. The company is based in Waltham, Massachusetts, and is currently a subsidiary of Kakao.

Exam Probability: **Low**

9. *Answer choices:*

(see index for correct answer)

- a. Dot-com company
- b. E-Dreams
- c. Internet time
- d. Dot com party

:: Commerce ::

_____ relates to "the exchange of goods and services, especially on a large scale". It includes legal, economic, political, social, cultural and technological systems that operate in a country or in international trade.

Exam Probability: **Medium**

10. *Answer choices:*

(see index for correct answer)

- a. Grain trade
- b. Social gravity
- c. Netflix
- d. Commerce

:: Project management ::

A _____ is a source or supply from which a benefit is produced and it has some utility. _____ s can broadly be classified upon their availability—they are classified into renewable and non-renewable _____ s.Examples of non renewable _____ s are coal ,crude oil natural gas nuclear energy etc. Examples of renewable _____ s are air,water,wind,solar energy etc. They can also be classified as actual and potential on the basis of level of development and use, on the basis of origin they can be classified as biotic and abiotic, and on the basis of their distribution, as ubiquitous and localized . An item becomes a _____ with time and developing technology. Typically, _____ s are materials, energy, services, staff, knowledge, or other assets that are transformed to produce benefit and in the process may be consumed or made unavailable. Benefits of _____ utilization may include increased wealth, proper functioning of a system, or enhanced well-being. From a human perspective a natural _____ is anything obtained from the environment to satisfy human needs and wants. From a broader biological or ecological perspective a _____ satisfies the needs of a living organism .

Exam Probability: **Medium**

11. *Answer choices:*

(see index for correct answer)

- a. Project initiation document
- b. Constructability
- c. Resource
- d. Value breakdown structure

Guidance: level 1

:: Business models ::

A _____ is "an autonomous association of persons united voluntarily to meet their common economic, social, and cultural needs and aspirations through a jointly-owned and democratically-controlled enterprise". _____ s may include.

Exam Probability: **Low**

12. *Answer choices:*

(see index for correct answer)

- a. Subsidiary
- b. InnovationXchange
- c. Entreship
- d. Organizational architecture

Guidance: level 1

:: Meetings ::

A _____ is a body of one or more persons that is subordinate to a deliberative assembly. Usually, the assembly sends matters into a _____ as a way to explore them more fully than would be possible if the assembly itself were considering them. _____ s may have different functions and their type of work differ depending on the type of the organization and its needs.

Exam Probability: **Medium**

13. *Answer choices:*

- a. Meeting point
- b. 2006 Russian March
- c. Committee
- d. Agenda

Guidance: level 1

:: ::

An _____ is the production of goods or related services within an economy. The major source of revenue of a group or company is the indicator of its relevant _____ . When a large group has multiple sources of revenue generation, it is considered to be working in different industries. Manufacturing _____ became a key sector of production and labour in European and North American countries during the Industrial Revolution, upsetting previous mercantile and feudal economies. This came through many successive rapid advances in technology, such as the production of steel and coal.

Exam Probability: **High**

14. *Answer choices:*

- a. empathy
- b. interpersonal communication

- c. functional perspective
- d. Character

Guidance: level 1

:: Payments ::

A _____ or government incentive is a form of financial aid or support extended to an economic sector generally with the aim of promoting economic and social policy. Although commonly extended from government, the term _____ can relate to any type of support – for example from NGOs or as implicit subsidies. Subsidies come in various forms including: direct and indirect .

Exam Probability: **Medium**

15. *Answer choices:*

(see index for correct answer)

- a. Subsidy
- b. Thirty pieces of silver
- c. Market transition payments
- d. Deficiency payments

Guidance: level 1

:: Monopoly (economics) ::

A _____ exists when a specific person or enterprise is the only supplier of a particular commodity. This contrasts with a monopsony which relates to a single entity's control of a market to purchase a good or service, and with oligopoly which consists of a few sellers dominating a market. Monopolies are thus characterized by a lack of economic competition to produce the good or service, a lack of viable substitute goods, and the possibility of a high _____ price well above the seller's marginal cost that leads to a high _____ profit. The verb monopolise or monopolize refers to the process by which a company gains the ability to raise prices or exclude competitors. In economics, a _____ is a single seller. In law, a _____ is a business entity that has significant market power, that is, the power to charge overly high prices. Although monopolies may be big businesses, size is not a characteristic of a _____ . A small business may still have the power to raise prices in a small industry .

Exam Probability: **High**

16. *Answer choices:*

(see index for correct answer)

- a. Network effect
- b. Average cost pricing
- c. Monopoly
- d. Coercive monopoly

Guidance: level 1

:: Accounting source documents ::

An _____ , bill or tab is a commercial document issued by a seller to a buyer, relating to a sale transaction and indicating the products, quantities, and agreed prices for products or services the seller had provided the buyer.

Exam Probability: **Medium**

17. *Answer choices:*

(see index for correct answer)

- a. Purchase order
- b. Remittance advice
- c. Invoice
- d. Parcel audit

Guidance: level 1

:: ::

_____ , also referred to as orthostasis, is a human position in which the body is held in an upright position and supported only by the feet.

Exam Probability: **Low**

18. *Answer choices:*

(see index for correct answer)

- a. Sarbanes-Oxley act of 2002
- b. imperative
- c. open system
- d. deep-level diversity

Guidance: level 1

:: Management accounting ::

_____ s are costs that change as the quantity of the good or service that a business produces changes. _____ s are the sum of marginal costs over all units produced. They can also be considered normal costs. Fixed costs and _____ s make up the two components of total cost. Direct costs are costs that can easily be associated with a particular cost object. However, not all _____ s are direct costs. For example, variable manufacturing overhead costs are _____ s that are indirect costs, not direct costs. _____ s are sometimes called unit-level costs as they vary with the number of units produced.

Exam Probability: **Low**

19. *Answer choices:*

(see index for correct answer)

- a. Chartered Institute of Management Accountants
- b. Variable cost
- c. Bridge life-cycle cost analysis
- d. Entity-level controls

:: Regulators ::

A _____ is a public authority or government agency responsible for exercising autonomous authority over some area of human activity in a regulatory or supervisory capacity. An independent _____ is a _____ that is independent from other branches or arms of the government.

Exam Probability: **Low**

20. *Answer choices:*

(see index for correct answer)

- a. Regulatory agency
- b. Croatian Regulatory Authority for Network Industries
- c. Independent regulatory agencies in Turkey
- d. Crofters Commission

Guidance: level 1

:: Marketing ::

_____ or stock control can be broadly defined as "the activity of checking a shop's stock." However, a more focused definition takes into account the more science-based, methodical practice of not only verifying a business' inventory but also focusing on the many related facets of inventory management "within an organisation to meet the demand placed upon that business economically." Other facets of _____ include supply chain management, production control, financial flexibility, and customer satisfaction. At the root of _____ , however, is the _____ problem, which involves determining when to order, how much to order, and the logistics of those decisions.

Exam Probability: **Medium**

21. *Answer choices:*

(see index for correct answer)

- a. Accreditation in Public Relations
- b. Inventory control
- c. Market share
- d. Personalized marketing

Guidance: level 1

:: Commerce ::

_____ , also known as duty _____ is defined by the United States Customs and Border Protection as the refund of certain duties, internal and revenue taxes and certain fees collected upon the importation of goods. Such refunds are only allowed upon the exportation or destruction of goods under U.S. Customs and Border Protection supervision. Duty _____ is an export promotions program sanctioned by the World Trade Organization and allows the refund of certain duties taxes and fees paid upon importation which was established in 1789 in order to promote U.S. innovation and manufacturing across the global market.

Exam Probability: **Low**

22. *Answer choices:*

(see index for correct answer)

- a. Drawback
- b. Oniomania
- c. Church sale
- d. International Marketmakers Combination

Guidance: level 1

:: Customs duties ::

A _____ is a tax on imports or exports between sovereign states. It is a form of regulation of foreign trade and a policy that taxes foreign products to encourage or safeguard domestic industry. _____ s are the simplest and oldest instrument of trade policy. Traditionally, states have used them as a source of income. Now, they are among the most widely used instruments of protection, along with import and export quotas.

Exam Probability: **High**

23. *Answer choices:*
(see index for correct answer)

- a. Canada Corn Act
- b. Specific rate duty
- c. Import Surtaxes
- d. World Customs Organization

Guidance: level 1

:: Service industries ::

_____ are the economic services provided by the finance industry, which encompasses a broad range of businesses that manage money, including credit unions, banks, credit-card companies, insurance companies, accountancy companies, consumer-finance companies, stock brokerages, investment funds, individual managers and some government-sponsored enterprises. _____ companies are present in all economically developed geographic locations and tend to cluster in local, national, regional and international financial centers such as London, New York City, and Tokyo.

24. *Answer choices:*

(see index for correct answer)

- a. Maid service
- b. Inn sign
- c. Tourism
- d. Language industry

Guidance: level 1

:: Summary statistics ::

_____ is the number of occurrences of a repeating event per unit of time. It is also referred to as temporal _____ , which emphasizes the contrast to spatial _____ and angular _____ . The period is the duration of time of one cycle in a repeating event, so the period is the reciprocal of the _____ . For example: if a newborn baby's heart beats at a _____ of 120 times a minute, its period—the time interval between beats—is half a second . _____ is an important parameter used in science and engineering to specify the rate of oscillatory and vibratory phenomena, such as mechanical vibrations, audio signals , radio waves, and light.

Exam Probability: **Medium**

25. *Answer choices:*

(see index for correct answer)

- a. Frequency
- b. Seven-number summary
- c. Mean percentage error
- d. Five-number summary

Guidance: level 1

:: Income ::

_____ is a ratio between the net profit and cost of investment resulting from an investment of some resources. A high ROI means the investment's gains favorably to its cost. As a performance measure, ROI is used to evaluate the efficiency of an investment or to compare the efficiencies of several different investments. In purely economic terms, it is one way of relating profits to capital invested. _____ is a performance measure used by businesses to identify the efficiency of an investment or number of different investments.

Exam Probability: **Low**

26. *Answer choices:*

(see index for correct answer)

- a. Trinity study
- b. National average salary
- c. Implied level of government service
- d. Return on investment

:: Industrial automation ::

_____ is the technology by which a process or procedure is performed with minimal human assistance. _____ or automatic control is the use of various control systems for operating equipment such as machinery, processes in factories, boilers and heat treating ovens, switching on telephone networks, steering and stabilization of ships, aircraft and other applications and vehicles with minimal or reduced human intervention.

Exam Probability: **Medium**

27. *Answer choices:*

(see index for correct answer)

- a. RAPIEnet
- b. CANopen
- c. Automation
- d. DirectLOGIC

:: E-commerce ::

_____ is a United States-based payment gateway service provider allowing merchants to accept credit card and electronic check payments through their website and over an Internet Protocol connection. Founded in 1996, _____ is now a subsidiary of Visa Inc. Its service permits customers to enter credit card and shipping information directly onto a web page, in contrast to some alternatives that require the customer to sign up for a payment service before performing a transaction.

Exam Probability: **Medium**

28. *Answer choices:*

(see index for correct answer)

- a. Alternative currency
- b. Authorize.Net
- c. Eagle Cash
- d. EBay API

Guidance: level 1

:: Organizational structure ::

An _____ defines how activities such as task allocation, coordination, and supervision are directed toward the achievement of organizational aims.

Exam Probability: **High**

29. *Answer choices:*

(see index for correct answer)

- a. Organization of the New York City Police Department
- b. Followership
- c. The Starfish and the Spider
- d. Organizational structure

Guidance: level 1

:: Management ::

The term _____ refers to measures designed to increase the degree of autonomy and self-determination in people and in communities in order to enable them to represent their interests in a responsible and self-determined way, acting on their own authority. It is the process of becoming stronger and more confident, especially in controlling one's life and claiming one's rights. _____ as action refers both to the process of self- _____ and to professional support of people, which enables them to overcome their sense of powerlessness and lack of influence, and to recognize and use their resources. To do work with power.

Exam Probability: **Medium**

30. *Answer choices:*

(see index for correct answer)

- a. Gemba
- b. Pomodoro Technique

- c. Empowerment
- d. Maryland StateStat

Guidance: level 1

:: ::

_____ is the social science that studies the production, distribution, and consumption of goods and services.

Exam Probability: **High**

31. *Answer choices:*

(see index for correct answer)

- a. hierarchical
- b. process perspective
- c. Economics
- d. open system

Guidance: level 1

:: Information technology management ::

B2B is often contrasted with business-to-consumer . In B2B commerce, it is often the case that the parties to the relationship have comparable negotiating power, and even when they do not, each party typically involves professional staff and legal counsel in the negotiation of terms, whereas B2C is shaped to a far greater degree by economic implications of information asymmetry. However, within a B2B context, large companies may have many commercial, resource and information advantages over smaller businesses. The United Kingdom government, for example, created the post of Small Business Commissioner under the Enterprise Act 2016 to "enable small businesses to resolve disputes" and "consider complaints by small business suppliers about payment issues with larger businesses that they supply."

Exam Probability: **Medium**

32. *Answer choices:*

(see index for correct answer)

- a. Imaging for Windows
- b. Ekatva
- c. Business-to-business
- d. Infra Corporation

Guidance: level 1

:: Supply chain management ::

_____ is the process of finding and agreeing to terms, and acquiring goods, services, or works from an external source, often via a tendering or competitive bidding process. _____ is used to ensure the buyer receives goods, services, or works at the best possible price when aspects such as quality, quantity, time, and location are compared. Corporations and public bodies often define processes intended to promote fair and open competition for their business while minimizing risks such as exposure to fraud and collusion.

Exam Probability: **Medium**

33. *Answer choices:*

(see index for correct answer)

- a. Supply-Chain Council
- b. Procurement
- c. TXT e-solutions
- d. Scan-based trading

Guidance: level 1

:: Auctioneering ::

Unlike sealed-bid auctions , an _____ is "open" or fully transparent, as the identity of all bidders is disclosed to each other during the auction. More generally, an auction mechanism is considered "English" if it involves an iterative process of adjusting the price in a direction that is unfavorable to the bidders . In contrast, a Dutch auction would adjust the price in a direction that favored the bidders .

34. *Answer choices:*

(see index for correct answer)

- a. Online auction
- b. Calor licitantis
- c. English auction
- d. Virginity auction

Guidance: level 1

:: ::

An _____ is a systematic and independent examination of books, accounts, statutory records, documents and vouchers of an organization to ascertain how far the financial statements as well as non-financial disclosures present a true and fair view of the concern. It also attempts to ensure that the books of accounts are properly maintained by the concern as required by law. _____ ing has become such a ubiquitous phenomenon in the corporate and the public sector that academics started identifying an " _____ Society". The _____ or perceives and recognises the propositions before them for examination, obtains evidence, evaluates the same and formulates an opinion on the basis of his judgement which is communicated through their _____ ing report.

Exam Probability: **Low**

35. *Answer choices:*

(see index for correct answer)

- a. hierarchical
- b. empathy
- c. information systems assessment
- d. Sarbanes-Oxley act of 2002

Guidance: level 1

:: ::

_____ is the collection of techniques, skills, methods, and processes used in the production of goods or services or in the accomplishment of objectives, such as scientific investigation. _____ can be the knowledge of techniques, processes, and the like, or it can be embedded in machines to allow for operation without detailed knowledge of their workings. Systems applying _____ by taking an input, changing it according to the system's use, and then producing an outcome are referred to as _____ systems or technological systems.

Exam Probability: **Low**

36. *Answer choices:*
(see index for correct answer)

- a. Technology
- b. similarity-attraction theory
- c. corporate values

- d. deep-level diversity

Guidance: level 1

:: Business law ::

The _____ , first published in 1952, is one of a number of Uniform Acts that have been established as law with the goal of harmonizing the laws of sales and other commercial transactions across the United States of America through UCC adoption by all 50 states, the District of Columbia, and the Territories of the United States.

Exam Probability: **Medium**

37. *Answer choices:*

(see index for correct answer)

- a. Participation
- b. Starting a Business Index
- c. Uniform Commercial Code
- d. Leave of absence

Guidance: level 1

:: Market research ::

_____ is an organized effort to gather information about target markets or customers. It is a very important component of business strategy. The term is commonly interchanged with marketing research; however, expert practitioners may wish to draw a distinction, in that marketing research is concerned specifically about marketing processes, while _____ is concerned specifically with markets.

Exam Probability: **Low**

38. *Answer choices:*

(see index for correct answer)

- a. Consumer neuroscience
- b. Cume
- c. Market research
- d. Competitor analysis

Guidance: level 1

:: Marketing ::

The _____ is a foundation model for businesses. The _____ has been defined as the "set of marketing tools that the firm uses to pursue its marketing objectives in the target market". Thus the _____ refers to four broad levels of marketing decision, namely: product, price, place, and promotion. Marketing practice has been occurring for millennia, but marketing theory emerged in the early twentieth century. The contemporary _____ , or the 4 Ps, which has become the dominant framework for marketing management decisions, was first published in 1960. In services marketing, an extended _____ is used, typically comprising 7 Ps, made up of the original 4 Ps extended by process, people, and physical evidence. Occasionally service marketers will refer to 8 Ps, comprising these 7 Ps plus performance.

Exam Probability: **High**

39. *Answer choices:*

(see index for correct answer)

- a. Adobe Target
- b. Call centre
- c. Marketing mix
- d. Cultural consumer

Guidance: level 1

:: ::

_____ is a marketing communication that employs an openly sponsored, non-personal message to promote or sell a product, service or idea. Sponsors of _____ are typically businesses wishing to promote their products or services. _____ is differentiated from public relations in that an advertiser pays for and has control over the message. It differs from personal selling in that the message is non-personal, i.e., not directed to a particular individual. _____ is communicated through various mass media, including traditional media such as newspapers, magazines, television, radio, outdoor _____ or direct mail; and new media such as search results, blogs, social media, websites or text messages. The actual presentation of the message in a medium is referred to as an advertisement, or "ad" or advert for short.

Exam Probability: **Low**

40. *Answer choices:*

(see index for correct answer)

- a. Advertising
- b. hierarchical perspective
- c. imperative
- d. process perspective

Guidance: level 1

:: Marketing ::

_____ is the percentage of a market accounted for by a specific entity. In a survey of nearly 200 senior marketing managers, 67% responded that they found the revenue- "dollar _____ " metric very useful, while 61% found "unit _____ " very useful.

Exam Probability: **Medium**

41. *Answer choices:*

(see index for correct answer)

- a. Market share
- b. Cult brand
- c. Purchase funnel
- d. Mobile marketing

Guidance: level 1

:: ::

In Western musical notation, the staff or stave is a set of five horizontal lines and four spaces that each represent a different musical pitch or in the case of a percussion staff, different percussion instruments. Appropriate music symbols, depending on the intended effect, are placed on the staff according to their corresponding pitch or function. Musical notes are placed by pitch, percussion notes are placed by instrument, and rests and other symbols are placed by convention.

Exam Probability: **High**

42. *Answer choices:*

(see index for correct answer)

- a. Staff position
- b. Character
- c. cultural
- d. information systems assessment

Guidance: level 1

:: ::

A _____ or _____ s is a type of footwear and not a specific type of shoe. Most _____ s mainly cover the foot and the ankle, while some also cover some part of the lower calf. Some _____ s extend up the leg, sometimes as far as the knee or even the hip. Most _____ s have a heel that is clearly distinguishable from the rest of the sole, even if the two are made of one piece. Traditionally made of leather or rubber, modern _____ s are made from a variety of materials. _____ s are worn both for their functionality protecting the foot and leg from water, extreme cold, mud or hazards or providing additional ankle support for strenuous activities with added traction requirements , or may have hobnails on their undersides to protect against wear and to get better grip; and for reasons of style and fashion.

Exam Probability: **Low**

43. *Answer choices:*

(see index for correct answer)

- a. imperative
- b. Character
- c. deep-level diversity
- d. Boot

Guidance: level 1

:: Materials ::

A _____ , also known as a feedstock, unprocessed material, or primary commodity, is a basic material that is used to produce goods, finished products, energy, or intermediate materials which are feedstock for future finished products. As feedstock, the term connotes these materials are bottleneck assets and are highly important with regard to producing other products. An example of this is crude oil, which is a _____ and a feedstock used in the production of industrial chemicals, fuels, plastics, and pharmaceutical goods; lumber is a _____ used to produce a variety of products including all types of furniture. The term " _____ " denotes materials in minimally processed or unprocessed in states; e.g., raw latex, crude oil, cotton, coal, raw biomass, iron ore, air, logs, or water i.e. "...any product of agriculture, forestry, fishing and any other mineral that is in its natural form or which has undergone the transformation required to prepare it for internationally marketing in substantial volumes."

Exam Probability: **High**

44. *Answer choices:*

(see index for correct answer)

- a. Mesoporous material

- b. Three-dimensional quartz phenolic
- c. Raw material
- d. Intumescent

Guidance: level 1

:: Business terms ::

_____ ning is an organization`s process of defining its strategy, or direction, and making decisions on allocating its resources to pursue this strategy. It may also extend to control mechanisms for guiding the implementation of the strategy. _____ ning became prominent in corporations during the 1960s and remains an important aspect of strategic management. It is executed by _____ ners or strategists, who involve many parties and research sources in their analysis of the organization and its relationship to the environment in which it competes.

Exam Probability: **Medium**

45. *Answer choices:*

(see index for correct answer)

- a. Strategic plan
- b. Mission statement
- c. granular
- d. operating cost

Guidance: level 1

:: ::

A _____ is a fund into which a sum of money is added during an employee's employment years, and from which payments are drawn to support the person's retirement from work in the form of periodic payments. A _____ may be a "defined benefit plan" where a fixed sum is paid regularly to a person, or a "defined contribution plan" under which a fixed sum is invested and then becomes available at retirement age. _____ s should not be confused with severance pay; the former is usually paid in regular installments for life after retirement, while the latter is typically paid as a fixed amount after involuntary termination of employment prior to retirement.

Exam Probability: **Low**

46. *Answer choices:*

(see index for correct answer)

- a. similarity-attraction theory
- b. surface-level diversity
- c. Character
- d. interpersonal communication

Guidance: level 1

:: Logistics ::

_____ is generally the detailed organization and implementation of a complex operation. In a general business sense, _____ is the management of the flow of things between the point of origin and the point of consumption in order to meet requirements of customers or corporations. The resources managed in _____ may include tangible goods such as materials, equipment, and supplies, as well as food and other consumable items. The _____ of physical items usually involves the integration of information flow, materials handling, production, packaging, inventory, transportation, warehousing, and often security.

Exam Probability: **High**

47. *Answer choices:*

(see index for correct answer)

- a. Design for availability
- b. Logistics
- c. Logistics center
- d. Low Altitude Parachute Extraction System

Guidance: level 1

:: Public relations ::

_____ is the public visibility or awareness for any product, service or company. It may also refer to the movement of information from its source to the general public, often but not always via the media. The subjects of _____ include people , goods and services, organizations, and works of art or entertainment.

48. *Answer choices:*

(see index for correct answer)

- a. Kompromat
- b. Aneta Avramova
- c. Publicity
- d. Vantage PR

Guidance: level 1

:: ::

Senior management, executive management, upper management, or a _____
is generally a team of individuals at the highest level of management of an
organization who have the day-to-day tasks of managing that organization —
sometimes a company or a corporation.

Exam Probability: **High**

49. *Answer choices:*

(see index for correct answer)

- a. Character
- b. empathy
- c. cultural

- d. process perspective

Guidance: level 1

:: Marketing ::

A _____ is an overall experience of a customer that distinguishes an organization or product from its rivals in the eyes of the customer. _____ s are used in business, marketing, and advertising. Name _____ s are sometimes distinguished from generic or store _____ s.

Exam Probability: **Medium**

50. *Answer choices:*
(see index for correct answer)

- a. Green marketing
- b. Counteradvertising
- c. Audience development
- d. Channel conflict

Guidance: level 1

:: ::

In a supply chain, a _____ , or a seller, is an enterprise that contributes goods or services. Generally, a supply chain _____ manufactures inventory/stock items and sells them to the next link in the chain. Today, these terms refer to a supplier of any good or service.

Exam Probability: **Medium**

51. *Answer choices:*

(see index for correct answer)

- a. functional perspective
- b. Vendor
- c. open system
- d. co-culture

Guidance: level 1

:: ::

_____ is the principled guide to action taken by the administrative executive branches of the state with regard to a class of issues, in a manner consistent with law and institutional customs.

Exam Probability: **High**

52. *Answer choices:*

(see index for correct answer)

- a. similarity-attraction theory
- b. functional perspective
- c. corporate values
- d. hierarchical

Guidance: level 1

:: Behavior modification ::

In psychotherapy and mental health, _____ has a positive sense of empowering individuals, or a negative sense of encouraging dysfunctional behavior.

Exam Probability: **Low**

53. *Answer choices:*
(see index for correct answer)

- a. behavioural change
- b. Enabling

Guidance: level 1

:: Insolvency ::

_____ is a legal process through which people or other entities who cannot repay debts to creditors may seek relief from some or all of their debts. In most jurisdictions, _____ is imposed by a court order, often initiated by the debtor.

Exam Probability: **High**

54. *Answer choices:*

(see index for correct answer)

- a. Personal Insolvency Arrangement
- b. Bankruptcy
- c. Debt consolidation
- d. George Samuel Ford

Guidance: level 1

:: Free market ::

In economics, a _____ is a system in which the prices for goods and services are determined by the open market and by consumers. In a _____ , the laws and forces of supply and demand are free from any intervention by a government or other authority and from all forms of economic privilege, monopolies and artificial scarcities. Proponents of the concept of _____ contrast it with a regulated market in which a government intervenes in supply and demand through various methods, such as tariffs, used to restrict trade and to protect the local economy. In an idealized free-market economy, prices for goods and services are set freely by the forces of supply and demand and are allowed to reach their point of equilibrium without intervention by government policy.

Exam Probability: **Medium**

55. *Answer choices:*
(see index for correct answer)

- a. Regulated market
- b. Piece rate

Guidance: level 1

:: Project management ::

Contemporary business and science treat as a _____ any undertaking, carried out individually or collaboratively and possibly involving research or design, that is carefully planned to achieve a particular aim.

Exam Probability: **Medium**

56. *Answer choices:*

(see index for correct answer)

- a. Burn down chart
- b. Project
- c. Project management 2.0
- d. TELOS

Guidance: level 1

:: Commerce ::

An _____ is a bank that offers card association branded payment cards directly to consumers. The name is derived from the practice of issuing payment to the acquiring bank on behalf of its customer .

Exam Probability: **Low**

57. *Answer choices:*

(see index for correct answer)

- a. Issuing bank
- b. Car boot sale
- c. Purchasing manager
- d. Perfect tender rule

Guidance: level 1

:: ::

In law, a _____ is a coming together of parties to a dispute, to present information in a tribunal, a formal setting with the authority to adjudicate claims or disputes. One form of tribunal is a court. The tribunal, which may occur before a judge, jury, or other designated trier of fact, aims to achieve a resolution to their dispute.

Exam Probability: **Low**

58. *Answer choices:*

(see index for correct answer)

- a. interpersonal communication
- b. functional perspective
- c. empathy
- d. corporate values

Guidance: level 1

:: ::

According to the philosopher Piyush Mathur , "Tangibility is the property that a phenomenon exhibits if it has and/or transports mass and/or energy and/or momentum".

59. *Answer choices:*

(see index for correct answer)

- a. information systems assessment
- b. imperative
- c. Character
- d. Tangible

Guidance: level 1

Business ethics

Business ethics (also known as corporate ethics) is a form of applied ethics or professional ethics, that examines ethical principles and moral or ethical problems that can arise in a business environment. It applies to all aspects of business conduct and is relevant to the conduct of individuals and entire organizations. These ethics originate from individuals, organizational statements or from the legal system. These norms, values, ethical, and unethical practices are what is used to guide business. They help those businesses maintain a better connection with their stakeholders.

:: United Kingdom labour law ::

The _____ was a series of programs, public work projects, financial reforms, and regulations enacted by President Franklin D. Roosevelt in the United States between 1933 and 1936. It responded to needs for relief, reform, and recovery from the Great Depression. Major federal programs included the Civilian Conservation Corps , the Civil Works Administration , the Farm Security Administration , the National Industrial Recovery Act of 1933 and the Social Security Administration . They provided support for farmers, the unemployed, youth and the elderly. The _____ included new constraints and safeguards on the banking industry and efforts to re-inflate the economy after prices had fallen sharply. _____ programs included both laws passed by Congress as well as presidential executive orders during the first term of the presidency of Franklin D. Roosevelt.

Exam Probability: **Low**

1. *Answer choices:*

(see index for correct answer)

- a. Employment Act 2008
- b. New Deal
- c. Enterprise Allowance Scheme
- d. Transnational Works Council Directive

Guidance: level 1

:: Social philosophy ::

The " _____ " is a method of determining the morality of issues. It asks a decision-maker to make a choice about a social or moral issue, and assumes that they have enough information to know the consequences of their possible decisions for everyone but would not know, or would not take into account, which person he or she is. The theory contends that not knowing one's ultimate position in society would lead to the creation of a just system, as the decision-maker would not want to make decisions which benefit a certain group at the expense of another, because the decision-maker could theoretically end up in either group. The idea has been present in moral philosophy at least since the eighteenth century. The _____ is part of a long tradition of thinking in terms of a social contract that includes the writings of Immanuel Kant, Thomas Hobbes, John Locke, Jean Jacques Rousseau, and Thomas Jefferson. Prominent modern names attached to it are John Harsanyi and John Rawls.

Exam Probability: **Medium**

2. *Answer choices:*

(see index for correct answer)

- a. vacancy chain
- b. Societal attitudes towards abortion
- c. Freedom to contract
- d. Invisible hand

Guidance: level 1

:: Socialism ::

_____ is a label used to define the first currents of modern socialist thought as exemplified by the work of Henri de Saint-Simon, Charles Fourier, Étienne Cabet and Robert Owen.

Exam Probability: **Medium**

3. *Answer choices:*

(see index for correct answer)

- a. Socialist economics
- b. Democratic Youth
- c. Edinburgh University Socialist Society
- d. The Ragged-Trousered Philanthropists

Guidance: level 1

:: Natural gas ::

_____ is a naturally occurring hydrocarbon gas mixture consisting primarily of methane, but commonly including varying amounts of other higher alkanes, and sometimes a small percentage of carbon dioxide, nitrogen, hydrogen sulfide, or helium. It is formed when layers of decomposing plant and animal matter are exposed to intense heat and pressure under the surface of the Earth over millions of years. The energy that the plants originally obtained from the sun is stored in the form of chemical bonds in the gas.

Exam Probability: **Medium**

4. *Answer choices:*

(see index for correct answer)

- a. Acid gas
- b. Twister Supersonic Separator
- c. Natural gas
- d. Associated petroleum gas

Guidance: level 1

:: Offshoring ::

A _____ is the temporary suspension or permanent termination of employment of an employee or, more commonly, a group of employees for business reasons, such as personnel management or downsizing an organization. Originally, _____ referred exclusively to a temporary interruption in work, or employment but this has evolved to a permanent elimination of a position in both British and US English, requiring the addition of "temporary" to specify the original meaning of the word. A _____ is not to be confused with wrongful termination. Laid off workers or displaced workers are workers who have lost or left their jobs because their employer has closed or moved, there was insufficient work for them to do, or their position or shift was abolished. Downsizing in a company is defined to involve the reduction of employees in a workforce. Downsizing in companies became a popular practice in the 1980s and early 1990s as it was seen as a way to deliver better shareholder value as it helps to reduce the costs of employers. Indeed, recent research on downsizing in the U.S., UK, and Japan suggests that downsizing is being regarded by management as one of the preferred routes to help declining organizations, cutting unnecessary costs, and improve organizational performance. Usually a _____ occurs as a cost cutting measure.

Exam Probability: **Medium**

5. *Answer choices:*

(see index for correct answer)

- a. Advanced Contact Solutions
- b. Layoff
- c. Antex
- d. Programmers Guild

Guidance: level 1

:: Labour law ::

An _____ is special or specified circumstances that partially or fully exempt a person or organization from performance of a legal obligation so as to avoid an unreasonable or disproportionate burden or obstacle.

Exam Probability: **Medium**

6. *Answer choices:*

(see index for correct answer)

- a. Occupational exposure limit
- b. Greenfield agreement
- c. Undue hardship
- d. Unreported employment

:: ::

An _____ is the release of a liquid petroleum hydrocarbon into the environment, especially the marine ecosystem, due to human activity, and is a form of pollution. The term is usually given to marine _____ s, where oil is released into the ocean or coastal waters, but spills may also occur on land. _____ s may be due to releases of crude oil from tankers, offshore platforms, drilling rigs and wells, as well as spills of refined petroleum products and their by-products, heavier fuels used by large ships such as bunker fuel, or the spill of any oily refuse or waste oil.

Exam Probability: **High**

7. *Answer choices:*

(see index for correct answer)

- a. levels of analysis
- b. Oil spill
- c. information systems assessment
- d. empathy

:: Industry ::

_____ is the manner in which a given entity has decided to address issues of energy development including energy production, distribution and consumption. The attributes of _____ may include legislation, international treaties, incentives to investment, guidelines for energy conservation, taxation and other public policy techniques. Energy is a core component of modern economies. A functioning economy requires not only labor and capital but also energy, for manufacturing processes, transportation, communication, agriculture, and more.

Exam Probability: **Low**

8. *Answer choices:*

(see index for correct answer)

- a. Secondary sector of the economy
- b. Light industry
- c. Energy policy
- d. Modelling of particle breakage

Guidance: level 1

:: Business ethics ::

_____ is a persistent pattern of mistreatment from others in the workplace that causes either physical or emotional harm. It can include such tactics as verbal, nonverbal, psychological, physical abuse and humiliation. This type of workplace aggression is particularly difficult because, unlike the typical school bully, workplace bullies often operate within the established rules and policies of their organization and their society. In the majority of cases, bullying in the workplace is reported as having been by someone who has authority over their victim. However, bullies can also be peers, and occasionally subordinates. Research has also investigated the impact of the larger organizational context on bullying as well as the group-level processes that impact on the incidence and maintenance of bullying behaviour. Bullying can be covert or overt. It may be missed by superiors; it may be known by many throughout the organization. Negative effects are not limited to the targeted individuals, and may lead to a decline in employee morale and a change in organizational culture. It can also take place as overbearing supervision, constant criticism, and blocking promotions.

Exam Probability: **Low**

9. *Answer choices:*

(see index for correct answer)

- a. Bribery Act 2010
- b. Workplace bullying
- c. Conscious business
- d. Corporate social entrepreneurship

Guidance: level 1

:: Electronic waste ::

_____ or e-waste describes discarded electrical or electronic devices. Used electronics which are destined for refurbishment, reuse, resale, salvage, recycling through material recovery, or disposal are also considered e-waste. Informal processing of e-waste in developing countries can lead to adverse human health effects and environmental pollution.

10. *Answer choices:*

(see index for correct answer)

- a. E-Stewards
- b. Computer liquidator
- c. Electronic waste
- d. Global waste trade

Guidance: level 1

:: Majority–minority relations ::

It was established as axiomatic in anthropological research by Franz Boas in the first few decades of the 20th century and later popularized by his students. Boas first articulated the idea in 1887: "civilization is not something absolute, but ... is relative, and ... our ideas and conceptions are true only so far as our civilization goes". However, Boas did not coin the term.

11. *Answer choices:*

(see index for correct answer)

- a. positive discrimination
- b. Affirmative action
- c. cultural dissonance

Guidance: level 1

:: Corporate scandals ::

_____ was a bank based in the Caribbean, which operated from 1986 to 2009 when it went into receivership. It was an affiliate of the Stanford Financial Group and failed when the its parent was seized by United States authorities in early 2009 as part of the investigation into Allen Stanford.

Exam Probability: **Medium**

12. *Answer choices:*

(see index for correct answer)

- a. ExtenZe
- b. Petters Group Worldwide
- c. Patent encumbrance of large automotive NiMH batteries
- d. Stanford International Bank

Guidance: level 1

:: Office work ::

_____ is the process and behavior in human interactions involving power and authority. It is also a tool to assess the operational capacity and to balance diverse views of interested parties. It is also known as office politics and organizational politics.It is the use of power and social networking within an organization to achieve changes that benefit the organization or individuals within it. Influence by individuals may serve personal interests without regard to their effect on the organization itself. Some of the personal advantages may include access to tangible assets, or intangible benefits such as status or pseudo-authority that influences the behavior of others. On the other hand, organizational politics can increase efficiency, form interpersonal relationships, expedite change, and profit the organization and its members simultaneously.Both individuals and groups may engage in office politics which can be highly destructive, as people focus on personal gains at the expense of the organization. "Self-serving political actions can negatively influence our social groupings, cooperation, information sharing, and many other organizational functions." Thus, it is vital to pay attention to organizational politics and create the right political landscape. "Politics is the lubricant that oils your organization's internal gears." Office politics has also been described as "simply how power gets worked out on a practical, day-to-day basis."

Exam Probability: **High**

13. *Answer choices:*

(see index for correct answer)

- a. Workplace politics
- b. White-collar worker
- c. Office humor
- d. Electronic office

:: Corporate scandals ::

Exxon Mobil Corporation, doing business as _____ , is an American multinational oil and gas corporation headquartered in Irving, Texas. It is the largest direct descendant of John D. Rockefeller's Standard Oil Company, and was formed on November 30, 1999 by the merger of Exxon and Mobil . _____ 's primary brands are Exxon, Mobil, Esso, and _____ Chemical.

Exam Probability: **High**

14. *Answer choices:*

(see index for correct answer)

- a. ExxonMobil
- b. Lynn Brewer
- c. Cookie Jar Group
- d. Michael Bailey

:: Public relations terminology ::

_____ , also called "green sheen", is a form of spin in which green PR or green marketing is deceptively used to promote the perception that an organization's products, aims or policies are environmentally friendly. Evidence that an organization is _____ often comes from pointing out the spending differences: when significantly more money or time has been spent advertising being "green" , than is actually spent on environmentally sound practices. _____ efforts can range from changing the name or label of a product to evoke the natural environment on a product that contains harmful chemicals to multimillion-dollar marketing campaigns portraying highly polluting energy companies as eco-friendly.Publicized accusations of _____ have contributed to the term's increasing use.

Exam Probability: **Low**

15. *Answer choices:*

(see index for correct answer)

- a. Corporate pathos
- b. Junk science
- c. PR Gallery
- d. Greenwashing

Guidance: level 1

:: ::

Competition law is a law that promotes or seeks to maintain market competition by regulating anti-competitive conduct by companies. Competition law is implemented through public and private enforcement. Competition law is known as "_____ law" in the United States for historical reasons, and as "anti-monopoly law" in China and Russia. In previous years it has been known as trade practices law in the United Kingdom and Australia. In the European Union, it is referred to as both _____ and competition law.

16. *Answer choices:*

(see index for correct answer)

- a. imperative
- b. hierarchical
- c. cultural
- d. information systems assessment

Guidance: level 1

:: Corporate scandals ::

The _____ was a privately held international group of financial services companies controlled by Allen Stanford, until it was seized by United States authorities in early 2009. Headquartered in the Galleria Tower II in Uptown Houston, Texas, it had 50 offices in several countries, mainly in the Americas, included the Stanford International Bank, and said it managed US$8.5 billion of assets for more than 30,000 clients in 136 countries on six continents. On February 17, 2009, U.S. Federal agents placed the company into receivership due to charges of fraud. Ten days later, the U.S. Securities and Exchange Commission amended its complaint to accuse Stanford of turning the company into a "massive Ponzi scheme".

Exam Probability: **Low**

17. *Answer choices:*

(see index for correct answer)

- a. Aluminium price-fixing conspiracy
- b. Stanford Financial Group
- c. Crawford Texas Peace House
- d. Yield Burning

Guidance: level 1

:: Mortgage ::

In finance, _____ means making loans to people who may have difficulty maintaining the repayment schedule, sometimes reflecting setbacks, such as unemployment, divorce, medical emergencies, etc. Historically, subprime borrowers were defined as having FICO scores below 600, although "this has varied over time and circumstances."

Exam Probability: **High**

18. *Answer choices:*

(see index for correct answer)

- a. Subprime lending
- b. Adjustable-rate mortgage
- c. Foreclosure
- d. PITI

Guidance: level 1

:: Renewable energy ::

_____ is the conversion of energy from sunlight into electricity, either directly using photovoltaics, indirectly using concentrated _____, or a combination. Concentrated _____ systems use lenses or mirrors and tracking systems to focus a large area of sunlight into a small beam. Photovoltaic cells convert light into an electric current using the photovoltaic effect.

Exam Probability: **Low**

19. *Answer choices:*

(see index for correct answer)

- a. RETScreen
- b. Wind power
- c. Solar power
- d. Electric aircraft

Guidance: level 1

:: ::

_____ is a bundle of characteristics, including ways of thinking, feeling, and acting, which humans are said to have naturally. The term is often regarded as capturing what it is to be human, or the essence of humanity. The term is controversial because it is disputed whether or not such an essence exists. Arguments about _____ have been a mainstay of philosophy for centuries and the concept continues to provoke lively philosophical debate. The concept also continues to play a role in science, with neuroscientists, psychologists and social scientists sometimes claiming that their results have yielded insight into _____ . _____ is traditionally contrasted with characteristics that vary among humans, such as characteristics associated with specific cultures. Debates about _____ are related to, although not the same as, debates about the comparative importance of genes and environment in development .

Exam Probability: **Low**

20. *Answer choices:*

(see index for correct answer)

- a. deep-level diversity
- b. empathy
- c. Human nature
- d. functional perspective

Guidance: level 1

:: Auditing ::

_____ , as defined by accounting and auditing, is a process for assuring of an organization's objectives in operational effectiveness and efficiency, reliable financial reporting, and compliance with laws, regulations and policies. A broad concept, _____ involves everything that controls risks to an organization.

Exam Probability: **Low**

21. *Answer choices:*

(see index for correct answer)

- a. Utility bill audit
- b. Internal control
- c. RSM International
- d. Negative assurance

Guidance: level 1

:: Law ::

_____ is a body of law which defines the role, powers, and structure of different entities within a state, namely, the executive, the parliament or legislature, and the judiciary; as well as the basic rights of citizens and, in federal countries such as the United States and Canada, the relationship between the central government and state, provincial, or territorial governments.

Exam Probability: **Low**

22. *Answer choices:*

(see index for correct answer)

- a. Constitutional law
- b. Comparative law

Guidance: level 1

:: Timber industry ::

The _____ is an international non-profit, multi-stakeholder organization established in 1993 to promote responsible management of the world's forests. The FSC does this by setting standards on forest products, along with certifying and labeling them as eco-friendly.

Exam Probability: **Medium**

23. *Answer choices:*

- a. Forest product
- b. Q-pit
- c. Lumber
- d. Forest Stewardship Council

Guidance: level 1

:: ::

The _____ , founded in 1912, is a private, nonprofit organization whose self-described mission is to focus on advancing marketplace trust, consisting of 106 independently incorporated local BBB organizations in the United States and Canada, coordinated under the Council of _____ s in Arlington, Virginia.

Exam Probability: **Low**

24. *Answer choices:*

- a. personal values
- b. hierarchical perspective
- c. interpersonal communication
- d. cultural

:: Business ethics ::

_____ is a type of harassment technique that relates to a sexual nature and the unwelcome or inappropriate promise of rewards in exchange for sexual favors. _____ includes a range of actions from mild transgressions to sexual abuse or assault. Harassment can occur in many different social settings such as the workplace, the home, school, churches, etc. Harassers or victims may be of any gender.

Exam Probability: **Medium**

25. *Answer choices:*

(see index for correct answer)

- a. Corruption of Foreign Public Officials Act
- b. Salad Oil Scandal
- c. Journal of Business Ethics
- d. Sexual harassment

:: Social responsibility ::

The United Nations Global Compact is a non-binding United Nations pact to encourage businesses worldwide to adopt sustainable and socially responsible policies, and to report on their implementation. The _____ is a principle-based framework for businesses, stating ten principles in the areas of human rights, labor, the environment and anti-corruption. Under the Global Compact, companies are brought together with UN agencies, labor groups and civil society. Cities can join the Global Compact through the Cities Programme.

Exam Probability: **Medium**

26. *Answer choices:*

(see index for correct answer)

- a. Socially responsible marketing
- b. Creating shared value
- c. Footprints network
- d. Stakeholder engagement

Guidance: level 1

:: Agricultural labor ::

The _____ of America, or more commonly just _____ , is a labor union for farmworkers in the United States. It originated from the merger of two workers' rights organizations, the Agricultural Workers Organizing Committee led by organizer Larry Itliong, and the National Farm Workers Association led by César Chávez and Dolores Huerta. They became allied and transformed from workers' rights organizations into a union as a result of a series of strikes in 1965, when the mostly Filipino farmworkers of the AWOC in Delano, California initiated a grape strike, and the NFWA went on strike in support. As a result of the commonality in goals and methods, the NFWA and the AWOC formed the _____ Organizing Committee on August 22, 1966. This organization was accepted into the AFL-CIO in 1972 and changed its name to the _____ Union.

Exam Probability: **Medium**

27. *Answer choices:*

(see index for correct answer)

- a. Teikei
- b. Texas Farm Workers Union
- c. Harvest excursion
- d. Bracero program

Guidance: level 1

:: ::

_____ , O.S.A. was a German professor of theology, composer, priest, monk, and a seminal figure in the Protestant Reformation.

28. *Answer choices:*

(see index for correct answer)

- a. personal values
- b. Martin Luther
- c. Sarbanes-Oxley act of 2002
- d. empathy

Guidance: level 1

:: ::

The Federal National Mortgage Association , commonly known as _____ , is a United States government-sponsored enterprise and, since 1968, a publicly traded company. Founded in 1938 during the Great Depression as part of the New Deal, the corporation`s purpose is to expand the secondary mortgage market by securitizing mortgage loans in the form of mortgage-backed securities , allowing lenders to reinvest their assets into more lending and in effect increasing the number of lenders in the mortgage market by reducing the reliance on locally based savings and loan associations . Its brother organization is the Federal Home Loan Mortgage Corporation , better known as Freddie Mac. As of 2018, _____ is ranked #21 on the Fortune 500 rankings of the largest United States corporations by total revenue.

Exam Probability: **Medium**

29. *Answer choices:*

- a. Fannie Mae
- b. Sarbanes-Oxley act of 2002
- c. imperative
- d. interpersonal communication

Guidance: level 1

:: Management ::

_____ is the identification, evaluation, and prioritization of risks followed by coordinated and economical application of resources to minimize, monitor, and control the probability or impact of unfortunate events or to maximize the realization of opportunities.

Exam Probability: **High**

30. *Answer choices:*

- a. Risk management
- b. Event chain methodology
- c. Real property administrator
- d. Earned value management

Guidance: level 1

_____ generally refers to a focus on the needs or desires of one's self. A number of philosophical, psychological, and economic theories examine the role of _____ in motivating human action.

Exam Probability: **Low**

31. *Answer choices:*

(see index for correct answer)

- a. surface-level diversity
- b. interpersonal communication
- c. Self-interest
- d. empathy

Guidance: level 1

:: White-collar criminals ::

_____ refers to financially motivated, nonviolent crime committed by businesses and government professionals. It was first defined by the sociologist Edwin Sutherland in 1939 as "a crime committed by a person of respectability and high social status in the course of their occupation". Typical _____ s could include wage theft, fraud, bribery, Ponzi schemes, insider trading, labor racketeering, embezzlement, cybercrime, copyright infringement, money laundering, identity theft, and forgery. Lawyers can specialize in _____ .

Exam Probability: **Medium**

32. *Answer choices:*

(see index for correct answer)

- a. White-collar crime
- b. Tongsun Park

Guidance: level 1

:: ::

_____ is a naturally occurring, yellowish-black liquid found in geological formations beneath the Earth's surface. It is commonly refined into various types of fuels. Components of _____ are separated using a technique called fractional distillation, i.e. separation of a liquid mixture into fractions differing in boiling point by means of distillation, typically using a fractionating column.

Exam Probability: **Medium**

33. *Answer choices:*

(see index for correct answer)

- a. imperative
- b. Petroleum
- c. co-culture
- d. functional perspective

Guidance: level 1

:: Electronic feedback ::

_____ occurs when outputs of a system are routed back as inputs as part of a chain of cause-and-effect that forms a circuit or loop. The system can then be said to feed back into itself. The notion of cause-and-effect has to be handled carefully when applied to _____ systems.

Exam Probability: **High**

34. *Answer choices:*

(see index for correct answer)

- a. feedback loop
- b. Feedback

Guidance: level 1

Sustainability is the process of people maintaining change in a balanced environment, in which the exploitation of resources, the direction of investments, the orientation of technological development and institutional change are all in harmony and enhance both current and future potential to meet human needs and aspirations. For many in the field, sustainability is defined through the following interconnected domains or pillars: environment, economic and social, which according to Fritjof Capra is based on the principles of Systems Thinking. Sub-domains of _____ development have been considered also: cultural, technological and political. While _____ development may be the organizing principle for sustainability for some, for others, the two terms are paradoxical . _____ development is the development that meets the needs of the present without compromising the ability of future generations to meet their own needs. Brundtland Report for the World Commission on Environment and Development introduced the term of _____ development.

Exam Probability: **High**

35. *Answer choices:*

(see index for correct answer)

- a. hierarchical
- b. levels of analysis
- c. empathy
- d. open system

Guidance: level 1

A _____ is a form of business network, for example, a local organization of businesses whose goal is to further the interests of businesses. Business owners in towns and cities form these local societies to advocate on behalf of the business community. Local businesses are members, and they elect a board of directors or executive council to set policy for the chamber. The board or council then hires a President, CEO or Executive Director, plus staffing appropriate to size, to run the organization.

Exam Probability: **Medium**

36. *Answer choices:*

(see index for correct answer)

- a. Chamber of Commerce
- b. co-culture
- c. hierarchical perspective
- d. deep-level diversity

Guidance: level 1

:: International trade ::

_____ involves the transfer of goods or services from one person or entity to another, often in exchange for money. A system or network that allows _____ is called a market.

Exam Probability: **High**

37. *Answer choices:*

(see index for correct answer)

- a. Indo-Roman relations
- b. Export subsidy
- c. Trade
- d. Parallel import

Guidance: level 1

:: ::

Bernard Lawrence _____ is an American former market maker, investment advisor, financier, fraudster, and convicted felon, who is currently serving a federal prison sentence for offenses related to a massive Ponzi scheme. He is the former non-executive chairman of the NASDAQ stock market, the confessed operator of the largest Ponzi scheme in world history, and the largest financial fraud in U.S. history. Prosecutors estimated the fraud to be worth $64.8 billion based on the amounts in the accounts of _____ 's 4,800 clients as of November 30, 2008.

Exam Probability: **Low**

38. *Answer choices:*

(see index for correct answer)

- a. Madoff
- b. empathy

- c. surface-level diversity
- d. hierarchical

Guidance: level 1

:: Types of marketing ::

_____ is an advertisement strategy in which a company uses surprise and/or unconventional interactions in order to promote a product or service. It is a type of publicity. The term was popularized by Jay Conrad Levinson's 1984 book _____ .

Exam Probability: **High**

39. *Answer choices:*

(see index for correct answer)

- a. Guerrilla Marketing
- b. Project SCUM
- c. Community marketing
- d. Megamarketing

Guidance: level 1

:: ::

_____ is the collection of mechanisms, processes and relations by which corporations are controlled and operated. Governance structures and principles identify the distribution of rights and responsibilities among different participants in the corporation and include the rules and procedures for making decisions in corporate affairs. _____ is necessary because of the possibility of conflicts of interests between stakeholders, primarily between shareholders and upper management or among shareholders.

Exam Probability: **Low**

40. *Answer choices:*

(see index for correct answer)

- a. Sarbanes-Oxley act of 2002
- b. levels of analysis
- c. surface-level diversity
- d. Corporate governance

Guidance: level 1

:: Cognitive biases ::

In personality psychology, _____ is the degree to which people believe that they have control over the outcome of events in their lives, as opposed to external forces beyond their control. Understanding of the concept was developed by Julian B. Rotter in 1954, and has since become an aspect of personality studies. A person's "locus" is conceptualized as internal or external .

41. *Answer choices:*

(see index for correct answer)

- a. Fluency heuristic
- b. Locus of control
- c. Contrast effect
- d. Woozle effect

Guidance: level 1

:: Business ethics ::

_____ is a type of international private business self-regulation. While once it was possible to describe CSR as an internal organisational policy or a corporate ethic strategy, that time has passed as various international laws have been developed and various organisations have used their authority to push it beyond individual or even industry-wide initiatives. While it has been considered a form of corporate self-regulation for some time, over the last decade or so it has moved considerably from voluntary decisions at the level of individual organisations, to mandatory schemes at regional, national and even transnational levels.

Exam Probability: **High**

42. *Answer choices:*

(see index for correct answer)

- a. Whistleblower
- b. Walmarting
- c. Institute of Business Ethics
- d. Price discrimination

Guidance: level 1

:: ::

_____ was a philosopher during the Classical period in Ancient Greece, the founder of the Lyceum and the Peripatetic school of philosophy and Aristotelian tradition. Along with his teacher Plato, he is considered the "Father of Western Philosophy". His writings cover many subjects – including physics, biology, zoology, metaphysics, logic, ethics, aesthetics, poetry, theatre, music, rhetoric, psychology, linguistics, economics, politics and government. _____ provided a complex synthesis of the various philosophies existing prior to him, and it was above all from his teachings that the West inherited its intellectual lexicon, as well as problems and methods of inquiry. As a result, his philosophy has exerted a unique influence on almost every form of knowledge in the West and it continues to be a subject of contemporary philosophical discussion.

Exam Probability: **High**

43. *Answer choices:*

(see index for correct answer)

- a. hierarchical perspective
- b. functional perspective

- c. open system
- d. Aristotle

Guidance: level 1

:: Monopoly (economics) ::

A _____ is a form of intellectual property that gives its owner the legal right to exclude others from making, using, selling, and importing an invention for a limited period of years, in exchange for publishing an enabling public disclosure of the invention. In most countries _____ rights fall under civil law and the _____ holder needs to sue someone infringing the _____ in order to enforce his or her rights. In some industries _____ s are an essential form of competitive advantage; in others they are irrelevant.

Exam Probability: **Medium**

44. *Answer choices:*

(see index for correct answer)

- a. De facto monopoly
- b. Natural monopoly
- c. Patent
- d. Ramsey problem

Guidance: level 1

The _____ is an agency of the United States Department of Labor. Congress established the agency under the Occupational Safety and Health Act , which President Richard M. Nixon signed into law on December 29, 1970. OSHA`s mission is to "assure safe and healthy working conditions for working men and women by setting and enforcing standards and by providing training, outreach, education and assistance". The agency is also charged with enforcing a variety of whistleblower statutes and regulations. OSHA is currently headed by Acting Assistant Secretary of Labor Loren Sweatt. OSHA`s workplace safety inspections have been shown to reduce injury rates and injury costs without adverse effects to employment, sales, credit ratings, or firm survival.

Exam Probability: **Low**

45. *Answer choices:*

(see index for correct answer)

- a. corporate values
- b. co-culture
- c. functional perspective
- d. levels of analysis

Guidance: level 1

:: Management ::

_____ or executive pay is composed of the financial compensation and other non-financial awards received by an executive from their firm for their service to the organization. It is typically a mixture of salary, bonuses, shares of or call options on the company stock, benefits, and perquisites, ideally configured to take into account government regulations, tax law, the desires of the organization and the executive, and rewards for performance.

Exam Probability: **Medium**

46. *Answer choices:*

(see index for correct answer)

- a. Executive compensation
- b. Intelligent customer
- c. Business-oriented architecture
- d. Project cost management

Guidance: level 1

:: ::

Revenge is a form of justice enacted in the absence or defiance of the norms of formal law and jurisprudence. Often, revenge is defined as being a harmful action against a person or group in response to a grievance, be it real or perceived . It is used to punish a wrong by going outside the law. Francis Bacon described revenge as a kind of "wild justice" that "does... offend the law [and] putteth the law out of office." Primitive justice or retributive justice is often differentiated from more formal and refined forms of justice such as distributive justice and divine judgment.

47. *Answer choices:*

(see index for correct answer)

- a. empathy
- b. cultural
- c. Retaliation
- d. levels of analysis

Guidance: level 1

:: Water law ::

The _____ is the primary federal law in the United States governing water pollution. Its objective is to restore and maintain the chemical, physical, and biological integrity of the nation's waters; recognizing the responsibilities of the states in addressing pollution and providing assistance to states to do so, including funding for publicly owned treatment works for the improvement of wastewater treatment; and maintaining the integrity of wetlands. It is one of the United States' first and most influential modern environmental laws. As with many other major U.S. federal environmental statutes, it is administered by the U.S. Environmental Protection Agency , in coordination with state governments. Its implementing regulations are codified at 40 C.F.R. Subchapters D, N, and O .

48. *Answer choices:*

- a. The Helsinki Rules on the Uses of the Waters of International Rivers
- b. Return flow
- c. Water law
- d. Clean Water Act

Guidance: level 1

:: Auditing ::

_____ refers to the independence of the internal auditor or of the external auditor from parties that may have a financial interest in the business being audited. Independence requires integrity and an objective approach to the audit process. The concept requires the auditor to carry out his or her work freely and in an objective manner.

Exam Probability: **Low**

49. *Answer choices:*

- a. Insolvency auditor
- b. Communication audit
- c. Lease audit
- d. Quality audit

:: Human resource management ::

_____ is the ethics of an organization, and it is how an organization responds to an internal or external stimulus. _____ is interdependent with the organizational culture. Although it is akin to both organizational behavior and industrial and organizational psychology as well as business ethics on the micro and macro levels, _____ is neither OB or I/O psychology, nor is it solely business ethics. _____ express the values of an organization to its employees and/or other entities irrespective of governmental and/or regulatory laws.

Exam Probability: **High**

50. *Answer choices:*

(see index for correct answer)

- a. Organizational ethics
- b. Human resource accounting
- c. Professional employer organization
- d. Autonomous work group

:: Industrial ecology ::

_____ is a strategy for reducing the amount of waste created and released into the environment, particularly by industrial facilities, agriculture, or consumers. Many large corporations view P2 as a method of improving the efficiency and profitability of production processes by technology advancements. Legislative bodies have enacted P2 measures, such as the _____ Act of 1990 and the Clean Air Act Amendments of 1990 by the United States Congress.

Exam Probability: **Medium**

51. *Answer choices:*

(see index for correct answer)

- a. Material flow management
- b. Life-cycle assessment
- c. Biomimetics
- d. Rebound effect

Guidance: level 1

:: Fraud ::

In law, _____ is intentional deception to secure unfair or unlawful gain, or to deprive a victim of a legal right. _____ can violate civil law, a criminal law, or it may cause no loss of money, property or legal right but still be an element of another civil or criminal wrong. The purpose of _____ may be monetary gain or other benefits, for example by obtaining a passport, travel document, or driver's license, or mortgage _____, where the perpetrator may attempt to qualify for a mortgage by way of false statements.

Exam Probability: **High**

52. *Answer choices:*

(see index for correct answer)

- a. Secret profit
- b. Check washing
- c. Lottery scam
- d. Long firm

Guidance: level 1

:: ::

_____ is the practice of deliberately managing the spread of information between an individual or an organization and the public. _____ may include an organization or individual gaining exposure to their audiences using topics of public interest and news items that do not require direct payment. This differentiates it from advertising as a form of marketing communications. _____ is the idea of creating coverage for clients for free, rather than marketing or advertising. But now, advertising is also a part of greater PR Activities.An example of good _____ would be generating an article featuring a client, rather than paying for the client to be advertised next to the article. The aim of _____ is to inform the public, prospective customers, investors, partners, employees, and other stakeholders and ultimately persuade them to maintain a positive or favorable view about the organization, its leadership, products, or political decisions. _____ professionals typically work for PR and marketing firms, businesses and companies, government, and public officials as PIOs and nongovernmental organizations, and nonprofit organizations. Jobs central to _____ include account coordinator, account executive, account supervisor, and media relations manager.

Exam Probability: **Medium**

53. *Answer choices:*

(see index for correct answer)

- a. deep-level diversity
- b. similarity-attraction theory
- c. Public relations
- d. Sarbanes-Oxley act of 2002

Guidance: level 1

:: ::

The _____ of 1906 was the first of a series of significant consumer protection laws which was enacted by Congress in the 20th century and led to the creation of the Food and Drug Administration. Its main purpose was to ban foreign and interstate traffic in adulterated or mislabeled food and drug products, and it directed the U.S. Bureau of Chemistry to inspect products and refer offenders to prosecutors. It required that active ingredients be placed on the label of a drug's packaging and that drugs could not fall below purity levels established by the United States Pharmacopeia or the National Formulary. The Jungle by Upton Sinclair with its graphic and revolting descriptions of unsanitary conditions and unscrupulous practices rampant in the meatpacking industry, was an inspirational piece that kept the public's attention on the important issue of unhygienic meat processing plants that later led to food inspection legislation. Sinclair quipped, "I aimed at the public's heart and by accident I hit it in the stomach," as outraged readers demanded and got the pure food law.

Exam Probability: **Low**

54. *Answer choices:*

(see index for correct answer)

- a. Sarbanes-Oxley act of 2002
- b. surface-level diversity
- c. corporate values
- d. personal values

Guidance: level 1

:: Organizational structure ::

An _____ defines how activities such as task allocation, coordination, and supervision are directed toward the achievement of organizational aims.

Exam Probability: **Low**

55. *Answer choices:*

(see index for correct answer)

- a. Organizational structure
- b. Followership
- c. Unorganisation
- d. The Starfish and the Spider

Guidance: level 1

:: Euthenics ::

_____ is an ethical framework and suggests that an entity, be it an organization or individual, has an obligation to act for the benefit of society at large. _____ is a duty every individual has to perform so as to maintain a balance between the economy and the ecosystems. A trade-off may exist between economic development, in the material sense, and the welfare of the society and environment, though this has been challenged by many reports over the past decade. _____ means sustaining the equilibrium between the two. It pertains not only to business organizations but also to everyone whose any action impacts the environment. This responsibility can be passive, by avoiding engaging in socially harmful acts, or active, by performing activities that directly advance social goals. _____ must be intergenerational since the actions of one generation have consequences on those following.

Exam Probability: **Medium**

56. *Answer choices:*

(see index for correct answer)

- a. Family and consumer science
- b. Social responsibility
- c. Home economics
- d. Euthenics

Guidance: level 1

:: Monopoly (economics) ::

The _____ of 1890 was a United States antitrust law that regulates competition among enterprises, which was passed by Congress under the presidency of Benjamin Harrison.

Exam Probability: **Medium**

57. *Answer choices:*

(see index for correct answer)

- a. Economies of scope
- b. Sherman Antitrust Act
- c. Quasi-rent
- d. Statute of Monopolies

Guidance: level 1

:: False advertising law ::

The Lanham Act is the primary federal trademark statute of law in the United States. The Act prohibits a number of activities, including trademark infringement, trademark dilution, and false advertising.

Exam Probability: **Low**

58. *Answer choices:*

(see index for correct answer)

- a. Rebecca Tushnet
- b. Lanham Act

Guidance: level 1

:: Private equity ::

In finance, a high-yield bond is a bond that is rated below investment grade. These bonds have a higher risk of default or other adverse credit events, but typically pay higher yields than better quality bonds in order to make them attractive to investors.

Exam Probability: **High**

59. *Answer choices:*

(see index for correct answer)

- a. High-yield
- b. Public Market Equivalent
- c. SVOX
- d. Early history of private equity

Guidance: level 1

Accounting

Accounting or accountancy is the measurement, processing, and communication of financial information about economic entities such as businesses and corporations. The modern field was established by the Italian mathematician Luca Pacioli in 1494. Accounting, which has been called the "language of business", measures the results of an organization's economic activities and conveys this information to a variety of users, including investors, creditors, management, and regulators.

:: International Financial Reporting Standards ::

_____ , usually called IFRS, are standards issued by the IFRS Foundation and the International Accounting Standards Board to provide a common global language for business affairs so that company accounts are understandable and comparable across international boundaries. They are a consequence of growing international shareholding and trade and are particularly important for companies that have dealings in several countries. They are progressively replacing the many different national accounting standards. They are the rules to be followed by accountants to maintain books of accounts which are comparable, understandable, reliable and relevant as per the users internal or external. IFRS, with the exception of IAS 29 Financial Reporting in Hyperinflationary Economies and IFRIC 7 Applying the Restatement Approach under IAS 29, are authorized in terms of the historical cost paradigm. IAS 29 and IFRIC 7 are authorized in terms of the units of constant purchasing power paradigm.IAS 2 is related to inventories in this standard we talk about the stock its production process etcIFRS began as an attempt to harmonize accounting across the European Union but the value of harmonization quickly made the concept attractive around the world. However, it has been debated whether or not de facto harmonization has occurred. Standards that were issued by IASC are still within use today and go by the name International Accounting Standards , while standards issued by IASB are called IFRS. IAS were issued between 1973 and 2001 by the Board of the International Accounting Standards Committee . On 1 April 2001, the new International Accounting Standards Board took over from the IASC the responsibility for setting International Accounting Standards. During its first meeting the new Board adopted existing IAS and Standing Interpretations Committee standards . The IASB has continued to develop standards calling the new standards " _____ ".

Exam Probability: **Low**

1. *Answer choices:*

(see index for correct answer)

- a. International Financial Reporting Standards
- b. Convergence of accounting standards
- c. IAS 2

- d. IAS 39

Guidance: level 1

:: ::

A _____ is the period used by governments for accounting and budget purposes, which varies between countries. It is also used for financial reporting by business and other organizations. Laws in many jurisdictions require company financial reports to be prepared and published on an annual basis, but generally do not require the reporting period to align with the calendar year . Taxation laws generally require accounting records to be maintained and taxes calculated on an annual basis, which usually corresponds to the _____ used for government purposes. The calculation of tax on an annual basis is especially relevant for direct taxation, such as income tax. Many annual government fees—such as Council rates, licence fees, etc.—are also levied on a _____ basis, while others are charged on an anniversary basis.

Exam Probability: **High**

2. *Answer choices:*
(see index for correct answer)

- a. surface-level diversity
- b. co-culture
- c. Fiscal year
- d. deep-level diversity

Guidance: level 1

:: Bank regulation ::

_____ is a measure implemented in many countries to protect bank depositors, in full or in part, from losses caused by a bank`s inability to pay its debts when due. _____ systems are one component of a financial system safety net that promotes financial stability.

Exam Probability: **Medium**

3. *Answer choices:*

(see index for correct answer)

- a. Stress test
- b. Bank regulation
- c. Deposit insurance
- d. Risk-weighted asset

Guidance: level 1

:: ::

_____ is a process whereby a person assumes the parenting of another, usually a child, from that person`s biological or legal parent or parents. Legal _____ s permanently transfers all rights and responsibilities, along with filiation, from the biological parent or parents.

4. *Answer choices:*

(see index for correct answer)

- a. surface-level diversity
- b. hierarchical perspective
- c. interpersonal communication
- d. Adoption

Guidance: level 1

:: Management accounting ::

_____ is the process of reviewing and analyzing a company's financial statements to make better economic decisions to earn income in future. These statements include the income statement, balance sheet, statement of cash flows, notes to accounts and a statement of changes in equity . _____ is a method or process involving specific techniques for evaluating risks, performance, financial health, and future prospects of an organization.

Exam Probability: **Low**

5. *Answer choices:*

(see index for correct answer)

- a. Extended cost
- b. Semi-variable cost

- c. Revenue center
- d. Financial statement analysis

Guidance: level 1

:: Information systems ::

_____ are formal, sociotechnical, organizational systems designed to collect, process, store, and distribute information. In a sociotechnical perspective, _____ are composed by four components: task, people, structure , and technology.

Exam Probability: **High**

6. *Answer choices:*

(see index for correct answer)

- a. European Research Center for Information Systems
- b. Cold start
- c. Information systems
- d. Electronic markets

Guidance: level 1

:: E-commerce ::

A _____ is a plastic payment card that can be used instead of cash when making purchases. It is similar to a credit card, but unlike a credit card, the money is immediately transferred directly from the cardholder's bank account when performing a transaction.

Exam Probability: **Medium**

7. *Answer choices:*

(see index for correct answer)

- a. Spamvertising
- b. Paid content
- c. Government-to-business
- d. Infomediary

Guidance: level 1

:: Budgets ::

A _____ is a financial plan for a defined period, often one year. It may also include planned sales volumes and revenues, resource quantities, costs and expenses, assets, liabilities and cash flows. Companies, governments, families and other organizations use it to express strategic plans of activities or events in measurable terms.

Exam Probability: **Low**

8. *Answer choices:*

(see index for correct answer)

- a. Marginal budgeting for bottlenecks
- b. Zero deficit budget
- c. Public budgeting
- d. Budget constraint

Guidance: level 1

:: Investment ::

In economics, _____ is spending which increases the availability of fixed capital goods or means of production and goods inventories. It is the total spending on newly produced physical capital and on inventories —that is, gross investment—minus replacement investment, which simply replaces depreciated capital goods. It is productive capital formation plus net additions to the stock of housing and the stock of inventories.

Exam Probability: **Low**

9. *Answer choices:*

(see index for correct answer)

- a. Investment broker
- b. Manager of managers fund
- c. Net investment
- d. Foreign portfolio investment

:: International trade ::

In finance, an _____ is the rate at which one currency will be exchanged for another. It is also regarded as the value of one country's currency in relation to another currency. For example, an interbank _____ of 114 Japanese yen to the United States dollar means that ¥114 will be exchanged for each US$1 or that US$1 will be exchanged for each ¥114. In this case it is said that the price of a dollar in relation to yen is ¥114, or equivalently that the price of a yen in relation to dollars is $1/114.

Exam Probability: **Low**

10. *Answer choices:*

(see index for correct answer)

- a. Special drawing rights
- b. Franz Oppenheimer
- c. Exchange rate
- d. Trade in Services Agreement

:: Management accounting ::

_____ accounting is a traditional cost accounting method introduced in the 1920s, as an alternative for the traditional cost accounting method based on historical costs.

Exam Probability: **High**

11. *Answer choices:*

(see index for correct answer)

- a. Investment center
- b. Certified Management Accountant
- c. Average per-bit delivery cost
- d. Standard cost

Guidance: level 1

:: Marketing ::

_____ or stock is the goods and materials that a business holds for the ultimate goal of resale .

Exam Probability: **High**

12. *Answer choices:*

(see index for correct answer)

- a. Adobe Target
- b. Kronos Effect
- c. Advertising media selection
- d. Gift suite

Guidance: level 1

:: ::

An _____ is a contingent motivator. Traditional _____ s are extrinsic motivators which reward actions to yield a desired outcome. The effectiveness of traditional _____ s has changed as the needs of Western society have evolved. While the traditional _____ model is effective when there is a defined procedure and goal for a task, Western society started to require a higher volume of critical thinkers, so the traditional model became less effective. Institutions are now following a trend in implementing strategies that rely on intrinsic motivations rather than the extrinsic motivations that the traditional _____ s foster.

Exam Probability: **Low**

13. *Answer choices:*

(see index for correct answer)

- a. Character
- b. empathy
- c. similarity-attraction theory
- d. Incentive

:: Taxation in the United States ::

The Modified Accelerated Cost Recovery System is the current tax depreciation system in the United States. Under this system, the capitalized cost of tangible property is recovered over a specified life by annual deductions for depreciation. The lives are specified broadly in the Internal Revenue Code. The Internal Revenue Service publishes detailed tables of lives by classes of assets. The deduction for depreciation is computed under one of two methods at the election of the taxpayer, with limitations. See IRS Publication 946 for a 120-page guide to _____ .

Exam Probability: **Low**

14. *Answer choices:*

(see index for correct answer)

- a. User fee
- b. KETRA
- c. MACRS
- d. Carryover basis

:: Management accounting ::

_____ is accounting which tracks the costs and revenues by "job" and enables standardized reporting of profitability by job. For an accounting system to support _____ , it must allow job numbers to be assigned to individual items of expenses and revenues. A job can be defined to be a specific project done for one customer, or a single unit of product manufactured, or a batch of units of the same type that are produced together.

Exam Probability: **High**

15. *Answer choices:*

(see index for correct answer)

- a. Target income sales
- b. Standard cost
- c. Invested capital
- d. Double counting

Guidance: level 1

:: Inventory ::

_____ is the amount of inventory a company has in stock at the end of its fiscal year. It is closely related with _____ cost, which is the amount of money spent to get these goods in stock. It should be calculated at the lower of cost or market.

Exam Probability: **Low**

16. *Answer choices:*

(see index for correct answer)

- a. Cost of goods available for sale
- b. Inventory optimization
- c. Stock-taking
- d. Reorder point

Guidance: level 1

:: ::

_____ is the income that is gained by governments through taxation. Taxation is the primary source of income for a state. Revenue may be extracted from sources such as individuals, public enterprises, trade, royalties on natural resources and/or foreign aid. An inefficient collection of taxes is greater in countries characterized by poverty, a large agricultural sector and large amounts of foreign aid.

Exam Probability: **Medium**

17. *Answer choices:*

(see index for correct answer)

- a. levels of analysis
- b. surface-level diversity
- c. similarity-attraction theory
- d. Tax revenue

:: Income ::

_____ is a ratio between the net profit and cost of investment resulting from an investment of some resources. A high ROI means the investment's gains favorably to its cost. As a performance measure, ROI is used to evaluate the efficiency of an investment or to compare the efficiencies of several different investments. In purely economic terms, it is one way of relating profits to capital invested. _____ is a performance measure used by businesses to identify the efficiency of an investment or number of different investments.

Exam Probability: **High**

18. *Answer choices:*

(see index for correct answer)

- a. Aggregate expenditure
- b. Salary inversion
- c. Mandatory tipping
- d. Income Per User

:: United States Generally Accepted Accounting Principles ::

In the United States, the _____, Subpart F of the OMB Uniform Guidance, is a rigorous, organization-wide audit or examination of an entity that expends $750,000 or more of federal assistance received for its operations. Usually performed annually, the _____'s objective is to provide assurance to the US federal government as to the management and use of such funds by recipients such as states, cities, universities, non-profit organizations, and Indian Tribes. The audit is typically performed by an independent certified public accountant and encompasses both financial and compliance components. The _____s must be submitted to the Federal Audit Clearinghouse along with a data collection form, Form SF-SAC.

Exam Probability: **High**

19. *Answer choices:*

(see index for correct answer)

- a. Cost segregation study
- b. FIN 46
- c. Working Group on Financial Markets
- d. Single Audit

Guidance: level 1

:: Types of business entity ::

A sole _____ , also known as the sole trader, individual entrepreneurship or _____ , is a type of enterprise that is owned and run by one person and in which there is no legal distinction between the owner and the business entity. A sole trader does not necessarily work `alone`—it is possible for the sole trader to employ other people.

Exam Probability: **Low**

20. *Answer choices:*

(see index for correct answer)

- a. Proprietorship
- b. Kommanditselskab
- c. Mochibun kaisha
- d. Value-added reseller

Guidance: level 1

:: Labour law ::

In law, _____ is to give an immediately secured right of present or future deployment. One has a vested right to an asset that cannot be taken away by any third party, even though one may not yet possess the asset. When the right, interest, or title to the present or future possession of a legal estate can be transferred to any other party, it is termed a vested interest.

Exam Probability: **Low**

21. *Answer choices:*

(see index for correct answer)

- a. International labour law
- b. Carl Degenkolb
- c. Core Labor Standards
- d. Conditional dismissal

Guidance: level 1

:: Financial economics ::

A _____ is defined to include property of any kind held by an assessee, whether connected with their business or profession or not connected with their business or profession. It includes all kinds of property, movable or immovable, tangible or intangible, fixed or circulating. Thus, land and building, plant and machinery, motorcar, furniture, jewellery, route permits, goodwill, tenancy rights, patents, trademarks, shares, debentures, securities, units, mutual funds, zero-coupon bonds etc. are _____ s.

Exam Probability: **High**

22. *Answer choices:*

(see index for correct answer)

- a. Financialization
- b. Capital asset
- c. Consumer leverage ratio

- d. Market trend

Guidance: level 1

:: Generally Accepted Accounting Principles ::

The _____ principle is a cornerstone of accrual accounting together with the matching principle. They both determine the accounting period in which revenues and expenses are recognized. According to the principle, revenues are recognized when they are realized or realizable, and are earned , no matter when cash is received. In cash accounting – in contrast – revenues are recognized when cash is received no matter when goods or services are sold.

Exam Probability: **High**

23. *Answer choices:*

(see index for correct answer)

- a. Closing entries
- b. Revenue recognition
- c. Historical cost
- d. Net profit

Guidance: level 1

:: Credit cards ::

The _____ Company, also known as Amex, is an American multinational financial services corporation headquartered in Three World Financial Center in New York City. The company was founded in 1850 and is one of the 30 components of the Dow Jones Industrial Average. The company is best known for its charge card, credit card, and traveler's cheque businesses.

Exam Probability: **High**

24. *Answer choices:*

(see index for correct answer)

- a. Payoneer
- b. BC Card
- c. Card scheme
- d. American Express

Guidance: level 1

:: Generally Accepted Accounting Principles ::

_____ s is an accounting term that refers to groups of accounts serving to express the cost of goods and service allocatable within a business or manufacturing organization. The principle behind the pool is to correlate direct and indirect costs with a specified cost driver, so to find out the total sum of expenses related to the manufacture of a product.

Exam Probability: **Medium**

25. *Answer choices:*

(see index for correct answer)

- a. Construction in progress
- b. Insurance asset management
- c. Cash method of accounting
- d. Paid in capital

Guidance: level 1

:: Accounting software ::

_____ describes a type of application software that records and processes accounting transactions within functional modules such as accounts payable, accounts receivable, journal, general ledger, payroll, and trial balance. It functions as an accounting information system. It may be developed in-house by the organization using it, may be purchased from a third party, or may be a combination of a third-party application software package with local modifications. _____ may be on-line based, accessed anywhere at any time with any device which is Internet enabled, or may be desktop based. It varies greatly in its complexity and cost.

Exam Probability: **Low**

26. *Answer choices:*

(see index for correct answer)

- a. Passport Software
- b. Moneydance

- c. Outright
- d. Accounting software

Guidance: level 1

:: Management accounting ::

In _____ or managerial accounting, managers use the provisions of accounting information in order to better inform themselves before they decide matters within their organizations, which aids their management and performance of control functions.

Exam Probability: **Medium**

27. *Answer choices:*

(see index for correct answer)

- a. Owner earnings
- b. Construction accounting
- c. Management accounting
- d. Spend management

Guidance: level 1

:: Accounting source documents ::

_____ is a letter sent by a customer to a supplier to inform the supplier that their invoice has been paid. If the customer is paying by cheque, the _____ often accompanies the cheque. The advice may consist of a literal letter or of a voucher attached to the side or top of the cheque.

Exam Probability: **Medium**

28. *Answer choices:*

(see index for correct answer)

- a. Credit memo
- b. Credit memorandum
- c. Remittance advice
- d. Air waybill

Guidance: level 1

:: Stock market ::

A _____ , equity market or share market is the aggregation of buyers and sellers of stocks , which represent ownership claims on businesses; these may include securities listed on a public stock exchange, as well as stock that is only traded privately. Examples of the latter include shares of private companies which are sold to investors through equity crowdfunding platforms. Stock exchanges list shares of common equity as well as other security types, e.g. corporate bonds and convertible bonds.

Exam Probability: **Medium**

29. *Answer choices:*

(see index for correct answer)

- a. Share
- b. Bagholder
- c. FTSE Global Equity Index Series
- d. Stock Market

Guidance: level 1

:: Business law ::

An _____ is a natural person, business, or corporation that provides goods or services to another entity under terms specified in a contract or within a verbal agreement. Unlike an employee, an _____ does not work regularly for an employer but works as and when required, during which time they may be subject to law of agency. _____ s are usually paid on a freelance basis. Contractors often work through a limited company or franchise, which they themselves own, or may work through an umbrella company.

Exam Probability: **Low**

30. *Answer choices:*

(see index for correct answer)

- a. Limited liability limited partnership
- b. Participation
- c. Process agent

- d. Independent contractor

Guidance: level 1

:: Cash flow ::

In corporate finance, _____ or _____ to firm is a way of looking at a business's cash flow to see what is available for distribution among all the securities holders of a corporate entity. This may be useful to parties such as equity holders, debt holders, preferred stock holders, and convertible security holders when they want to see how much cash can be extracted from a company without causing issues to its operations.

Exam Probability: **Low**

31. *Answer choices:*

(see index for correct answer)

- a. Free cash flow
- b. First Chicago Method
- c. Propequity
- d. Discounted cash flow

Guidance: level 1

:: Generally Accepted Accounting Principles ::

_____ , or non-current liabilities, are liabilities that are due beyond a year or the normal operation period of the company. The normal operation period is the amount of time it takes for a company to turn inventory into cash. On a classified balance sheet, liabilities are separated between current and _____ to help users assess the company's financial standing in short-term and long-term periods. _____ give users more information about the long-term prosperity of the company, while current liabilities inform the user of debt that the company owes in the current period. On a balance sheet, accounts are listed in order of liquidity, so _____ come after current liabilities. In addition, the specific long-term liability accounts are listed on the balance sheet in order of liquidity. Therefore, an account due within eighteen months would be listed before an account due within twenty-four months. Examples of _____ are bonds payable, long-term loans, capital leases, pension liabilities, post-retirement healthcare liabilities, deferred compensation, deferred revenues, deferred income taxes, and derivative liabilities.

Exam Probability: **Low**

32. *Answer choices:*

(see index for correct answer)

- a. Generally Accepted Accounting Practice
- b. Long-term liabilities
- c. Deprival value
- d. Expense

Guidance: level 1

:: Expense ::

_____ relates to the cost of borrowing money. It is the price that a lender charges a borrower for the use of the lender's money. On the income statement, _____ can represent the cost of borrowing money from banks, bond investors, and other sources. _____ is different from operating expense and CAPEX, for it relates to the capital structure of a company, and it is usually tax-deductible.

Exam Probability: **Medium**

33. *Answer choices:*

(see index for correct answer)

- a. Freight expense
- b. Tax expense
- c. Expense account
- d. Interest expense

Guidance: level 1

:: ::

A _____ is a tax paid to a governing body for the sales of certain goods and services. Usually laws allow the seller to collect funds for the tax from the consumer at the point of purchase. When a tax on goods or services is paid to a governing body directly by a consumer, it is usually called a use tax. Often laws provide for the exemption of certain goods or services from sales and use tax.

34. *Answer choices:*

(see index for correct answer)

- a. functional perspective
- b. Sales tax
- c. imperative
- d. Character

Guidance: level 1

:: Macroeconomics ::

_____ is a change in a price of a good or product, or especially of a currency, in which case it is specifically an official rise of the value of the currency in relation to a foreign currency in a fixed exchange rate system. Under floating exchange rates, by contrast, a rise in a currency's value is an appreciation. Altering the face value of a currency without changing its purchasing power is a redenomination, not a _____ .

Exam Probability: **High**

35. *Answer choices:*

(see index for correct answer)

- a. Robot economics
- b. Macroeconomic model

- c. Asset-based economy
- d. Country attractiveness

Guidance: level 1

:: Tax reform ::

_____ is the process of changing the way taxes are collected or managed by the government and is usually undertaken to improve tax administration or to provide economic or social benefits. _____ can include reducing the level of taxation of all people by the government, making the tax system more progressive or less progressive, or simplifying the tax system and making the system more understandable or more accountable.

Exam Probability: **Medium**

36. *Answer choices:*

(see index for correct answer)

- a. Tax reform
- b. Joseph A. Pechman
- c. Goods and Services Tax
- d. Single tax

Guidance: level 1

:: ::

A _____ is a form of public administration which, in a majority of contexts, exists as the lowest tier of administration within a given state. The term is used to contrast with offices at state level, which are referred to as the central government, national government, or federal government and also to supranational government which deals with governing institutions between states. _____ s generally act within powers delegated to them by legislation or directives of the higher level of government. In federal states, _____ generally comprises the third tier of government, whereas in unitary states, _____ usually occupies the second or third tier of government, often with greater powers than higher-level administrative divisions.

Exam Probability: **Medium**

37. *Answer choices:*

(see index for correct answer)

- a. Sarbanes-Oxley act of 2002
- b. interpersonal communication
- c. imperative
- d. Local government

Guidance: level 1

:: Asset ::

In accounting, a _____ is any asset which can reasonably be expected to be sold, consumed, or exhausted through the normal operations of a business within the current fiscal year or operating cycle . Typical _____ s include cash, cash equivalents, short-term investments , accounts receivable, stock inventory, supplies, and the portion of prepaid liabilities which will be paid within a year.In simple words, assets which are held for a short period are known as _____ s. Such assets are expected to be realised in cash or consumed during the normal operating cycle of the business.

Exam Probability: **High**

38. *Answer choices:*

(see index for correct answer)

- a. Current asset
- b. Fixed asset

Guidance: level 1

:: Accounting ::

It is the period for which books are balanced and the financial statements are prepared. Generally, the _____ consists of 12 months. However the beginning of the _____ differs according to the jurisdiction. For example, one entity may follow the regular calendar year, i.e. January to December as the accounting year, while another entity may follow April to March as the _____ .

Exam Probability: **High**

39. *Answer choices:*

(see index for correct answer)

- a. KashFlow
- b. amortisation
- c. Accounting period
- d. Accountant General

Guidance: level 1

:: Real estate ::

Amortisation is paying off an amount owed over time by making planned, incremental payments of principal and interest. To amortise a loan means "to kill it off". In accounting, amortisation refers to charging or writing off an intangible asset's cost as an operational expense over its estimated useful life to reduce a company's taxable income.

Exam Probability: **Medium**

40. *Answer choices:*

(see index for correct answer)

- a. Automated valuation model
- b. Domania
- c. Deeds registration
- d. Crown land

:: ::

_____ are electronic transfer of money from one bank account to another, either within a single financial institution or across multiple institutions, via computer-based systems, without the direct intervention of bank staff.

Exam Probability: **Low**

41. *Answer choices:*

(see index for correct answer)

- a. co-culture
- b. similarity-attraction theory
- c. functional perspective
- d. personal values

:: Accounting ::

_____ are key sources of information and evidence used to prepare, verify and/or audit the financial statements. They also include documentation to prove asset ownership for creation of liabilities and proof of monetary and non monetary transactions.

Exam Probability: **Medium**

42. *Answer choices:*

(see index for correct answer)

- a. INPACT International
- b. Engineering Accounting
- c. Accounting records
- d. Comfort letter

Guidance: level 1

:: Banking terms ::

An _____ occurs when money is withdrawn from a bank account and the available balance goes below zero. In this situation the account is said to be "overdrawn". If there is a prior agreement with the account provider for an _____ , and the amount overdrawn is within the authorized _____ limit, then interest is normally charged at the agreed rate. If the negative balance exceeds the agreed terms, then additional fees may be charged and higher interest rates may apply.

Exam Probability: **Low**

43. *Answer choices:*

(see index for correct answer)

- a. Allowance for Loan and Lease Losses
- b. Collection item
- c. Overdraft
- d. Suspense account

Guidance: level 1

:: Real estate valuation ::

_____ or OMV is the price at which an asset would trade in a competitive auction setting. _____ is often used interchangeably with open _____ , fair value or fair _____ , although these terms have distinct definitions in different standards, and may or may not differ in some circumstances.

Exam Probability: **Medium**

44. *Answer choices:*

(see index for correct answer)

- a. Real estate benchmarking
- b. Sales comparison approach
- c. Market value
- d. Uniform Standards of Professional Appraisal Practice

:: ::

_____ is the field of accounting concerned with the summary, analysis and reporting of financial transactions related to a business. This involves the preparation of financial statements available for public use. Stockholders, suppliers, banks, employees, government agencies, business owners, and other stakeholders are examples of people interested in receiving such information for decision making purposes.

Exam Probability: **Low**

45. *Answer choices:*

(see index for correct answer)

- a. empathy
- b. Sarbanes-Oxley act of 2002
- c. corporate values
- d. Financial accounting

:: Accounting terminology ::

In management accounting or _____ , managers use the provisions of accounting information in order to better inform themselves before they decide matters within their organizations, which aids their management and performance of control functions.

Exam Probability: **High**

46. *Answer choices:*

(see index for correct answer)

- a. Accrual
- b. Accounts payable
- c. Managerial accounting
- d. Record to report

Guidance: level 1

:: Taxation ::

_____ is a type of tax law that allows a person to give assets to his or her spouse with reduced or no tax imposed upon the transfer. Some _____ laws even apply to transfers made postmortem. The right to receive property conveys ownership for tax purposes. A decree of divorce transfers the right to that property by reason of the marriage and is also a transfer within a marriage. It makes no difference whether the property itself or equivalent compensation is transferred before, or after the decree dissolves the marriage. There is no U.S. estate and gift tax on transfers of any amount between spouses, whether during their lifetime or at death. There is an important exceptions for non-citizens. The U.S. federal Estate and gift tax _____ is only available if the surviving spouse is a U.S. citizen. For a surviving spouse who is not a U.S. citizen a bequest through a Qualified Domestic Trust defers estate tax until principal is distributed by the trustee, a U.S. citizen or corporation who also withholds the estate tax. Income on principal distributed to the surviving spouse is taxed as individual income. If the surviving spouse becomes a U.S. citizen, principal remaining in a Qualifying Domestic Trust may then be distributed without further tax.

Exam Probability: **Medium**

47. *Answer choices:*

(see index for correct answer)

- a. Average tax rate
- b. Optimal taxation
- c. Privilege tax
- d. Seigniorage

Guidance: level 1

:: Finance ::

_____ is a notional asset or liability to reflect corporate income taxation on a basis that is the same or more similar to recognition of profits than the taxation treatment. _____ liabilities can arise as a result of corporate taxation treatment of capital expenditure being more rapid than the accounting depreciation treatment. _____ assets can arise due to net loss carry-overs, which are only recorded as asset if it is deemed more likely than not that the asset will be used in future fiscal periods. Different countries may also allow or require discounting of the assets or particularly liabilities. There are often disclosure requirements for potential liabilities and assets that are not actually recognised as an asset or liability.

Exam Probability: **High**

48. *Answer choices:*

(see index for correct answer)

- a. Creative industries
- b. Deferred tax
- c. Short
- d. Seven Pillars Institute

Guidance: level 1

:: Generally Accepted Accounting Principles ::

_____ is, in accrual accounting, money received for goods or services which have not yet been delivered. According to the revenue recognition principle, it is recorded as a liability until delivery is made, at which time it is converted into revenue.

49. *Answer choices:*

(see index for correct answer)

- a. Deferred income
- b. Gross income
- c. Access to finance
- d. Provision

Guidance: level 1

:: Fundamental analysis ::

_____ is the monetary value of earnings per outstanding share of common stock for a company.

50. *Answer choices:*

(see index for correct answer)

- a. Goldman Sachs asset management factor model
- b. Public float
- c. Trading Advantage
- d. Earnings per share

:: Competition (economics) ::

In taxation and accounting, _____ refers to the rules and methods for pricing transactions within and between enterprises under common ownership or control. Because of the potential for cross-border controlled transactions to distort taxable income, tax authorities in many countries can adjust intragroup transfer prices that differ from what would have been charged by unrelated enterprises dealing at arm's length . The OECD and World Bank recommend intragroup pricing rules based on the arm's-length principle, and 19 of the 20 members of the G20 have adopted similar measures through bilateral treaties and domestic legislation, regulations, or administrative practice. Countries with _____ legislation generally follow the OECD _____ Guidelines for Multinational Enterprises and Tax Administrations in most respects, although their rules can differ on some important details.

Exam Probability: **Low**

51. *Answer choices:*

(see index for correct answer)

- a. Currency competition
- b. Transfer pricing
- c. Regulatory competition
- d. Level playing field

:: Foreign exchange market ::

A currency , in the most specific sense is money in any form when in use or circulation as a medium of exchange, especially circulating banknotes and coins. A more general definition is that a currency is a system of money in common use, especially for people in a nation. Under this definition, US dollars , pounds sterling , Australian dollars , European euros , Russian rubles and Indian Rupees are examples of currencies. These various currencies are recognized as stores of value and are traded between nations in foreign exchange markets, which determine the relative values of the different currencies. Currencies in this sense are defined by governments, and each type has limited boundaries of acceptance.

Exam Probability: **Medium**

52. *Answer choices:*

(see index for correct answer)

- a. Petrodollar recycling
- b. Chiang Mai Initiative
- c. Floating exchange rate
- d. Exchange-rate regime

Guidance: level 1

:: Payment systems ::

An _____ is an electronic telecommunications device that enables customers of financial institutions to perform financial transactions, such as cash withdrawals, deposits, transfer funds, or obtaining account information, at any time and without the need for direct interaction with bank staff.

Exam Probability: **Medium**

53. *Answer choices:*

(see index for correct answer)

- a. Automated teller machine
- b. Post-dated cheque
- c. NetSpend Corporation
- d. Freedompay

Guidance: level 1

:: Hazard analysis ::

Broadly speaking, a _____ is the combined effort of 1. identifying and analyzing potential events that may negatively impact individuals, assets, and/or the environment ; and 2. making judgments "on the tolerability of the risk on the basis of a risk analysis" while considering influencing factors . Put in simpler terms, a _____ analyzes what can go wrong, how likely it is to happen, what the potential consequences are, and how tolerable the identified risk is. As part of this process, the resulting determination of risk may be expressed in a quantitative or qualitative fashion. The _____ is an inherent part of an overall risk management strategy, which attempts to, after a _____ , "introduce control measures to eliminate or reduce" any potential risk-related consequences.

Exam Probability: **High**

54. *Answer choices:*

(see index for correct answer)

- a. Risk assessment
- b. Hazard identification
- c. Hazardous Materials Identification System
- d. Swiss cheese model

Guidance: level 1

:: Accounting terminology ::

_____ is money owed by a business to its suppliers shown as a liability on a company's balance sheet. It is distinct from notes payable liabilities, which are debts created by formal legal instrument documents.

55. *Answer choices:*

(see index for correct answer)

- a. double-entry bookkeeping
- b. Accounts payable
- c. Accrual
- d. Basis of accounting

Guidance: level 1

:: Financial ratios ::

The _____ or dividend-price ratio of a share is the dividend per share, divided by the price per share. It is also a company's total annual dividend payments divided by its market capitalization, assuming the number of shares is constant. It is often expressed as a percentage.

56. *Answer choices:*

(see index for correct answer)

- a. Dividend yield
- b. Information ratio
- c. K-factor

- d. Alpha

Guidance: level 1

:: Auditing ::

An _____ is a security-relevant chronological record, set of records, and/or destination and source of records that provide documentary evidence of the sequence of activities that have affected at any time a specific operation, procedure, or event. Audit records typically result from activities such as financial transactions, scientific research and health care data transactions, or communications by individual people, systems, accounts, or other entities.

Exam Probability: **High**

57. *Answer choices:*
(see index for correct answer)

- a. Utility bill audit
- b. Circulation Verification Council
- c. Mazars
- d. Audit trail

Guidance: level 1

:: Generally Accepted Accounting Principles ::

A _____ or reacquired stock is stock which is bought back by the issuing company, reducing the amount of outstanding stock on the open market .

Exam Probability: **Low**

58. *Answer choices:*

(see index for correct answer)

- a. Treasury stock
- b. Net profit
- c. Operating statement
- d. Paid in capital

Guidance: level 1

:: Accounting organizations ::

The _____ promotes accounting education, research and practice. Founded in 1916 as the American Association of University Instructors in Accounting, its present name was adopted in 1936. The Association is a voluntary group of persons interested in accounting education and research.

Exam Probability: **Medium**

59. *Answer choices:*

(see index for correct answer)

- a. American Accounting Association
- b. Accounting Hall of Fame
- c. The Siegfried Group
- d. Professional accounting body

Guidance: level 1

INDEX: Correct Answers

Foundations of Business

1. b: Solution

2. a: Exercise

3. b: Debt

4. c: Employment

5. : Marketing strategy

6. d: Joint venture

7. a: American Express

8. c: Competition

9. a: Direct investment

10. : System

11. d: Life

12. : Marketing

13. a: Variable cost

14. a: Mission statement

15. c: Business plan

16. d: SWOT analysis

17. : Initiative

18. : Inventory

19. : Small business

20. c: Capitalism

21. b: Industrial Revolution

22. : Project management

23. b: Risk

24. a: Financial services

25. c: Regulation

26. d: Logistics

27. c: Business

28. d: Law

29. b: Payment

30. c: Case study

31. b: Tool

32. b: Insurance

33. : Free trade

34. : Income statement

35. b: Specification

36. : Description

37. c: Corporate governance

38. d: Social security

39. c: Benchmarking

40. d: Empowerment

41. b: Best practice

42. a: Supply chain

43. c: ITeM

44. c: Accounting

45. b: Balance sheet

46. b: Buyer

47. b: Analysis

48. : Selling

49. : Business model

50. a: Demand

51. d: Risk management

52. : Review

53. a: Finance

54. c: Focus group

55. b: Evaluation

56. d: Loan

57. a: Globalization

58. : Trade

59. d: Good

Management

1. : Review

2. : Mission statement

3. b: Statistical process control

4. d: Philosophy

5. : Knowledge management

6. : Good

7. b: Feedback

8. a: Compromise

9. d: Choice

10. d: Explanation

11. : Forecasting

12. d: Strategic management

13. c: Human capital

14. b: Income

15. d: Research and development

16. c: International trade

17. b: Empowerment

18. d: Continuous improvement

19. : 360-degree feedback

20. : Transformational leadership

21. : Theory X

22. a: Market research

23. c: Resource

24. c: Shareholder

25. b: Standard deviation

26. c: Variable cost

27. c: Description

28. a: Quality control

29. b: Decentralization

30. a: Policy

31. : Product life cycle

32. b: Job design

33. b: Labor relations

34. : Code

35. : Time management

36. d: Incentive

37. b: Control chart

38. d: Recession

39. : Employment

40. c: Referent power

41. : Performance appraisal

42. d: Human resources

43. b: Assessment center

44. d: Reputation

45. d: Evaluation

46. a: Grievance

47. : Insurance

48. c: Hotel

49. b: Business model

50. d: Strategic alliance

51. : Mediation

52. : Efficiency

53. d: Simulation

54. c: Business process

55. d: Performance

56. : Contingency theory

57. c: Affirmative action

58. : Management by objectives

59. d: Franchising

Business law

1. b: Joint venture

2. : Lien

3. c: Constitutional law

4. d: Presentment

5. c: Anticipatory repudiation

6. c: Summary judgment

7. : World Trade Organization

8. d: Commerce Clause

9. : Apparent authority

10. c: Mortgage

11. c: Punitive damages

12. a: Arbitration clause

13. c: Consumer credit

14. a: Real property

15. d: Internal Revenue Service

16. b: Offeree

17. b: Health insurance

18. d: Securities Act

19. : Purchasing

20. d: Sole proprietorship

21. b: Precedent

22. b: Management

23. d: Mirror image rule

24. c: Computer fraud

25. : Rescind

26. c: Trustee

27. a: Advertisement

28. c: Contract law

29. a: Prima facie

30. d: Hearing

31. b: Oral contract

32. d: Federal Arbitration Act

33. b: Service mark

34. b: Broker

35. b: Appeal

36. c: Disparagement

37. : Perfection

38. : Executory contract

39. : Statute of frauds

40. d: Accord and satisfaction

41. b: Estoppel

42. b: Consideration

43. d: Property

44. b: Commerce

45. a: Sherman Act

46. b: Disclaimer

47. c: Incentive

48. c: Criminal procedure

49. d: Acceleration clause

50. a: Adoption

51. b: Plaintiff

52. a: Collective bargaining

53. a: Procedural law

54. d: Warehouse

55. b: Preference

56. b: Merchant

57. a: Secured transaction

58. c: Beneficiary

59. : Antitrust

Finance

1. d: Future value

2. : Bank reconciliation

3. c: Sinking fund

4. : Investor

5. : Financial analysis

6. : Fraud

7. c: Accounts payable

8. d: Income statement

9. b: Adjusting entries

10. : Schedule

11. a: Accounts receivable

12. : Hedge fund

13. b: Choice

14. b: Financial risk

15. b: Chart of accounts

16. a: Common stock

17. c: Corporate governance

18. d: Convertible bond

19. : Stockholder

20. b: Limited liability

21. c: Purchasing

22. a: Advertising

23. : Contribution margin

24. : Net profit

25. : Technology

26. d: General journal

27. c: Public Company Accounting Oversight Board

28. b: Risk assessment

29. c: Capital expenditure

30. c: Market value

31. d: Accrued interest

32. c: Internal Revenue Service

33. b: Operating leverage

34. d: Firm

35. c: Write-off

36. b: Pricing

37. c: Expected return

38. c: Credit card

39. : Patent

40. b: Shareholder

41. c: S corporation

42. : Capital asset

43. a: Property

44. d: Sole proprietorship

45. a: Coupon

46. a: Securities and Exchange Commission

47. : Rate risk

48. d: Amortization

49. c: Currency

50. d: Finished good

51. b: Fiscal year

52. c: Intangible asset

53. : Preference

54. d: Specific identification

55. b: General ledger

56. b: Government bond

57. d: Cash equivalent

58. a: Conservatism

59. d: Income tax

Human resource management

1. d: Realistic job preview

2. a: Strategy map

3. a: Service Employees International Union

4. b: Ownership

5. : Total Reward

6. : Hazard

7. b: Asset

8. c: Six Sigma

9. d: Assessment center

10. b: Social network

11. c: Skill

12. c: Socialization

13. a: Self-assessment

14. a: Reinforcement

15. b: Employee Free Choice Act

16. b: Drug test

17. d: Job rotation

18. a: Part-time

19. : Salary

20. b: Job enlargement

21. c: Human resources

22. a: Balance sheet

23. : Picketing

24. c: Criterion validity

25. : Career

26. a: Organizational learning

27. c: Background check

28. b: Needs analysis

29. d: Hazard analysis

30. d: E-HRM

31. c: Mergers and acquisitions

32. : Structured interview

33. d: Hostile work environment

34. d: Retraining

35. d: Unfair labor practice

36. d: New Deal

37. : Phantom stock

38. a: Behavior modification

39. a: Sweatshop

40. a: Deferred compensation

41. d: Management

42. a: Online assessment

43. d: Material safety data sheet

44. : Cafeteria plan

45. b: Decentralization

46. d: Disability insurance

47. c: Locus of control

48. a: Persuasion

49. a: Cost leadership

50. a: Tacit knowledge

51. a: Employee engagement

52. : Performance improvement

53. d: Content validity

54. d: Layoff

55. c: Competitive advantage

56. a: Task force

57. c: Severance package

58. d: Predictive validity

59. c: Health Reimbursement Account

Information systems

1. b: Copyright

2. c: Sustainable

3. a: Electronic funds transfer

4. b: Balanced scorecard

5. a: Payment card

6. a: Flash memory

7. c: Yelp

8. b: Transport Layer Security

9. d: Long tail

10. : Decision support system

11. d: Manifesto

12. b: Text mining

13. c: Cookie

14. b: Smart card

15. d: Downtime

16. d: Geocoding

17. : Phishing

18. d: Competitive advantage

19. c: Groupware

20. a: Backup

21. a: Automated teller machine

22. a: Consumer-to-business

23. b: PageRank

24. b: Vulnerability

25. b: Service level

26. a: Business model

27. d: Data element

28. b: Google

29. d: Critical success factor

30. d: Bit rate

31. b: Statistics

32. : Master data management

33. c: Government-to-citizen

34. c: Total cost of ownership

35. c: Content management

36. d: Strategic planning

37. : Data warehouse

38. : Authentication protocol

39. b: Input device

40. : Edge computing

41. a: Chart

42. d: YouTube

43. b: Fraud

44. c: Porter five forces analysis

45. : Dashboard

46. c: Web analytics

47. : Cybersquatting

48. : Service level agreement

49. a: Wide Area Network

50. a: Galileo

51. c: Availability

52. b: Questionnaire

53. b: Data governance

54. b: Network interface card

55. a: Google Maps

56. c: Identity theft

57. : Metadata

58. : Supply chain management

59. d: Read-only memory

Marketing

1. a: Merchandising

2. d: Psychographic

3. b: Distribution channel

4. d: Utility

5. b: Inflation

6. : Data collection

7. b: Blog

8. d: Advertising

9. : Economy

10. : Loyalty

11. d: Copyright

12. c: American Express

13. : Early adopter

14. d: Green marketing

15. b: Entrepreneur

16. a: Small business

17. : Creative brief

18. b: Warehouse

19. : Supply chain management

20. d: Problem Solving

21. b: Stock

22. : Universal Product Code

23. c: Reinforcement

24. : Technology

25. a: Market research

26. d: Contract

27. d: Policy

28. a: Interactive marketing

29. : Infomercial

30. d: Marketing management

31. b: Data analysis

32. d: Strategic planning

33. c: Manager

34. : Sales management

35. : Customer satisfaction

36. c: Cognitive dissonance

37. b: Trademark

38. b: Commerce

39. d: Situation analysis

40. c: Marketing communication

41. b: Services marketing

42. d: Clayton Act

43. d: Life

44. : Auction

45. c: Competition

46. a: Adoption

47. b: Frequency

48. a: Industry

49. b: North American Free Trade Agreement

50. d: Respondent

51. d: Loyalty program

52. : Globalization

53. d: Product concept

54. b: Economies of scale

55. c: Attention

56. c: Partnership

57. d: Public

58. d: Accounting

59. c: Testimonial

Manufacturing

1. d: Glass

2. d: Obsolescence

3. : Project

4. c: Root cause

5. d: Remanufacturing

6. a: Voice of the customer

7. : PDCA

8. b: Change management

9. : Reverse auction

10. : Lead

11. d: Licensed production

12. c: Check sheet

13. : Financial plan

14. : Resource allocation

15. : Raw material

16. c: Furnace

17. a: Virtual team

18. b: Vendor relationship management

19. c: Steering committee

20. a: Total cost

21. b: Knowledge management

22. : Certification

23. b: Bill of materials

24. : Kaizen

25. d: American Society for Quality

26. c: Sputnik

27. : Planning

28. c: Sunk costs

29. c: Schedule

30. b: Interaction

31. d: Throughput

32. a: Service level

33. : Property

34. a: Expediting

35. d: Extended enterprise

36. b: Metal

37. : Sensitivity analysis

38. : Information management

39. d: Forecasting

40. a: Project team

41. a: Process management

42. d: Mary Kay

43. b: Thomas Register

44. c: Concurrent engineering

45. : Materials management

46. b: Total productive maintenance

47. b: Quality assurance

48. : Resource management

49. c: Value engineering

50. b: Quality Engineering

51. d: Procurement

52. : Perfect competition

53. a: Purchasing

54. a: Dimension

55. c: Blanket

56. b: Clay

57. a: Cost

58. c: Request for quotation

59. : Acceptance sampling

Commerce

1. a: Product mix

2. c: Export

3. : Quality management

4. a: Teamwork

5. a: Phishing

6. a: Purchasing manager

7. c: Payment card

8. a: Hospitality

9. : Lycos

10. d: Commerce

11. c: Resource

12. : Cooperative

13. c: Committee

14. : Industry

15. a: Subsidy

16. c: Monopoly

17. c: Invoice

18. : Standing

19. b: Variable cost

20. a: Regulatory agency

21. b: Inventory control

22. a: Drawback

23. : Tariff

24. : Financial services

25. a: Frequency

26. d: Return on investment

27. c: Automation

28. b: Authorize.Net

29. d: Organizational structure

30. c: Empowerment

31. c: Economics

32. c: Business-to-business

33. b: Procurement

34. c: English auction

35. : Audit

36. a: Technology

37. c: Uniform Commercial Code

38. c: Market research

39. c: Marketing mix

40. a: Advertising

41. a: Market share

42. a: Staff position

43. d: Boot

44. c: Raw material

45. a: Strategic plan

46. : Pension

47. b: Logistics

48. c: Publicity

49. : Management team

50. : Brand

51. b: Vendor

52. : Public policy

53. b: Enabling

54. b: Bankruptcy

55. c: Free market

56. b: Project

57. a: Issuing bank

58. : Trial

59. d: Tangible

Business ethics

1. b: New Deal

2. : Veil of ignorance

3. : Utopian socialism

4. c: Natural gas

5. b: Layoff

6. c: Undue hardship

7. b: Oil spill

8. c: Energy policy

9. b: Workplace bullying

10. c: Electronic waste

11. d: Cultural relativism

12. d: Stanford International Bank

13. a: Workplace politics

14. a: ExxonMobil

15. d: Greenwashing

16. : Antitrust

17. b: Stanford Financial Group

18. a: Subprime lending

19. c: Solar power

20. c: Human nature

21. b: Internal control

22. a: Constitutional law

23. d: Forest Stewardship Council

24. : Better Business Bureau

25. d: Sexual harassment

26. : UN Global Compact

27. : United Farm Workers

28. b: Martin Luther

29. a: Fannie Mae

30. a: Risk management

31. c: Self-interest

32. a: White-collar crime

33. b: Petroleum

34. b: Feedback

35. : Sustainable

36. a: Chamber of Commerce

37. c: Trade

38. a: Madoff

39. a: Guerrilla Marketing

40. d: Corporate governance

41. b: Locus of control

42. : Corporate social responsibility

43. d: Aristotle

44. c: Patent

45. : Occupational Safety and Health Administration

46. a: Executive compensation

47. c: Retaliation

48. d: Clean Water Act

49. : Auditor independence

50. a: Organizational ethics

51. : Pollution Prevention

52. : Fraud

53. c: Public relations

54. : Pure Food and Drug Act

55. a: Organizational structure

56. b: Social responsibility

57. b: Sherman Antitrust Act

58. b: Lanham Act

59. : Junk bond

Accounting

1. a: International Financial Reporting Standards

2. c: Fiscal year

3. c: Deposit insurance

4. d: Adoption

5. d: Financial statement analysis

6. c: Information systems

7. : Debit card

8. : Budget

9. c: Net investment

10. c: Exchange rate

11. d: Standard cost

12. : Inventory

13. d: Incentive

14. c: MACRS

15. : Job costing

16. : Ending inventory

17. d: Tax revenue

18. : Return on investment

19. d: Single Audit

20. a: Proprietorship

21. : Vesting

22. b: Capital asset

23. b: Revenue recognition

24. d: American Express

25. : Cost pool

26. d: Accounting software

27. c: Management accounting

28. c: Remittance advice

29. d: Stock Market

30. d: Independent contractor

31. a: Free cash flow

32. b: Long-term liabilities

33. d: Interest expense

34. b: Sales tax

35. : Revaluation

36. a: Tax reform

37. d: Local government

38. a: Current asset

39. c: Accounting period

40. : Amortization

41. : Electronic funds transfer

42. c: Accounting records

43. c: Overdraft

44. c: Market value

45. d: Financial accounting

46. c: Managerial accounting

47. : Marital deduction

48. b: Deferred tax

49. a: Deferred income

50. d: Earnings per share

51. b: Transfer pricing

52. : Monetary unit

53. a: Automated teller machine

54. a: Risk assessment

55. b: Accounts payable

56. a: Dividend yield

57. d: Audit trail

58. a: Treasury stock

59. a: American Accounting Association

CPSIA information can be obtained
at www.ICGtesting.com
Printed in the USA
LVHW041025301019
635717LV00002B/26/P